MILITANT

MILITANT

Michael Crick

Biteback Publishing

This edition published in Great Britain in 2016 by
Biteback Publishing Ltd
Westminster Tower
3 Albert Embankment
London SE1 7SP
Copyright © Michael Crick 1984, 1986, 2016

First published as *The March of Militant* in Great Britain in 1986 by Faber & Faber Ltd

Michael Crick has asserted his right under the Copyright, Designs and
Patents Act 1988 to be identified as the author of this work.

Portions of this book previously appeared in *Militant*,
published by Faber & Faber Ltd in 1984

ISBN 978-1-78590-029-7

10 9 8 7 6 5 4 3 2 1

A CIP catalogue record for this book is available from the British Library.

Set in Arno Pro and Gotham by Adrian McLaughlin

Printed and bound in Great Britain by
CPI Group (UK) Ltd, Croydon CR0 4YY

MIX
Paper from
responsible sources
FSC® C020471

CONTENTS

PREFACE AND ACKNOWLEDGEMENTS

For the Leader of Her Majesty's Opposition to miss the twice-weekly Prime Minister's Questions in the Commons is quite rare. It happens perhaps five or six times a year, usually when the opposition leader is away on a foreign visit. Normally his or her deputy will take over. In Neil Kinnock's case, of course, the stand-in is Roy Hattersley. But on Thursday 22 May 1986 not only did Neil Kinnock miss the twice-weekly confrontation with Mrs Thatcher, so too did Mr Hattersley. In an almost unprecedented move, it was a somewhat unprepared Denis Healey who had to face the Prime Minister across the dispatch boxes.

However, neither Neil Kinnock nor Roy Hattersley were on a foreign trip that day. Nor had illness or bad weather prevented them from making it to the Commons. Both men were well, and indeed working in central London, but felt they had more important business to see to. The National Executive Committee of the Labour Party was in the twenty-first hour of its hearings against certain members of the Liverpool Labour Party. Kinnock and Hattersley feared that if either of them left the meeting there might not be enough votes to secure a majority for expelling from party membership the chairman of Liverpool Council's Joint Shop Stewards' Committee, Ian Lowes.

It was not that Lowes was particularly important, but that for Kinnock the whole issue of Militant was. The Labour leader wanted finally to deal with the Trotskyist group once and for all. It was more than a decade since Militant's presence within the party had been brought to the attention of the party leadership. During that decade the party had first chosen not to take any action, and then failed to take effective action. Meanwhile Militant had grown from obscurity to national fame, from several hundred members to several thousand. All had been operating secretly within the structure of the Labour Party, and yet in reality operating as an independent revolutionary party. Indeed, with probably more influence and publicity than the Communist Party, and arguably more members, by 1986 Militant was effectively Britain's fifth most important political party.

This book is the story of that party, probably Trotsky's most successful group of followers in Britain, known internally as the Revolutionary Socialist League, publicly called the Militant tendency.* Militant is more than just a well-organised and successful

---

* The political organisation associated with the newspaper *Militant* was originally called the Revolutionary Socialist League (RSL). Indeed, the RSL preceded *Militant* itself by nine years. The editors of *Militant* have always publicly denied the existence of the RSL, and nowadays the name has largely fallen into disuse inside the organisation. Many journalists refer to the organisation as 'Militant Tendency' (with a capital 'T' and often without the definite article). This is wrong. Although Militant does refer to itself,

far-left Labour Party pressure group: its programme, aims and policies are not just a more extreme version of the views of Tony Benn or Eric Heffer. Its philosophy descends directly from Marx, Engels, Lenin and Trotsky, and virtually nobody else. As a result the tendency believes in the kinds of methods, policies and goals that would be rejected totally by most ordinary Labour Party members. Because it is a revolutionary group, membership involves far more than just licking envelopes, arranging public meetings and sending out newsletters. To be a member of Militant is almost to adopt a new way of life, which consumes most of one's spare time, energy and cash. Many who eventually leave the tendency are burned out and never again become involved in politics. In some ways Militant has more in common with religion than with democratic politics.

The Labour Party battle over Militant has received a great deal of coverage in the press, on radio and on television, and media treatment has itself played an important part in the drama. But in spite of this extensive publicity few members of the public understand who or what the Militant tendency is. Militant with a capital 'M' is often confused with militants with a small 'm'. Some people may still think the term 'Militant tendency' refers to the whole of the Labour far left and includes people such as Tony Benn. This false picture is often created, even encouraged, by certain parts of the press.

internally and externally, as 'the tendency', or 'our tendency', this term is used only in the same way that internally it occasionally calls itself a 'group' or an 'organisation'. The word 'tendency' is never given a capital 'T'. Throughout the book I will refer to the organisation simply as Militant, or as the Militant tendency (without a capital 'T') or, in the early stages, as the Revolutionary Socialist League. I shall use *Militant,* in italics, when referring to the tendency's newspaper.

I first encountered Militant when I helped to set up a Labour Party Young Socialists branch in Stockport in 1974. It was only weeks before Militant took the branch over, and I watched with a mixture of annoyance and admiration as Militant carried out its operation. I realised then that Militant was more than just a newspaper, but I was not quite sure what. Frustrated by my work in the Young Socialists, I decided thereafter to concentrate on the Labour Party itself.

I did not really encounter Militant again until I became a journalist with ITN in January 1980, at a time when the Labour Party National Executive was being urged to take action against the tendency. It struck me then that Militant was a good story waiting to be told, and as the Militant saga continued over the next few years I became increasingly surprised that no journalist had ever made a serious attempt to tell it. Eventually I came to the conclusion that I would have to do the job myself.

So what is the Militant tendency? How exactly is Militant organised? Where does it get its funds? What precisely does it stand for? What is its ultimate goal? Why has it had so much success? To what extent has that success been exaggerated? How influential is the organisation? How will Militant do in the future? How effective has Neil Kinnock been in tackling the tendency? This book aims to deal with these questions, but it is also a book about the Labour Party itself, revealing much about how the party works at all levels and detailing the events that led to the leadership's eventual decision to take disciplinary action against Militant. The book is not meant to be a hatchet job on Militant.

Certainly it contains things the tendency will not like to see in print, but Militant's leaders will admit, I hope, if only to themselves, that it is a fair account.

The work is based partly on *Militant*, the tendency's newspaper, its other official publications and a large number of secret internal documents which have leaked out of the organisation. The most important source, however, has been a series of discussions and interviews with more than seventy people, nearly all of them Labour Party members. These have included Militant members, Labour Party officials, MPs, trade union officers and journalists. Particularly helpful have been more than twenty-five Militant defectors, former members of the tendency who have been prepared to talk about the organisation and their lives in it.

Militant's leaders have given me only limited assistance. They did arrange interviews for me for the very first chapter I wrote, 'Militant Merseyside'. Afterwards it was made clear that further help would depend on the Militant leadership's seeing that chapter. With some reluctance I showed it to them. Since then, they have always been 'too busy' to meet me. However, perhaps I ought to thank *Militant* editor Peter Taaffe, if only for saving me considerable time and effort.

Many of the people I interviewed and who helped me wish to remain anonymous, for obvious reasons. I am grateful for the time they were able to spare me. Those whom I can thank publicly are, in alphabetical order: Graeme Atkinson, Mike Barnes, Robert Baxter, David Blunkett, Betty Boothroyd, Neil Brookes, Jeff Burns, Barrie Clarke, Tony Clarke, Ian Craig, Ken Cure, Sean

Davey, Jimmy Deane, John Dennis, Kieran Devaney, Pete Duncan, Pat Edlin, Keith Ellis, Frank Field, Rob Gibson, Alistair Graham, Michael Gregory, Peter Hadden, John Hamilton, Terry Harrison, Richard Hart, Millie Haston, Jom Heeren, Ellis Hillman, James Hogan, Steve Howe, David Hughes, Mike Hughes, Sean Hughes, Charles James, Patrick Jenkin, Robert Jones, Gavin Kennedy, Jane Kennedy, Laura Kirton, Tony Lane, Peter Lennard, Martin Linton, Terry McDonald, Stewart Maclennan, Sinna Mani, John Mann, David Mason, Pat Montague, Sally Morgan, Jim Mortimer, Dean Nelson, Tony Page, Greg Pope, Allan Roberts, Eddie Roderick, Tom Sawyer, Adrian Schwarz, Eric Shaw, Ken Smith, Pat Stacey, Nigel Stanley, Alfred Stocks, Paul Thompson, Els Tieman, Jonathan Timbers, Russell Tuck, Charles Turnock, Reg Underhill, Mitchell Upfold, Neil Vann, Richard Venton, Mark Walker, Frank Ward, John Ware, Larry Whitty, Alan Williams, Willie Wilson, Alex Wood, Frances Wood and Margaret Young.

For their assistance I must also thank the staff in the cuttings and photo libraries at ITN and the *Liverpool Post and Echo*; Stephen Bird, the archivist at Walworth Road; and the staff of the libraries at the universities of Oxford, Hull and Sussex, at the London School of Economics and Manchester Polytechnic, and at the British Newspaper Library at Colindale. My thanks also go to those who kindly read all or part of my manuscript and commented on it: my wife, Margaret, my father, John Crick, and mother, Patricia Crick; my ITN colleagues, Andrew Curry, Elinor Goodman, Lawrence McGinty, Paul McKee and David Walter; Simon Jenkins of *The Economist*; Michael Patchett-Joyce, Rosaleen Hughes, Jeremy

Mayhew and Bill Hamilton of A. M. Heath; and Tim Pearce, who did a lot of the detailed and painstaking research. Margaret Cornish eased my movements around Walworth Road. Caz Ratford and Ernie Holloway of ITN helped with the photographs. John Callaghan of Wolverhampton Polytechnic helped investigate the Deane Collection at Manchester Polytechnic. Finally, I am particularly grateful to Andrew Franklin, who encouraged the idea, and Sarah Hardie, who saw it through.

M. C.

June 1986

FOREWORD

It took one back to the 1980s. A sunny evening in early August 2015 – warm enough for politics *al fresco*. The street behind Camden Town Hall, just off the Euston Road in north London, had been transformed into a socialist bazaar. Along the pavement stood a row of stalls, in several cases converted wallpaper-pasting tables, selling the many different varieties of left-wing and Marxist newspaper, vying to catch the attention of the hundreds of Jeremy Corbyn supporters who were patiently queuing round three sides of the block, and beyond.

Jeremy Corbyn attracted about 2,000 people that night, far more than could be accommodated in the main hall of the Town Hall building. So Corbyn and his several supporting speakers worked on a shift system, doing the rounds of four separate gatherings on the site – in the main hall; in an annexe upstairs; in the canteen; and finally outside, addressing the 300 or so latecomers who hadn't been able to get into the building, from the roof of an old fire engine supplied by the Fire Brigades Union.

My editors at *Channel 4 News* had asked me to concentrate on talking to the young people energised that summer by the Corbyn campaign. What struck me, though, was just how old lots of the faces in the queue were – men and women in their sixties, seventies and eighties. These were people who would have gone to similar rallies three decades before, during the heyday of Tony Benn.

'It's unbelievable,' said a familiar figure, Chris Knight, who was out selling the *Labour Briefing* journal he's been editing since the late 1970s. 'I never thought I'd see scenes like this in my lifetime again.' For the Marxist newspaper-sellers in Camden, these, and similar crowds at other Corbyn campaign events, were an obvious source not just of one-off paper sales, but of potential long-term recruits. In several cases – notably *Socialist Worker* – their publications represented groups outside the Labour Party. 'Would they now join Labour if Corbyn was elected leader?' I asked, with a touch of mischief.

Just round the corner, I came across another table piled with copies of *The Socialist*. Trying to sell them was Sarah Sachs-Eldridge, national organiser of the Socialist Party. Here was the link with the subject of this book, for the Socialist Party are the main descendants of the Militant tendency, the Trotskyist group which for several decades successfully infiltrated the Labour Party, before hundreds of their members were expelled and most of the remainder left en masse in 1991.

Militant, in their prime, were brilliant at capturing newspaper and broadcast headlines. For many people unversed in the minu-tiae of Labour politics, the word Militant came to represent the hard or far left as a whole. Yet, the group was actually shunned by many others on the left – from the pro-Soviet elements in the Communist Party and left-wing unions such as the miners'; to the metropolitan, socially liberal left of Ken Livingstone and the old Greater London Council.

Jeremy Corbyn was never anywhere near being a member of Militant. And yet, in the mid-1980s, when Militant was fighting efforts by successive leaders Michael Foot and Neil Kinnock (aided by two pro-Labour barristers Derry Irvine and his young protégé Anthony Blair) to expel them, Corbyn defended Militant's right to remain in the Labour Party. Many Labour figures at that time – on both left and right – rather naively took Militant for what they claimed to be – a group of supporters of a Marxist newspaper. Jer-emy Corbyn, as an astute and active member of the London left, and a member of the editorial board of Chris Knight's magazine *London Labour Briefing*, would have known the truth as detailed in this book – that Militant were in effect a secret political party that had decided to operate clandestinely within the Labour Party. And Corbyn would also have known Militant's protestations, that it had no organisation, were utterly dishonest.

An article in the July 1982 edition of *London Labour Briefing* illustrated Corbyn's public stance: 'If expulsions are in order for Militant,' he wrote, 'they should apply to us too.' And Corbyn, a year before he became an MP, announced himself as 'provisional convenor' of the new 'Defeat the Witch-Hunt Campaign'. It was based at an address in Lausanne Road in Hornsey, north London, Corbyn's own home at that time.

This is the story of Militant, the Marxist, Trotskyist group whose presence inside the Labour Party Jeremy Corbyn tried to defend.

A NOTE ON THE TEXT

The first edition of this book was published under the title *Militant* in 1984. The second edition, which contained very substantial additions and updated the story, was published as *The March of Militant* two years later. For this edition, thirty years on, I have made a few small amendments to the 1986 text. Nearly all the changes are stylistic, or for greater clarity.

M. C.

JANUARY 2016

1

'I CALL THIS
AN OUTRAGE'

When the Labour Party National Executive Committee (NEC) decided, in February 1983, to expel five members of the Editorial Board of *Militant*, it was not the first time the Labour Party had tried to take action against a Marxist newspaper within its ranks. There was an important precedent and one that must have been disturbingly familiar to the then party leader, Michael Foot.

Nearly thirty years before, in the spring of 1954, the NEC had decided that 'Persons associated in any way with the editing and sale [of a journal called *Socialist Outlook*], or contributing to that journal, are declared to be ineligible for membership of the Labour Party.' The NEC minutes stated: 'From complaints that have been received it seems evident that a Trotskyist organisation is functioning within the Labour Party.'[1]

That decision in 1954 prompted a ferocious attack in *Tribune*, the leading journal of the Labour left. Under the heading 'I Call

This an Outrage', a former editor of *Tribune* wrote: 'For the first time in its history, so far as I am aware, the leaders of the Labour Party have taken steps to suppress a newspaper.' The article went on: 'Such a decree might fittingly be issued within a Fascist or Communist Party. That it should be issued by the leaders of a democratic party is an outrage.'[2]

The author of the article was Michael Foot. In 1982 *Tribune* was to reprint his words more than once, in a new campaign against the Labour Party NEC.[3] This time *Militant* was the Trotskyist paper the Executive was trying to suppress, and Michael Foot was leading the action.

Ever since the Labour Party established itself as the unchallenged representative of the British working class, the party leadership has constantly been in conflict with groups on the left who have felt that the party has not been sufficiently radical in its methods and policies. These groups range from revolutionary Marxists to what is often termed the 'legitimate left' (by those further to the right). They include groups, initially outside, who have decided deliberately to join the Labour Party in order to influence it from within, as well as groups of like-minded party members who have come together to press for some cause or other. But no matter how strong their dissent, and no matter how limited their prospects of advancement, these factions have usually preferred to remain inside the party – aware no doubt that groups which have left the party have always suffered drastically. The result has been a long history of disciplinary action by the party establishment against left-wing pressure groups and 'newspapers'. And one of the great ironies of this history has been that often the rebels of one generation have become the establishment of the next.

The history of Labour Party internal discipline did not really begin until the 1920s. In 1918 the party had introduced individual membership: until then it had been simply a federation of affiliated bodies, such as trade unions and socialist societies. One of the affiliated societies was a Marxist group, the Social Democratic Federation; another was the British Socialist Party, which later became the British Communist Party. Until 1918 all party members had to belong to an affiliated organisation rather than directly to the party. The advent of individual membership was to bring with it the problem of what to do when individual members grouped together in non-affiliated organisations outside the party's control. The same year, 1918, saw the Labour Party commit itself fully to socialism: the new constitution contained the famous Clause IV, which calls for common ownership. But while the party appeared to move leftwards, many felt that for electoral reasons, and in the wake of the Russian Revolution, Labour would have to distance itself from the ideas of Bolshevism if it was to become a serious party of government.

When the British Communist Party (CP) was formally established in 1920, it applied almost immediately for affiliation to the Labour Party. The Communist leaders pointed to the example of the left-wing Independent Labour Party which had been affiliated to the Labour Party since 1900; they argued that they should be allowed to join in the same way. But time and again in the early 1920s Labour conferences turned down the Communists' requests. The leadership argued that the CP's aims were not in accord with Labour's 'constitution, principles and programme' and said that the Communists would be loyal to the Soviet-led Communist International (Comintern) rather than to the Labour Party. Labour was perhaps right to be cautious: Lenin had urged his British comrades to support the Labour Party secretary Arthur Henderson 'as a rope supports the hanged'.[4]

It took some years for Labour to expel those Communists already inside its ranks. Under the existing rules Communists were for several years allowed to speak at conference and even to serve as Labour councillors and MPs: one case was Sharurji Saklatvala (one of Britain's first Asian MPs), who in 1922 was elected for Labour in Battersea North while openly being a Communist as well. Gradually, though, the loopholes were closed: Communists were barred from being individual Labour Party members and from selection as Labour candidates, and affiliated unions were asked not to choose Communists as delegates to the Labour conference. And in 1927 the NEC disbanded ten local Labour parties, most of them in London, because they had effectively been taken over by the CP.

Between 1928 and 1935 the problem of Communists in the party died down; the Comintern was now advising its supporters not to link up with the 'social fascists' in Western social democratic parties. After the 1935 election, though, the Communist general secretary, Harry Pollitt, once again applied for affiliation for his party. At one point it looked as though the Labour conference might agree, but a series of show trials staged by Stalin in the

Soviet Union ruined the British Communists' chances. They did not give up, however. A new tactic was employed instead. Over the next four years CP members secretly infiltrated hundreds of local Labour parties. Douglas Hyde, once news editor of the Communist *Daily Worker*, later revealed that he himself had organised a gradual Communist takeover of his local Labour Party in Surrey, secretly signing up the most promising members one by one. Eventually, when Hyde had recruited a large number of individuals to the CP, he gathered them together for what they all thought was just a meeting of local left-wing Labour Party members.

> When all had arrived I revealed that everyone present was already a Communist Party member, and suddenly they realised what had happened and just what strength the Party already had in the local Labour movement. Then we got down to business... From then on we functioned as a Communist Party group, continuing to keep our membership secret and working inside the Labour Party and Trades Council.[5]

After Munich, though, the CP decided that undercover members should leave as a political demonstration against the Labour leadership. 'Almost the whole of our group resigned from the Labour Party, getting maximum publicity for their action ... the Labour Party in that Division was all but wrecked, losing all its active and leading members at one move.'[6]

Another 'entrist' at this time was the young Denis Healey, chairman of the Oxford University Labour Club while openly carrying a CP card as well. 'I read all the basic books, but I never believed in it,' Healey said years later. 'It was more a reaction to Nazism. The really big issue was the rise of Hitler and the coming war. Any young man who was interested in stopping the war became a Communist at Oxford, whether he joined the party or not.'[7]

Towards the end of the 1930s disciplinary action was being taken not only against Communists but also against members who were working politically with the CP. Many socialists believed that the most important political priority at that time was to construct a United or Popular Front against fascism, involving socialists, Communists and even Liberals and Conservatives.

These were the years of Victor Gollancz's Left Book Club, the start of the newspaper *Tribune* and the sending of the International Brigade to fight against Franco in Spain. Thousands of socialists worked side by side with members of the CP: this did not necessarily mean that they were Communists themselves or that they were subject to every whim of Stalin's Communist International, much though some Labour Party officials may have believed that. True, the idea of 'Popular Fronts' with other parties had originated with the Communist International, but these socialists were not simply being manipulated by the CP. There was a genuine desire for unity against fascism; advocates of the 'Popular Front' were not necessarily Communist infiltrators.

At first the left-wing Socialist League, affiliated to the party, was the main proponent of 'unity' in the fight against fascism. The leaders of the League were Sir Stafford Cripps, the MP and wealthy barrister who provided most of the money; Aneurin Bevan and George Strauss, also MPs; Harold Laski; and G. D. H. Cole. Less well-known League leaders were two young journalists from *Tribune*: Michael Foot and Barbara Betts (the young Barbara Castle). Because it advocated 'unity', the League was disaffiliated in 1937 and, later, in January 1939, Cripps was expelled; a few months later four others followed, including Bevan and Strauss. It did not take long for the rebels to be rehabilitated, however. By 1942 Cripps was a Labour member of Churchill's Cabinet, and he later went on to be Chancellor of the Exchequer under Attlee. Bevan helped to draft the 1945 manifesto and served with distinction in the post-war Labour Cabinet. Strauss was to be a junior minister under Attlee and eventually Father of the House of Commons.

Members of the Labour Party youth section were also regarded as a 'nuisance' by the Labour leadership before the war. The majority left-wing group in the Labour League of Youth was led by Ted Willis, later to achieve fame as a writer. On the opposing side of the League was the young George Brown. The Willis faction of the Labour League of Youth Advisory Committee (its Executive Committee) decided to ignore the League's official paper, *New Nation*, because it was produced by Labour headquarters at Transport House. Instead they published their own journal, *Advance!*, which at one point achieved a remarkable circulation of 50,000. Naturally they supported Cripps and Bevan in their call for a 'Popular Front'. Their reward was suspension of their committee by Transport House; after months of argument Willis and most of his comrades eventually left the Labour Party and joined the Young Communist

League. After the war Willis re-joined Labour, and he has sat on the Labour benches in the House of Lords for the last twenty years.

Immediately after the war the CP hoped that its support of the wartime coalition would help its case for affiliation to the Labour Party, but its new application was rejected overwhelmingly by the 1946 Labour conference. That year conference also decided that no new national political organisation would ever be allowed to affiliate to the party. So CP tactics changed. Rather than infiltrate the Labour Party directly, the Communists built up a whole range of 'front organisations' designed to attract and influence Labour Party members. Some of these had been established before the war and often involved 'peace' or 'friendship' with a Communist country. Among such groups were the British–Romanian Association, the British Vietnam Committee, the British–China Friendship Committee and the World Peace Council. So as not to give the game away too obviously, each group had as its chairman not a CP member but a 'fellow-traveller', someone with Communist sympathies.

The Labour Party's response to these groups was the famous (perhaps notorious) List of Proscribed Organisations, originally established in 1930 to deal with Communist infiltration then. Labour Party members were not allowed to belong to groups on the list. Among the casualties was a trade union official, Jim Mortimer, who was forced to leave the party in the early 1950s for being vice-chairman of the British–China Friendship Association. Thirty years later, as Labour Party general secretary, Mortimer was to establish another kind of list, a 'List of Approved Organisations', in his fight against Militant.

Nearly all groups on the Proscribed List were CP bodies, but in 1951 the name of the Socialist Fellowship was added. This was a left-wing pressure group designed to bring together MPs, trade unionists and rank-and-file party members. It had several branches around the country, held national conferences and had its own policy. But in time the Socialist Fellowship increasingly came to be dominated by a secret Trotskyist organisation called The Club, which was run by Gerry Healy, a former member of the Trotskyist Revolutionary Communist Party and later leader of the Workers' Revolutionary Party. Closely associated with the Socialist Fellowship was the newspaper *Socialist Outlook*, which in 1954[8] was also banned on the grounds that some of its contributors were 'known for their previous association with the Trotskyist Revolutionary Communist Party'.[9] Among those expelled because of their links with *Socialist Outlook* was a 21-year-old called Ted Knight, nearly thirty years later to become Labour leader of Lambeth Council. The NEC's action led to the *Tribune* article by Michael Foot quoted above.

At the time Foot and the group around Aneurin Bevan – the Bevanites – worked closely with Gerry Healy and his newspaper. Indeed, when *Socialist Outlook* was eventually forced to fold because of a libel action, Gerry Healy began writing for *Tribune*. (Years later Michael Foot was to be reminded by Eric Heffer of his close associations with Healy, much to Foot's embarrassment.) The Bevanites argued that the banning of *Socialist Outlook* was just the first step in a large-scale witch-hunt against the Labour left. Foot told a meeting in London that if the NEC got away with banning *Socialist Outlook*, it would 'look around for the next one on the list'.[10] It was exactly the same argument as that used by the left today against the banning of *Militant*. In the 1950s the left's fears were understandable. The period saw several moves against Aneurin Bevan and his supporters, Foot included.

The accusations against the Bevanites will be familiar to observers of the modern Labour Party. Attlee spoke of them as 'a party within a party, with separate leadership, separate meetings, supported by its own press'.[11] In Parliament the Bevanite group of MPs was forced to open up its meetings to outsiders and in the end had to disband altogether. Quite apart from the action against *Socialist Outlook*, it was suggested by some on the right that *Tribune* should be outlawed as well.

Accounts of party meetings from the period show they were just as bitter, if not worse, than those of today. Richard Crossman said that the NEC had a 'detestable atmosphere'; according to Ian Mikardo, Tom Driberg was 'wrung out like a dish rag' after each meeting, 'desperate for a large drink'; Michael Foot described Parliamentary Labour Party (PLP) meetings as 'gruesome'.[12] Yet in the 1950s the policy differences between the two sides were minor compared with those of the Labour Party in recent times.

The feud reached its peak in the spring of 1955, as Bevan and Gaitskell squared up for the contest to succeed Attlee. In March Bevan attacked Attlee in a Commons debate on nuclear weapons and was promptly expelled from the PLP. Soon it looked almost certain that Bevan would also be expelled from the Labour Party itself – for the second time. Hugh Gaitskell and Arthur Deakin saw it as their chance finally to get rid of him. As the crucial NEC meeting approached, Bevan looked doomed. Deakin seemed to have sewn up most of the trade union and women members – the majority of the NEC. The episode had remarkable parallels with recent events. As with the expulsion of Militant members in both 1983 and 1986, the turmoil erupted when a general election was approaching, but the leadership, far from being reluctant to take action because of the prospect of going to the polls, believed that Bevan was an electoral liability and that his expulsion would increase the party's chances of victory. In the end, however, against the odds and almost by accident, Bevan survived by one vote.

Within two years Bevan was de facto second in command of the party.[13] In the poll for the new shadow Cabinet immediately after the 1955 election, the PLP voted Bevan into seventh position – just three months after having voted to eject him from their ranks. In the autumn of 1957, when the two former arch-enemies, Gaitskell and Bevan, had become leader of the party and shadow Foreign Secretary respectively, they gave the press a unique political photo. Just before the Brighton conference the two men could be seen walking arm in arm along the sea front at Brighton. 'Remarkable,' said journalist Leslie Hunter to a nearby trade unionist. 'Remarkable?' came the quick reply. 'That's not remarkable, it's a bloody miracle.'[14] And by 1959 Bevan was deputy leader.

Michael Foot, perhaps because he was less important, was luckier than Bevan and always managed to hold on to his party card. But he was less fortunate in the PLP. After Bevan's death in 1960 Foot returned to the Commons as MP for his hero's old seat, Ebbw Vale. But not long after, the future Labour leader was one of five left-wing MPs who lost the whip for voting against the Conservative defence estimates (the instructions were to abstain). Considering the widespread dissent within the PLP in modern times, it seems surprising that such extreme action should have been taken, but that was how the party worked under the leadership of Hugh Gaitskell. PLP membership was not restored to Foot and his colleagues until after Harold Wilson's election in 1963, which meant that Foot could not vote in the leadership poll. During his long career in Parliament Foot achieved the distinction of being perhaps the greatest rebel of them all: in the period from 1945 to 1970, when he joined the front bench, Foot probably voted against his party more than any other Labour MP; on the Tory side only Enoch Powell rebelled more often.[15]

This chapter has tried to put the events of the recent Militant story into historical perspective. The Labour Party has a long history of expulsions, of discipline by the leadership against left-wing rebel groups that have been considered electorally damaging or just politically irritating: Militant is only the most recent. What is so fascinating about the party's history is that rebels should so easily become leaders. As far as this story is concerned, it is particularly ironic that three of the main leaders of the recent campaign against Militant should themselves have all incurred the wrath of party officials at one time or another: Denis Healey, the Communist 'infiltrator' in the 1930s; Jim Mortimer, member of a proscribed organisation; and, above all, Michael Foot.

But perhaps more important, so far as the story of Militant is concerned, is that the memories of heavy-handed discipline in the 1930s and 1950s were to have a profound effect on the party in later years. Harold Wilson's Labour Party was to be much more tolerant than Hugh Gaitskell's; expulsions were rare, and the Proscribed List fell into disuse simply because nobody bothered to update it. Ron Hayward claims that when he became general secretary in 1972 he personally burned the Transport House files on left-wingers. By the 1970s the NEC contained many people who had once experienced party discipline themselves. They were determined not to allow a return to what they saw as the 'McCarthyism' of the past.

2

THE PERMANENT REVOLUTIONARY

From the late 1920s to the present day the history of British Trotskyism has been a tale of splits and mergers, of internal wrangling and bitterness, of argument rather than action. Each of the successive sects and factions seems to have detested its Trotskyist rivals far more than any of its natural enemies on the right of British politics. Uninitiated outsiders have considerable difficulty in working out the subtle political differences between the various groupings. The key point to grasp in studying the revolutionary left of British politics is that questions of tactics are often more divisive than ideology, personalities a more frequent cause of strife than policy. The followers of Leon Trotsky, like those of Jesus Christ, may all believe in the teachings of the same man, but they have rarely been united.

Trotsky's followers have suffered possibly more divisions in Britain than anywhere else. And what makes the progression particularly difficult to understand is that as one sect has replaced another, each has felt obliged to compose its name from a holy list of about twelve words, among them: Workers, Labour, Socialist, International, Revolutionary, Marxist, Communist, Militant, Group, Party, Tendency and League. According to the rules of the game of 'Select-a-Sect', you can pick any two or three from the above list and make yourself a new Trotskyist grouping. You might end up with the Workers' International League, the Militant Labour League, the International Marxist Group, the Revolutionary Socialist League, the Revolutionary Communist Party or the Workers' Revolutionary Party. All of these, and dozens more, exist now or have existed at one time or another.

After Stalin succeeded to the leadership of the Soviet Communist Party on Lenin's death in 1924, his opponents within the Soviet Union began to gather around Lenin's right-hand man during the Russian Revolution and founder of the Red Army, Leon Trotsky. They adopted the title of the Left opposition. Apart from personality differences, the division between the two men was over which course the revolution should follow from that point onwards. Since 1906 Trotsky had believed in the idea of permanent revolution and was convinced that his country could achieve socialism only if there were worldwide revolution. In Trotsky's view, it had been possible for the Bolsheviks to achieve power purely within national boundaries, but it would be impossible for the Soviet Union to proceed to socialism without revolutionary developments elsewhere. Stalin, on the other hand, proposed 'socialism in one country', partly in opposition to Trotsky's position. The Soviet leader believed that his country could create a socialist society on its own.

The division between the two men spread to the Communist International (the Comintern or Third International), the organisation founded in Moscow in 1919 to unite those parties formerly in the Second International that supported the Bolshevik Revolution. (The Second International had split in 1914 over the member parties' different attitudes to the First World War, and afterwards the 'reformist' members formed their own Socialist International.) In the Comintern Trotsky's supporters adopted the title of the International Left Opposition (ILO). Eventually the differences between Stalin and Trotsky became so great, however, that in 1929 Trotsky was banished to Turkey, and his supporters were purged from the Communist International, which had become totally dominated by Stalin. But the Trotskyists kept up their struggle.

In Britain Trotsky gained no significant support until the early 1930s, and then it was split into two groups. One group worked within the British Communist Party until it was expelled in 1932; the other operated inside the Independent Labour Party (ILP), which until 1932 was affiliated to the Labour Party. From the very beginning Trotskyists in this country were divided over how they should proceed. Such tactical differences have afflicted British Trotskyism to this day.

Long after his expulsion from the Soviet Union, Trotsky himself remained convinced that his followers should be loyal to the Communist International, even though they were actually banned from it, and that they should work within Communist parties. According to his biographer, Isaac Deutscher,

Trotsky was initially totally opposed to the idea that his supporters should form their own Fourth International to challenge the Comintern:

> Trotsky believed that with all their flaws and vices the Communist parties still represented the militant vanguard of the working classes. The opposition's place was with that vanguard. If he and his followers were to turn their backs on it, they would voluntarily go out into the wilderness into which Stalin was driving them.[1]

But from 1933 Trotsky's position changed. The failure of the German Communists (the KPD) to unite with the German Social Democrats against Nazism had finally convinced him that no further progress could be made inside Communist parties. From now on he was to recommend his famous policy of 'entrism' (sometimes spelt 'entryism' – strong advocates are said to have 'enteritis') to supporters in all Western countries: they should abandon Communist parties and instead 'enter' the mass social democratic parties. The most notable example of entrism by Trotskyists occurred in France, where Trotsky had a strong following. There he advised them to join the French socialist party, the SFIO, and to 'carry their revolutionary programme to the masses'. This radical change of tactics became known as the 'French turn', and Trotsky recommended the same entrist policy to his supporters in other countries: the United States, Chile, Belgium and Spain. In Britain he had advocated entrism as early as 1933 but did not, as might have been expected, recommend 'entering' the main mass party, the Labour Party. Since his British supporters were numerically very weak, Trotsky felt they would have more influence inside the smaller Independent Labour Party (ILP).

In 1932 the ILP had disaffiliated from the Labour Party in an argument over whether ILP MPs should be answerable to the Labour Party or to the ILP. Over the next few years the ILP started moving leftwards but also lost most of its members. Trotsky was confident, though, that at some future date a more left-wing ILP would come to reaffiliate to the Labour Party. He saw the potential situation in Britain as a series of levers. His followers could have a significant effect as a lever within the ILP;[2] in turn, he hoped, an ILP under their influence, once reaffiliated, would act as a radical lever inside the Labour Party itself.

But again Trotsky's British troops were divided: not all thought the ILP worth entering. Many favoured a more direct approach and entered the Labour Party instead. By 1936 Trotsky accepted that ILP entry should be abandoned: although Trotskyist numbers had increased sixfold, within the ILP there had been no political victories. Entrism within the Labour Party, it was now thought, might be politically more profitable. Trotsky wrote to his British supporters:

> It is understood that, regardless of how we enter, we will have a secret faction from the very beginning. Our subsequent actions will depend on our progress within the LP [Labour Party]. It is very important that we do not lay ourselves open at the beginning to attacks from the LP bureaucracy, which will result in our expulsion

without having gained any appreciable strength ... While it is necessary for the revolutionary party to maintain its independence at all times, a revolutionary group of a few hundred comrades is not a revolutionary party and can work most effectively at present by opposition to the social patriots within the mass parties.[3]

Independent existence for the Trotskyists at that time just would not work – the numbers were too small. Nevertheless, it is clear from Trotsky's writings that he saw entrism as very much a short-term tactic.

Modern Trotskyists are still divided over the purpose of entrism. Two types of entrism have evolved, both of which cite Trotsky's work as justification. One is the 'raiding party' type of entrism: Trotskyists go into a mass party to win converts and then leave as a much strengthened force. The work in the ILP in the 1930s had turned out to be of this type, and, as we have seen in Chapter 1, Lenin argued for a similar tactic in the Labour Party in the 1920s. The other sort of entrism, termed 'Waiting for Lefty' by Tariq Ali,[4] involves joining a party at a time of social and political upheaval in order to be in the forefront of the revolution when the right moment comes. The long-term secret entrism later adopted by Militant – sometimes called 'deep entrism' – seems to be a modified version of this.

In the mid-1930s in Britain one set of Trotskyists – called the Balham Group – operated within the Labour Party in south London and were active within the Socialist League. The party authorities knew what these Trotskyists were up to but did not pay them too much attention, since the NEC was concerned at that time about a much bigger problem: infiltration by members of the Communist Party.

Another Trotskyist group (internally known as the Revolutionary Socialist League) became active in the Labour Party youth section, the Labour League of Youth, rallying around a monthly paper called *Young Militant*. By 1937 this group was selling nearly 2,000 copies of its journal and was the biggest Trotskyist group yet seen in Britain. That year it publicly adopted the title of the Militant Labour League and later its paper was simply called *Militant*. Here was a 'Militant tendency' active in the Labour Party nearly twenty years before the present Militant tendency was even set up. This group, like its successor, quickly learned that young members of the Labour Party are a good source of recruits.

The Militant Labour League was not the first to use the name 'Militant': it had been borrowed from Trotsky's followers in America, who had been publishing a newspaper called *The Militant* since 1928. Several thousand copies of the paper had crossed the Atlantic to be sold here. But the name 'Militant' is not the only link with the present-day group. It is at this point in the story that we first meet the man who has been one of the leading figures of British Trotskyism for half a century and who today is the spiritual leader of the Militant tendency: Ted Grant.

In the mid-1930s a group of six South African Trotskyists arrived in ones and twos from Johannesburg. All had been involved in left-wing politics in their homeland, organising strikes among black workers and suffering police harassment and arrests.

But the prospects at home were extremely limited: even left-wing whites in South Africa did not trust them. Britain was a more likely starting-point for the revolution than South Africa and was obviously the place to go.

The first to take the boat trip from Johannesburg were Sid Frost and Ted Grant. Frost had been called Max Bosch but changed his name on arrival, and it is likely that Ted Grant had changed his name as well. After spending about a fortnight in Paris en route, where they met several leading French Trotskyists, Grant and Bosch arrived in London in December 1934. The first known record of Ted Grant's presence in Britain is a small advertisement in the March 1935 edition of the ILP paper, *New Leader*, for a party meeting in Clapham addressed by Grant on the subject of 'Workers' Movements in South Africa'.[5] Grant seems initially to have joined the ILP but within a few months followed other ILP Trotskyists into the Militant Labour League and the Labour Party.

Another to make the journey from Johannesburg was Millie Lee (later Millie Haston). Today, retired and living in Clapham, she reviews Ted Grant's subsequent career with astonishment:

> Ted had always been a full-time revolutionary, right from the age of seventeen when we first met him, but he was never an organiser. Ted never seemed to have the sort of personality which would attract his own following, but nevertheless he did. And he's saying exactly the same things now as he was saying then – like a gramophone record that got stuck forty years ago.[6]

Within a year of joining the Militant Labour League the six South Africans had broken away to form their own group, the Workers' International League (WIL). It occurred not so much because of political disagreements but as a result of personality clashes and resentment towards the South African newcomers. Others to leave with them were a Scotsman, Jock Haston, and Gerry Healy, a former Communist Party member who had joined the Militant Labour League after a violent argument with Haston at Speakers' Corner.

In September 1938 Trotsky and his followers from around the world held a conference at a house in Perigny, a village just outside Paris, called the 'Lausanne Conference' for security reasons. Present were twenty delegates from eleven countries. This was the founding conference of the Fourth International, a worldwide organisation of Trotskyists who saw it as the natural successor to the Second and Third (Communist) Internationals, which they now regarded as 'morally dead'. The British delegation to the conference came from the Militant Labour League, not the breakaway Workers' International League. Afterwards the Militant Labour League became the Fourth International's official British section. The Labour Party responded by proscribing it.

So during the key event in Trotskyist history Ted Grant and his comrades were left out in the cold. Furthermore, their Workers' International League was tiny – just nineteen members to start with – compared with the rival Militant Labour League, whose membership numbered several hundred. Grant's group was ignored by Trotsky and the Fourth International. Because of this disagreement Ted Grant never met the 'Old Man' in the period between Grant's arrival from South Africa and Trotsky's assassination in 1940.

Soon the Militant Labour League publicly adopted its internal title, the Revolutionary Socialist League (RSL). Meanwhile Grant and the small WIL set out on their own road, determined to wrest from the RSL the honour of being the Fourth International's British section. They started a new monthly journal, *Youth for Socialism* (later called *Socialist Appeal*), which Grant edited, and a newspaper, *Workers' International News*. Even though there was a war on, the WIL was very active and held regular public meetings. It is interesting to note that at one meeting in August 1941, on the anniversary of Trotsky's assassination, the two main speakers were Ted Grant and Gerry Healy. The chairman that evening was Syd Bidwell, who today is Labour MP for Ealing Southall.

In spite of its split with the official group, the WIL carried on for a while practising entrism within the Labour Party. Ted Grant himself must have been a member of the party at this time, although it is unlikely that he was very active. Today Grant boasts of having been a Labour Party member since 1950 but omits to mention any period of membership before the war. In any case, in 1941 the WIL abandoned entrism because it saw it as a good tactic only where the reformist party was 'in a state of flux, where political life is at a high pitch and where the members are steadily moving left. It is essentially a short-term perspective for work in a milieu where favourable prospects exist for a short space of time.'[7] The wartime coalition had, in the view of the WIL, made the Labour Party a 'moribund political force'. During the war both the

Labour Party and the trade unions had agreed to moderate political and industrial activities in support of the coalition. The WIL's departure from the Labour Party was a move which gave it scope for militant political and industrial action.

Within a few years Grant and his comrades had achieved a much stronger position than that of the rival RSL, which had remained entrist. By 1944, in fact, the RSL was so weak that the Fourth International persuaded it to merge with the WIL and to form the new Revolutionary Communist Party (RCP) – a title which greatly annoyed the official Communist Party. In effect, though, it was more of a takeover than a merger. Jock Haston became the RCP general secretary; *Socialist Appeal* became the party's paper, with Grant continuing as editor; and the WIL took the bulk of the places on the new RCP central committee. The RCP became the Fourth International's official British section, and the first two delegates were Haston and Grant. Grant and his comrades had worked their way back into the official Trotskyist fold, and they had done so mainly through their decision to leave the temporarily 'moribund' Labour Party.

For three years British Trotskyists were almost totally united for the only time in their history. The RCP was quite successful at first, at least by its own standards: it had twelve full-time workers and perhaps as many as 600 members. It played a leading role in the increasing number of industrial disputes. At one point three RCP leaders (though not Grant) were jailed for encouraging apprentices to resist ballots for selecting 'Bevin boys' to go down the mines. Questions were asked in the Commons about the sale of *Socialist Appeal* in the coalfields, and the Cabinet even considered banning the party.[8]

In April 1944 the Home Secretary, Herbert Morrison, prepared a paper on the RCP for the War Cabinet. Grant's name was fairly prominent:

> Edward Grant. Editor of *Socialist Appeal*, aged 30, is also South African and has been connected with the Workers' International League since its inception. He was posted to the Pioneer Corps but fractured his skull before joining up and was discharged. It has proved impossible, owing to the effects of his injury, to find him alternative employment.[9]

This meant that Grant was able to carry on working full-time at politics. Indeed, it seems he worked so hard that, according to the Cabinet papers, he suffered a nervous breakdown.[10]

Frank Ward was another leading member of both the WIL and then the RCP in this period. Until recently he was Information Officer at the Labour Party headquarters at Walworth Road. After the war Ward was an RCP organiser in Glasgow and then Manchester, earning a meagre £2 a week. Ward remembers that Grant and Haston worked side by side as leaders of the RCP. Haston was the main organiser, as opposed to Grant, whom he remembers as a 'writer' and 'lecturer':

> He was never organised. Millie [Haston] basically edited the paper, though Ted would make the decisions. Sometimes it was impossible

to get him to write the editorials; we had to lock him and Jock into a room to make them write them. On one occasion they climbed out of the window though, and nipped down to the local flea-pit.[11]

Sammy Bornstein also worked with Grant in the RCP. Today he is a Labour Party member in Finchley:

I haven't seen him in years. But I knew him quite well. Rather colourless, never struck me as a personality. But he was able to hold an audience when he spoke. Nobody really knew Ted. You'd have a drink, eye up the girls – but not Ted. He was very serious ... Ted's always been the same. Since 1945 he has been predicting a slump.[12]

As we shall see, the Ted Grant of the 1930s and 1940s was very much the same as the Ted Grant of today. People who knew him then say much the same things about him as those who work with him now. And his political outlook has hardly changed at all.

With the end of the Second World War the RCP went into decline. The wartime coalition was now over and the Labour Party was again on the political stage, making a spectacular comeback with its landslide victory in 1945. The RCP leaders, optimistic as always, predicted that Attlee would 'do a Ramsay MacDonald' and betray the Labour movement. They were to be disappointed. The post-war Labour government proceeded to nationalise the major industries and to build the welfare state. Arguments about 'betrayal' were difficult to sustain. The British economy soon moved back to full employment, and an era of growth began.

The RCP's belief that capitalism was on the point of collapse started to look somewhat unconvincing. And while one Trotskyist enemy, social democracy, was succeeding in Britain, the other, Stalinism, was flourishing abroad. The Soviet Union had emerged from the war with considerable international prestige and control of Eastern Europe. The 1949 revolution in China, backed by the Soviet Union, was regarded as another feather in Stalin's cap.

Slowly the RCP broke up. The Fourth International wanted its British comrades to readopt the entrist tactic, but most of the RCP argued that the time was not right. Since the formation of the RCP in 1944, a minority group, led by Gerry Healy, had practised entrism and for several years produced a journal called *Militant*. Later Healy's group began *Socialist Outlook* for its Labour Party work (see Chapter 1). The official RCP paper, Ted Grant's *Socialist Appeal*, appeared less frequently.

Gradually the minority faction had been gaining the upper hand, and for most RCP comrades entry now seemed the only option. Grant himself was not keen on the idea but did not think it worth causing internal strife over the issue. In a signed statement to a colleague he wrote:

Discussion in the party on the question of entry has naturally provoked a crisis in the organisation … under the given conditions, the best tactic for the party is the maintenance of the independent party.

The discussion has not convinced us that in the present situation entry would constitute a superior tactic. However, faced with the fact that the overwhelming majority of the leadership and the trained cadres, and a substantial section of the rank and file, are in favour of entering the Labour Party, and given that the objective situation will be a difficult one for the party, we believe that a struggle in the party [the RCP] would be sterile.[13]

So it was that when the RCP was finally disbanded in 1950 Ted Grant came to re-join the Labour Party.

Frank Ward looks back on those years in the WIL and the RCP, the late 1930s and 1940s, as 'the age when Trotskyism grew up'. 'It was an attempt', he says, 'to deal with what the world looked like on the limited evidence of the 1930s. Before the war it wasn't easy to see that Stalin would maintain his position in the Soviet Union, or that there would be economic expansion in the West after the war.'[14] In June 1950 the RCP general secretary, Jock Haston, and his wife, Millie, renounced Trotskyism and joined the Labour Party. Frank Ward went with them. The rest of the RCP had no choice but to join Healy's group inside the Labour Party, The Club. But soon Healy began expelling many of the leading individuals who had joined him. The result was that three separate groups quickly formed around three key figures: Gerry Healy himself, Tony Cliff, an immigrant from Palestine, and Ted Grant. These three factions have dominated British Trotskyism to this day. (It is interesting to note that none of the three was British. All came from former parts of the British Empire: Healy from Ireland, Cliff from Palestine and Grant from South Africa.)

Healy's group, The Club, later became the Socialist Labour

League and then the Workers' Revolutionary Party (WRP). For the time being, at least, Healy kept the Fourth International franchise. Cliff's faction, the *Socialist Review* group, who were known as the 'state caps' because of their belief that the Soviet Union was state capitalist, later became the International Socialists and eventually the Socialist Workers' Party (SWP). And Grant's group went on to become the Militant tendency. Relations between the three groups have often been bitter, especially between Healy and Grant. Only four years after the parting of the ways Grant abstained at a meeting of his local Labour Party in East Islington when it voted to expel two Healyites.

In the years since the collapse of the RCP all three groups have at one time or another practised entrism inside the Labour Party. Until recently both the Cliff group, the SWP, and the Healy group, the WRP, which split in 1985, rejected entrism. However, there is evidence that in recent years both parties have attempted entrism on a very small scale – the WRP through the London-based journal *Labour Herald*, whose commissioning editor was recently revealed to be a former member of the WRP's central committee.[15] Of the three, in terms of political outlook the Grant faction has changed the least from that of the old WIL and RCP.

But while the entrism of the Healy and Cliff groups eventually came up against Labour Party discipline in the 1950s and 1960s, Ted Grant and his colleagues survived this period virtually unscathed. This was largely because for a long period they were by far the least significant of the three factions. At one point in the early 1950s a Labour Party official did try to use Grant's past record to expel him from his local party in Islington, but without success. For fourteen years Grant carried on publishing insignificant Trotskyist newspapers and worked, almost unseen, within the Labour Party. Unlike Haston and Ward, but just like Healy and Cliff, Grant never gave up being a revolutionary. 'When the party disintegrated most of us found jobs and some dropped out of politics altogether,' says Frank Ward. 'But Ted had nowhere to go to. He needed a social grouping to carry on as a part-time revolutionary.'[16]

Grant stayed in London and began a small magazine, *International Socialist*, which declared itself a 'rallying centre for the left in the Labour Party'. In the first issue, in February 1952, Grant declared:

> The British masses in the upheavals and convulsions of tomorrow will find the way to a Marxist policy. Armed with this, the Labour movement will overthrow capitalism and together with the workers on the Continent organise a Socialist United States of Europe. The alternatives are either Fascism and war or the victory of the working class. There can be no middle road.[17]

Buy a copy of *Militant* more than thirty years later and there on the back page, at the bottom of a list of principles for which *Militant* stands, is the same call for a 'Socialist United States of Europe'.[18] However, *International Socialist* existed for only seven issues, the last of which came out in April 1954.

Associated with the magazine was the International Socialist

Group, which had actually been formed fifteen months before the first issue came out. The group had a formal organisation and held regular meetings above a restaurant in the Finchley Road, in north London. Its activities, such as they were, were confined almost entirely to London, and there were no more than fifty members at the most. The group was so weak, however, that meetings frequently had to be abandoned because there was not even a quorum. The Grantites were in a sorry state.

3

THE LIVERPOOL CONNECTION

On the first floor of the library of Manchester Polytechnic, next to the shelves holding politics material, is a small windowless room. Students probably hardly notice it, and the door is always kept locked. Inside is a desk, a chair, a typewriter, a wooden cabinet with card-indexes, and on the wall three metal shelves containing 104 green box files. These house the Jimmy Deane collection, an archive of letters, notes, minutes, articles, financial documents and other material that provides the most interesting and conclusive documentary evidence ever publicly discovered about the origins of Militant.

Access to the Deane Collection is not easy. The papers are divided into two parts – an open section, which anybody can look at, and a closed section that is available only to bona fide academic researchers, and then only after permission has been granted by the polytechnic lecturer who supervises the collection, Brian Ripley. Journalists are not given access, and Labour

Party members are not welcome either. Unpublished documents cannot be photocopied. Perhaps not surprisingly, according to the librarian only four outsiders have bothered to inspect it since the collection was donated by Jimmy Deane in 1982.

James Augustus Bargrave Deane was born in Liverpool in January 1921. He joined the British Trotskyist movement in 1937 while still a teenager, and met Ted Grant in the Workers' International League. On his father's side, Deane's family was descended from members of the Irish Protestant aristocracy, and Deane himself is a distant cousin of Hastings Fitzmaurice Tilson Deane, the 8th Baron Muskerry. On his mother's side, the family had a long Marxist tradition in the Liverpool Labour movement. Deane's maternal grandfather, Charles Carrick Wilson, was elected president of the Liverpool Trades Council in 1905, served for fourteen years as one of Liverpool's first Labour councillors, and was an organiser for the Marxist Social Democratic Federation. Deane's mother, Gertie, a former suffragette, often entertained leading socialists such as Jim Larkin and H. M. Hyndman at the Deane home, and is still a Labour Party member in Liverpool.[1] Jimmy's brothers, Brian and Arthur, also became active Trotskyists: Brian at one time served as a Liverpool councillor, while Arthur was also a councillor, in Hackney and then Croydon, and pursued a career as a union official. But the most important was Jimmy.

Today Jimmy Deane lives on the outskirts of Wigan. Divorced and now retired, he seems rather a sad figure. Deane went through several years of unemployment and illness before reaching sixty-five, and he looks at the achievements of Derek Hatton and his colleagues in Liverpool with what seems to be a mixture of admiration and envy. For if anybody can be described as the real founding father of Militant in Liverpool it is the unsung James Deane.

Deane formed his own branch of the Workers' International League in Liverpool in 1939 when still only eighteen. After the start of the war, Deane became a League organiser, first in Lancashire and Cheshire and then the north-west as a whole, though he was also employed as an apprentice electrician in the Cammell Laird shipyard in Birkenhead. When British Trotskyists united in the Revolutionary Communist Party in 1944, Deane went to London to work full time for the party, and joined the editorial board of *Socialist Appeal*, which was then edited by Ted Grant.[2]

After the war Deane returned to Merseyside, where he resumed work as an electrician, and the RCP again became a part-time activity. He became quite active in the Labour Party in the Walton constituency, north of the city centre, which at that time was the only left-wing Labour Party in Liverpool.

In 1948, Deane helped to start a Marxist magazine in the Birkenhead Labour League of Youth – the Labour Party youth section – called *Rally!* (which stood for 'Read All about the Labour League of Youth'). *Rally!* was to survive in Liverpool on and off for a remarkably long period (often under the name *Rally for Socialism*). Sometimes the magazine was properly printed; more often it was simply duplicated. It was essentially a paper for young members of the Labour Party and campaigned vigorously for a youth charter of rights for young people. This small, sporadic,

Merseyside-based magazine, first published sixteen years before *Militant*, can nevertheless be described as one of the two main forerunners of *Militant*.

In the late 1940s and 1950s the Marxist politics of *Rally!* found very limited support amid the robust old-style politics of the Liverpool Labour Party. At that time, as indeed it was for most of its history, the Liverpool Labour Party was a very right-wing body, and the unusual traditions of Liverpool Labour politics partly explain why Militant's politics were eventually to meet with success.

Only in recent times have Liverpool politics ceased to be dominated by religion. In the late nineteenth century, and during the first decade of this century, the sectarian divisions often became violent, with large-scale religious riots in 1909 and a state of emergency declared in Liverpool in 1910. Until the 1920s the main opposition to the Conservatives and Liberals had not been Labour but the Irish Nationalists, who had several Liverpool councillors and, remarkably, for many years even boasted a Liverpool MP. The Nationalists could always count on the Roman Catholic vote, but with the partition of Ireland in 1921 the party quickly died out, and nearly all its members and supporters switched to Labour.

This meant that the Labour Party was dominated by Catholics until well after the Second World War, and in the 1930s and 1940s was effectively run by a Catholic machine. But since only about a quarter of Liverpool voters were Catholic, such an overwhelmingly Catholic party could never take over the town hall. Rather than vote Labour, many working-class Protestants supported the Working Men's Conservative Association, and it was not until 1955 that Labour gained full control of Liverpool Council for the first time. Even recently the religious influence has remained: councillors standing as 'Protestants' were elected as late as 1972, while the Catholic Action group has only just ceased being a major force inside the Labour Party.

Liverpool University lecturer Tony Lane believes this Catholic inheritance created a style of Labour politics which has lasted ever since:

> There has always been a flavour of Tammany Hall about the Labour Party in Liverpool ... Where in other parts of Britain the Labour Party fell heir to the radical wing of the Liberal Party, no such process took place in Liverpool. The Labour Party, instead of inheriting the democratic, nonconformist tradition of the Liberal Party, acquired the conspiratorialism of Irish politics as practised in England.[3]

In the post-war years the Labour Party was dominated by the Braddocks. Jack Braddock was Labour leader on Liverpool Council, and his wife Bessie served as MP for Liverpool Exchange. The Braddocks in Liverpool have provided one of the best examples of local boss politics in Labour Party history; the *New Statesman* once compared Liverpool with Mayor Daley's Chicago, calling the city 'Cook County, UK'.[4] But Braddock was not the first Liverpool boss: Tory leaders such as Thomas White and Archibald Salvidge, and Luke Hogan for Labour in the 1930s and 1940s, developed a style of city leadership Liverpool seems to cultivate – the American-style city boss, a Mr Fixit, ruling with patronage and the promise of jobs, surrounded by a slight whiff of corruption. According to historian Robert Baxter:

> Braddock found his supporters among the politically illiterate working men of the city centre. From the slumland wards of the riverfront came councillors whose primary reason for being in politics was to obtain a social status and satisfaction that was denied them in their everyday lives. These people had little concern with the policies that the leadership pursued. They were interested in status and their support could be won by a leader who would reward their loyalty with prizes that were, in themselves, unimportant, but to the recipient they conferred prestige. Membership of the Parks and Gardens Committee is rarely of political significance, but to an unskilled labourer who is used to no social respect, the committee's lunches and tours of inspection can afford considerable satisfaction.[5]

And, of course, the particular Liverpool tradition of 'rewards' for political loyalty did not die with Jack Braddock.

In Braddock's day people who applied to join the Labour Party might be told it was 'full up' if their faces didn't fit.[6] Party membership in Liverpool was among the lowest in the country. That's how the Braddocks liked it. 'The organisation was poor and intentionally kept poor to keep out the "wrong" sort of candidate,' one party official revealed later.[7] On two occasions the national Labour Party carried out inquiries into the poor state of the organisation in Liverpool, but these had little effect. Braddock's decrepit organisation survived until the late 1970s, and would prove to be excellent soil for new plants to dig their roots.

The seeds were in Walton, a thriving constituency party with more than 2,000 members. It was also the one Liverpool local party that did not fall under the right-wing Labour machine. This left-wing independence dated from before the war, when Walton left-wingers had published their own newspaper, the *Walton Herald*. In this one constituency:

> The handful of Trotskyites had controlled the party for a while and had achieved the status almost of an 'establishment' of their own with 'fellow-travellers' – people who were left-wing but not 'Trotskyite', who wanted to keep the left wing as united as possible and were not particular about the company they kept. In some respects Walton represented the fortress of the left wing – it was impregnable and unconcerned with anything outside its boundaries.[8]

A key figure was Laura Kirton, then in her thirties. A lady of great energy and ability, she served as both secretary and agent for the Walton party until only a few years ago. In the 1950s, she and Jimmy Deane, who was chairman of Walton, helped nurture a young group of Marxists, and this group took over the publication of *Rally!*, when it moved across the Mersey from Birkenhead to Walton in 1952 and lost its exclamation mark. At that time *Rally* was edited by a Young Socialist called Pat Wall, who, at sixteen, in the Liverpool Garston constituency, had been the youngest party secretary in the country. Thirty years later, in 1982,

Wall was at the centre of controversy when Michael Foot tried to stop him becoming Labour candidate for Bradford North because of his Militant connections. Later in the 1950s *Rally* was edited by another who faced the wrath of the party leadership in the early 1980s, Keith Dickinson, one of the five Militant leaders expelled from the Labour Party in 1983.

Of course, if the Braddocks had had their way, many of these Walton Trotskyists would have been expelled from the party. In April 1959 Braddock sent a copy of *Rally* to the Labour Party general secretary, Morgan Phillips. Mentioning the involvement of Laura Kirton, Brian Deane and Pat Wall in the magazine, he called for *Rally* to be banned.[9] It wasn't.

Ted Grant, meanwhile, was still living in London, where he quickly moved from one flat to another, and even lived in a caravan at one time. He eventually found work as a night telephone operator, enabling him to carry on with political work during the day. He and Deane had often worked closely in the WIL and then the RCP; now, even though they lived 200 miles apart, they were probably closer than ever. 'You and I are really the last of the Old Guard and we must look after ourselves both personally and politically,' Grant told Deane in 1954.[10] Grant visited Liverpool often, and clearly saw it as the main springboard for future advances. In January 1955 Grant wrote about Liverpool: 'I think under certain circumstances it could be a base to spread out in Lancashire then London and nationally.'[11]

Shortly afterwards Deane very nearly got Walton to select Ted Grant as its parliamentary candidate for the 1955 election. At the first selection meeting in November 1954, Grant and a rival tied with an equal number of votes. A second selection meeting three months later produced another tie initially – twenty-two votes each. Then another vote at the same meeting gave Grant twenty-two votes to his opponent's twenty-one, but four blank voting papers deprived Grant of the necessary outright majority of the delegates. The regional organiser then deemed that new nominations should be called for, but before the new process could be got underway, the 1955 election was called. Because of the shortage of time, the party authorities imposed their own candidate on Walton – Sir Joseph Cleary, a former mayor of Liverpool. Though Cleary was on the right of the party, Grant hid his disappointment and happily stayed in Liverpool to work for Cleary during the election campaign.

While Grant would concern himself with theoretical matters, Deane was the more down-to-earth politician who dealt with practical problems: organisation and trade union work. In some ways Deane had the same relationship with Grant in the barren years of the 1950s as Jock Haston had with Grant in the 1940s. Laura Kirton feels they complemented each other. While Ted Grant was the 'boffin plodder' Deane was an excellent speaker and organiser – 'quite brilliant in many ways' she says. Yet Deane seemed to have little personal ambition.[12]

Deane himself says of that period in the early 1950s: 'After the RCP split up we kept up a whole series of publications. We did our best with the meagre resources we had. They wouldn't come out regularly – maybe every month, two months, three months.

We tried to keep the light burning.'[13] In 1955 came another important development for the Grantites.

Following the dissolution of the Revolutionary Communist Party, the Fourth International franchise had gone to Healy's group, The Club. But in 1953 the Fourth International had split and Healy had helped form a separate international grouping. For three years the Fourth International searched for a new group to hold their British franchise. (One story goes that they even advertised in *Tribune*.) Eventually, largely through the work of another former RCP member in London, Sammy Bornstein, Grant and his colleagues got the job. In return they agreed to publish English versions of Fourth International documents. More important, the Grantites also agreed in 1955 to form a new organisation, which they called the Revolutionary Socialist League. Jimmy Deane was its first general secretary. This was effectively the birth of what we know today as the Militant tendency.

In June 1956 Ted Grant wrote to Jimmy Deane in Liverpool to report on a meeting of the International's Executive. This had agreed that the RSL's collaboration with the Fourth International should begin at that point, though the RSL was not given full membership of the Fourth International until 1957. Grant also revealed that the Fourth International would pay for the RSL to publish a theoretical journal, starting in September 1956.[14]

The resulting magazine was *Workers' International Review*, edited by Sammy Bornstein, which came out regularly every two months for the next year, and published English versions of Fourth International documents. It was published under the business name of Workers' International Review (Publishers), and today, one of Militant's limited companies, WIR Publications Limited, is obviously the successor to that firm.

One issue of *Workers' International Review* contained a letter from another small Marxist group, which was partly operating inside the Labour Party at that time, the Socialist Workers' Federation (SWF). It called on all revolutionary groups to unite on a common programme that would include 'the rejection of the parliamentary "peaceful" road' and would affirm that Parliament was to be used 'merely as a soundingboard'.[15] The letter was signed by the National Secretary of the SWF, Eric S. Heffer. At that time Heffer was not a member of the Labour Party. He and Deane had known each other in Liverpool for several years and regularly wrote to each other. Earlier, in March 1957, Heffer had sent a letter to Deane arguing the need for an independent revolutionary party: 'We are definitely opposed to all the comrades being in the Labour Party,' Heffer said, though he did not reject the idea of a small entrist faction.[16] Heffer of course went on to join the Labour Party, quickly becoming Labour MP for Liverpool Walton in 1964, and in recent years he has been one of Militant's best allies on the Labour Party's National Executive. It should be stressed, though, that Heffer has never been a member of the RSL or Militant; indeed in private he has often been very critical of the organisation.

In 1958, *Workers' International Review* gave way to a new RSL theoretical magazine, *Fourth International*, which continued sporadically until 1962. The same year, following the RSL's first

National Congress in June 1957, the League began a new newspaper, as opposed to a theoretical magazine, called *Socialist Fight*.
A four-page broadsheet, it was designed to appeal to workers and
ordinary Labour Party members, not just committed Trotskyists.
By the late 1950s the name Revolutionary Socialist League was
being used only internally and *Socialist Fight* never mentioned
the RSL, presumably to avoid the kind of Labour Party discipline
meted out against Gerry Healy's Socialist Labour League, which
was proscribed in 1959. *Socialist Fight* was nevertheless an RSL
paper. In the first issue in January 1958, alongside an article from
Grant entitled 'Slump this Year', was a piece on the Young Socialists by Pat (Paddy) Wall.[17] A much later contributor was Peter
Taaffe.[18] Every issue of *Socialist Fight* advertised the Liverpool
youth paper, *Rally*, and similarly *Rally* in this period always advertised *Socialist Fight*. *Socialist Fight* was the other of the two main
forerunners of *Militant* and indeed was acknowledged as such by
Militant in 1970.[19]

During these early years the RSL made little progress, even
though it had the official Fourth International franchise. Good
opportunities were missed. The events in Hungary in 1956 presented British Trotskyists with an excellent chance for expansion,
as thousands left the British Communist Party. But it was Gerry
Healy who made most of this opportunity and his Socialist Labour
League grew quickly, becoming the dominant group within
the Labour Party's Young Socialists. The RSL remained small,
insignificant and unappealing. Ted Grant did approach several
ex-Communists personally to ask them to join the RSL, but with

little success. He even visited Frank Chapple of the electricians' union, who had just left the CP. Chapple found Grant likeable, but was not wooed: 'He turned up on my doorstep a few times and was always hungry; he got a cuppa and a bite from me but there was no political affinity, although I did once write an article for him.'[20]

By 1959 it seems that some RSL members were so depressed about that lack of progress that they were advocating pulling out of the Labour Party, but in an important internal RSL pamphlet written in 1959, 'Problems of Entrism', Grant rejected the idea of leaving the party:

> It is true that the conditions for entry, as Trotsky outlined them, are still not present. But it would be the height of stupidity to abandon work in the LP [Labour Party] now and launch into 'independent' adventures after a decade or more of work there … We have to establish ourselves a tendency in the Labour movement.[21]

Today, after more than three and a half decades of work inside the party, Grant's now-very-much-established tendency gives a republished version of the pamphlet to new members of Militant 'to cut their teeth on'.[22]

In London the RSL could boast two relatively distinguished supporters. John Baird had served as Labour MP for Wolverhampton North-East since 1945 without ever making any headlines, until his party dropped him as candidate, for reasons which are unclear, in 1963. Baird had a bad drink problem and was not a very active MP. The RSL cannot have regarded him as much of an asset: his speeches in Parliament were infrequent and rarely showed his Trotskyist beliefs. Baird died shortly after retiring from Parliament in 1964. Ellis Hillman, who today is a leading geologist and president of the Lewis Carroll Society, was then a London county councillor. 'I was simply being used by them,'[23] he argues now, and denies ever being an RSL member, but according to the Deane documents Hillman was once treasurer of the RSL. In February 1961, Hillman wrote a guide for RSL members who, like himself, were elected to councils. A quarter of a century later it is a useful guide to the attitude of Militant councillors:

> The Marxists ... do not accept the view that it is possible, within the framework of Parliament or the existing structure of local government, to achieve socialism. The parliamentary system has to be replaced by the soviet system. This applies on a local as well as a national level.

And, twenty years before any budget crisis in Liverpool, Councillor Hillman wrote:

> Marxists oppose all rent and rate increases on the grounds that the burden of these increases should not be imposed on the class which is least able to afford them but on the class whose system is responsible for the pressure on local government for high rents and high rates.[24]

It was really only in Liverpool that RSL members made much impact, and even then it was not great. For the 1959 election, Walton selected an RSL sympathiser, George McCartney, although the Braddocks tried to get him axed. Twenty years before Derek Hatton, Pat Wall and Brian Deane both served on Liverpool City Council. Walton would regularly send RSL members to the Labour Party conference.

Along the way the Liverpool RSL had recruited two young men who were to play leading roles in the organisation, Terry Harrison and Peter Taaffe. Harrison joined in 1958 after seeing a copy of *Rally*. A boilermaker by trade, and from a lower-middle-class family, Harrison had originally been a Young Conservative and remembers pulling Labour leaflets out of people's front doors as a child, but he left the party over Suez. Soon he was attending the Walton youth section, though he didn't live in the constituency, and he wrote regularly for *Rally*.

Peter James Taaffe did not arrive in Walton until 1960, even though he had lived across the water in Birkenhead. Harrison recalls how, while he was completing his National Service, he received a letter about Taaffe from a friend in Liverpool, in which the future Militant leader was described as a 'young lad' with 'promising ideas'.[25] But Laura Kirton says that he was 'nothing outstanding'.[26] It is perhaps amusing to note that at that time Taaffe actually worked for Liverpool Council – in the treasury department.

In 1962 *Rally* agreed to amalgamate with another, London-based, Young Socialist paper, *Rebel*, which was published by Tony Cliff's faction. The resulting journal was called *Young Guard*, and Keith Dickinson served as its business manager. But it was not long before the Cliff group in *Young Guard*, who included future television presenter Gus MacDonald and future *Guardian* journalist John Palmer, got the upper hand, rejecting the *Rally* group's call for a youth charter. Within a few months the Liverpool people left, and for a while they published yet another journal, *Youth for Socialism*, based in Garston in Liverpool, but this lasted for only four issues.

By 1964, after fourteen years of little success, Ted Grant and Jimmy Deane had done far worse than either of the two rival groups from the RCP days, the Healy and Cliff groups, who both had strong factions within the youth section of the Labour Party, even if they made little public impact. The RSL was still tiny. Its publications were irregular and badly produced. Two hundred miles separated one section in Liverpool from the other major section in London. Such was the Revolutionary Socialist League, the future Militant tendency, on the eve of Labour's return to government in 1964. But the RSL's fortunes would soon change.

On Sunday 1 March 1964 the Liverpool branch of the RSL had passed a crucial motion for submission to that year's RSL National Conference. The proposal was that *Socialist Fight* should be wound up and a new paper be started in its place. That paper would be *Militant*.

4

ENTER
MILITANT

It was a Saturday afternoon early in 1964. A prominent Labour MP and future Cabinet minister was entertaining a group of fellow socialists in the back garden of his home in west London. A parliamentary colleague, John Baird, Member for Wolverhampton North-East, had brought along some Marxist friends: Jimmy Deane, Ted Grant, Keith Dickinson and Peter Taaffe were among them. The comrades spent the afternoon discussing politics and the principles of socialism. Suddenly, after Taaffe had made a particularly perceptive remark, Baird turned to Deane and said: 'You've got a brilliant young fellow here, Jim.'[1]

According to Deane, it was then that he and Grant realised that Taaffe was the right man to be editor of the new paper they were thinking of starting later in the year. It was a crucial decision. In the years that followed, Taaffe was to be the organiser whom Grant had been lacking since the days when he had worked in successful co-operation with Jock Haston in the WIL and the RCP.

Jimmy Deane himself, though able in many ways and a brilliant speaker, had never really been an adequate replacement for Haston. Although Deane had been general secretary of the RSL since its formation in 1955, his job had frequently taken him abroad and he spent much of his time dealing with family problems at home.

At first Grant had not been convinced that a new, regular paper would work. Not since the days of the RCP had he managed to sustain a printed journal that came out on schedule, without fail. The man who was convinced that it would be possible was a young Indian, Sinna Mani, who was active in the Young Socialists in south London. Though Mani was a member of the RSL, Grant regarded him with some suspicion, since at one time he had been a member of Healy's Socialist Labour League. The idea was that the new RSL paper should have a broad outlook, extending beyond the narrow doctrines of the RSL and concentrating on the Young Socialists. Mani felt that such a paper could generate sufficient support from Young Socialist branches to keep going. In the early part of 1964, Mani finally persuaded Grant that the idea was workable, and the two made a trip to Liverpool to ask the comrades there for assistance.

Throughout the spring and summer of 1964, plans for the new journal were discussed at a whole series of RSL meetings, most of them in London. One problem was the choice of name. *Spark*, *Fight*, *New Chartist*, *Struggle* and *Vanguard* were all suggested. Ted Grant wanted to call it *Forward*, but at an Editorial Board meeting on 13 June 1964 he was outvoted by three to one.

The title the board decided on was *The Militant*. The meeting knew that the Trotskyist American Socialist Workers' Party had been producing a regular printed paper with that name since 1928, and they hoped that their new journal would be similarly successful. Indeed, one of the most famous pictures of Trotsky shows him reading a copy of the American *Militant*. The new paper's full title was in fact *The Militant – for Youth and Labour*; the extra words were a sign of the spirit behind the new venture and emphasised that it was primarily a paper for the Young Socialists. 'Youth' and 'Labour' represented the merging of two strands. The first, in essence the Taaffe–Dickinson strand, was from Liverpool and had been associated with the paper *Rally*, aimed at 'youth' within the Labour Party; the second strand represented the group associated with Grant and *Socialist Fight*, the paper that had been designed for the rank and file of the Labour movement, not committed Trotskyists, and which the early *Militant* greatly resembled.

Because of the new emphasis on youth, Militant's first Editorial Board was composed almost entirely of members of the Young Socialists. One exception was Grant himself, who became political editor to compensate for the fact that he could not be editor because he was well beyond Young Socialist age. At this stage the Editorial Board of *The Militant* was a separate, independent body from the Executive Committee of the RSL, though the RSL leadership held a firm grip over the new newspaper. The Editorial Board was elected by the RSL's National Committee, and the RSL Executive controlled the editorial line. In time, however, the Editorial Board of *Militant* and the RSL Executive would effectively become the same body.

Grant provided the paper with historical ballast, an almost religious link with the old RCP and ultimately with Trotsky himself. Taaffe, the editor, was the down-to-earth working-class boy from Birkenhead, who had the enthusiasm and youth. Taaffe would eventually show the RSL the key to success within the Labour Party that Grant had never understood – progress through the party's youth movement.

Although he was officially editor, Taaffe had very little to do with the first few issues of *Militant*, which probably explains why for several editions his name was misspelt (with only one 'f').[2] For three months *Militant* was effectively edited by Mani, who was nominally the business manager. Though Mani did belong to Ted Grant's RSL, the main group behind the paper, for the first few months *Militant* did not belong exclusively to the Grant group.

Issue number one came out in October 1964, a few days before Harold Wilson became Prime Minister after thirteen years of Conservative government. It cost 6d (2½p). 'Drive Out the Tories' read the front-page headline, and typically underneath was added, 'But Labour must have socialist policies.'[3] 'Our aim is to be the Marxist voice of the Young Socialists and the militants in the Labour movement,' the first editorial proclaimed. 'The sacrifice and collection of money among militant workers and Young Socialists has made possible the production of the paper ... Make it the mass journal of militant labour and socialist youth.'[4]

Taaffe's contribution was an article on 'The Mods and Rockers Problem'. Page three contained the first 'Fighting Fund' appeal, with a modest target of £500 (today Militant often raises more than that at a single public meeting). Perhaps emphasising the Liverpool connection, there was a review of the Beatles' film, *A Hard Day's Night*, by Roger Protz, a recent recruit to the RSL from Healy's Socialist Labour League. Protz had once edited the League's *Keep Left* and was initially responsible for *Militant*'s layout.

Under Mani's brief stewardship the early *Militant* displayed a much greater spirit of tolerance than it has in recent times. 'Signed articles express the views of their authors and not necessarily those of the Editorial Board,' it declared.[5] And Protz was even able to urge the comrades: 'Let's stop kidding ourselves that capitalism is about to quietly keel over and roll into its grave.' This was hardly the sort of thing to endear him to Grant, though it was also stated that the comments were 'solely those of the author'.[6]

Along with that air of tolerance – quite unlike anything in *Militant* today – was another important development in the RSL. A few days before publication of the first issue of *Militant* the International Secretariat of the Fourth International had persuaded Grant and his comrades to merge with some Marxists from Nottingham, known as the Nottingham Group or the International Group. They too practised entrism and had recently started a journal called *The Week* (only a duplicated publication at first), which was sponsored by several MPs and a trade union official called Jim Mortimer.[7] The merger was agreed one weekend in September 1964, at the end of a conference in Sevenoaks held by the National Association of Labour Student Organisations. It was accepted by the leaders of both groups that 'political agreement generally existed' between them, and that 'tactical agreement existed on 90 per cent of the problems'. Ken Tarbuck of the International Group and Jimmy Deane of the RSL were asked to draft a new joint constitution on the basis of both groups' existing constitutions.[8]

The leaders of the International Group were two former members of the Communist Party, Ken Coates and Pat Jordan, who ran a left-wing bookshop in Nottingham. Coates had long been in touch with Grant, and Jordan had sold both *Socialist Fight* and *Rally* in his shop. The International Secretariat hoped that this merger would strengthen their British group. 'This unification marks a very important step forward for the Trotskyist movement in Britain,' Jimmy Deane wrote at the time.[9]

It was a forced engagement, though, and it never worked. There were no tangible results: both groups carried on producing their own publications, *The Week* and *Militant*. Neither journal ever mentioned the other. A few weeks after the agreement Protz wrote to an RSL member in Scotland: 'Unfortunately factionalism is raising its head with Grant and Co.'s insistence not only that *Militant* should be a "tendency" paper but that it must also be a "youth and labour" paper, which adds up to them trying to cut *The Week*'s slender neck.'[10]

Not for the last time, Grant wanted to have it all his own way. Later Protz was to write about a *Militant* Editorial Board meeting:

We told Grant that he was hopelessly factional and sectarian, that his attitude would strangle *Militant* and that he had no right to read anybody else's articles until he had written his own. He began screaming and shouting, threatening that I had no rights at all as I wasn't active in the RSL, hadn't 'proven' myself, etc.[11]

By January 1965 Protz felt that he no longer cared about what happened to *Militant* but that *The Week* should be supported 'to the hilt': 'When I arrived for a *Militant* EB [Editorial Board] last night the Grantites were howling with laughter at the first printed *The Week* – "Look at this, ha, ha – isn't it dreadful? Ho, ho."'[12]

Not surprisingly, it wasn't long before the engagement was broken off. Early in 1965 the International Group became the International Marxist Group (IMG), and *The Week* continued as its paper. Before long the International Secretariat of the Fourth International had disenfranchised Grant and the RSL and had recognised the IMG instead. The young Tariq Ali, a wealthy Oxford undergraduate from Pakistan, who had just joined the IMG, was more their idea of a revolutionary than the ageing Ted Grant. Before their departure a future IMG secretary remarked: 'Grant and Co. should be put out of the International (they haven't paid a penny in subs for years) because they refuse to accept the politics of a majority and because they are not really a Trotskyist tendency.'[13]

The International Marxist Group stayed inside the Labour Party until 1968. Recently, as the Socialist League, the former IMG has been re-entering the party and in August 1983 achieved considerable publicity when thirteen League members were sacked by BL at Cowley.

One of the original leaders of the IMG, Ken Coates, was expelled from the Labour Party in 1965 for criticising the government's economic policy. By the time Coates had regained a party card in 1969, he had left the IMG. Since 1968 Coates has concentrated on running the Institute for Workers' Control, one of the important bodies within the Bennite left, and the Bertrand Russell Peace Foundation, both based in Nottingham. In 1983 Coates stood as Labour candidate in Nottingham South (and lost). His son Laurence, a Militant member, served as Young Socialist representative on the Labour NEC from 1981 to 1983.

After Taaffe had come down to London from Liverpool to fulfil his duties as editor of *Militant*, Protz and Mani separately broke with Grant and the RSL, though neither joined the IMG. The two men who had done so much to put the first few issues of *Militant* together had lost the battle to keep it a paper with a broad Marxist outlook within the Young Socialists. From that point onwards *Militant* was exclusively the paper of one particular Trotskyist tendency, the RSL. As if to illustrate the partial movement away from the emphasis on 'youth', in May 1965 the subtitle changed from 'for Youth and Labour' to 'for Labour and Youth'.[14] And, for the first time, Peter Taaffe's name was spelt with two 'f's.

As some people were leaving Militant, however, another significant group was emerging. While Liverpool and London had provided the new tendency with two important elements, a third now came from Brighton, based at the new University of Sussex. Two second-year students, Roger Silverman, son of the left-wing Labour MP Sydney Silverman, and Alan Woods from south Wales, had been selling *Militant* from the very first issue. Over the next few years the Sussex comrades were to provide the tendency with much needed financial contributions, but, more important, they were to play a leading role in Militant in the years ahead. Others from Sussex were two members of the present Militant Executive, Lynn Walsh and Clare Doyle, who were both expelled by the Labour Party in 1983; Pat Craven, a future RSL treasurer; and Bob Edwards, a Central Committee member. Militant was to remain strong in Brighton throughout the 1960s, and it produced its own Sussex University magazines, *Spark* and *International Perspectives*. Another important figure at Sussex was a physics lecturer, Geoff Jones, who provided continuity and an important link with the party in Brighton Kemptown, which was eventually taken over by Militant in the 1970s and chose a Militant member, Rod Fitch, as its parliamentary candidate for the 1983 election.

By early 1965 the modern Militant tendency was becoming recognisable. The RSL was still small – no more than 100 members – but it was well on the road to what it is today. Three important elements had come together around a single national newspaper, *Militant*: Grant and his colleagues from the RCP, providing the historic link with Trotsky; the Liverpool group, contributing the youth and working-class elements; and the students at Sussex, who would give the tendency an important young, middle-class and intellectual ingredient.

For the first few years of its existence Militant progressed almost unnoticed. Originally offices were rented from a Militant sympathiser at 374 Gray's Inn Road, London, above the Connolly Club. In 1965 Militant moved a few hundred yards, to 197 King's Cross Road, where it rented rooms from the Independent Labour

Party, which also lent Militant several thousands of pounds. But Militant was still a tiny organisation. Of the initial £500 Fighting Fund target, only £150 was raised in the first year. Some months the paper did not appear, and throughout the 1960s it never expanded beyond four pages. Meetings were badly attended: fifty was considered a good turnout; twenty was average.

It was to be several years before Militant made any significant progress within the Labour Party. In 1964 the Gerry Healy faction, around the newspaper *Keep Left*, was in control of the Young Socialists (YS); the Cliff group, around *Young Guard*, was its nearest rival in the YS. The RSL was puny in comparison.

Then the Labour Party youth section was going through a period of turmoil and conflict with party officials. The troubles were nothing new, as one historian has commented: 'The history of Labour youth is one of conflict, suppression and constant reorganisation.'[15]

On three occasions, in 1936, 1940 and 1955, the Labour Party had closed down its youth section at national level because it had been taken over by a Marxist faction that the leadership did not like. In 1960, after Labour's third successive general election defeat, the party once again re-established its national youth section, hoping to win more members and voters among the young. Gradually the new Young Socialists, as they were now called, were taken over by Trotskyists, and the YS conference called on party leader Hugh Gaitskell to resign. The result was again disciplinary action, instigated by the assistant national agent, Reg Underhill. In 1962 and 1963 several *Keep Left* supporters were expelled, and a number of branches were closed down. The factionalism within the YS reached a peak at its conference in 1964, when the chairman told delegates he would 'march to socialism over your dead bodies'.[16] He was later expelled.

In 1964 the YS National Conference was abolished for the fourth time, although the National Committee was maintained, now appointed by the party. Individual YS branches continued in the constituencies. The now dominant *Keep Left* faction went ahead and organised its own unofficial YS conference, at which it proclaimed *Keep Left* the YS paper. This meeting marked the departure of *Keep Left* and the Healyites from the Labour Party. The Young Socialists became the official youth section of the Socialist Labour League; and the youth section of the League's successor, the now divided Workers' Revolutionary Party, carried on with the same name, Young Socialists. To avoid confusion, in 1965 the Labour Party youth section became the Labour Party Young Socialists (LPYS).

Shortly afterwards the other major Trotskyist faction within the party's youth section, the Cliff group, around *Young Guard*, also quit the party. So by 1967 the Militant tendency, as it was now becoming known (the name Revolutionary Socialist League was used only internally) was the sole significant Trotskyist group left inside the LPYS. But Militant was still small, and the LPYS was now very weak.

In 1967 the NEC allowed the LPYS National Committee to carry out a review of its organisation. The following year the Simpson Committee on Labour Party organisation recommended changes in the LPYS which 'would give to the Young Socialists more control of their own organisation than the Labour Youth Movement has ever enjoyed before'.[17] Later the NEC agreed that the LPYS should publish its own newspaper, *Left*, which would for the first time be free from censorship and would have an editor chosen by the LPYS itself. In time *Left* (now called *Socialist Youth*) simply became a poorer version of *Militant*, subsidised by the party.

The way was now open for Militant. The tendency succeeded because nobody else in the LPYS was offering any credible alternative. The first Militant supporter on the National Committee was elected in 1967. By 1969 the LPYS conference had accepted Militant's 'Charter for Young Workers' (first proposed by *Rally* in 1950), and the following year Militant achieved a majority on the LPYS National Committee. The tendency has retained that majority to this day, virtually unchallenged.

Most young people in the late 1960s regarded the Labour Party as the last place in which to be politically active. It was an era that marked the rise of the single-issue pressure group, and Trotskyist organisations outside the party began to grow. The Vietnam war demonstrations, pop music and pot-smoking of the 1960s generation did not interest Militant, which saw the new culture as a distraction from the real issues. While thousands demonstrated in Grosvenor Square, Militant sought the nationalisation of the top 380 monopolies. Militant's growing influence within the LPYS went largely unremarked. Compared with previous generations of Young Socialists, from *Advance!* in the 1930s to *Keep Left* in the early 1960s, Militant was seen as less troublesome. The Young Liberals, protesting about Vietnam and apartheid, were far more of an embarrassment to Liberal leader Jeremy Thorpe at this time than the LPYS was to Harold Wilson. With a National Executive that was moving leftwards, it came as no surprise when the LPYS was rewarded with even more autonomy.

An important advantage for the tendency was that the unions have no involvement in the Labour Party youth section, whereas in the Labour Party itself the unions hold around 90 per cent of the conference votes and have often used this power to offset the leftward inclinations of the constituencies. In the LPYS all the votes came from individual branches.

Branches were the key to success, and taking them over was a simple task for Militant. The first necessary ingredient in Militant's formula is a Militant member within the LPYS branch. If necessary, one is asked to move into a constituency from elsewhere. This is easier if the LPYS branch is a new one, as many were in the late 1960s, when the LPYS was being revived. The Militant member sells copies of the paper to other LPYS members and at an early stage suggests a programme of Militant speakers. These speakers will be presented not as being from Militant but as experts on particular subjects, such as Chile or Spain. After a few weeks' work in a branch the key Militant member will assess its prospects. If further recruits look likely and takeover seems possible, then the other LPYS members will slowly be drawn into the tendency. But if other groups are strong and a takeover looks difficult, then the Militant member may abandon the struggle in that particular branch. He or she will stop going to meetings and may move elsewhere. In some cases, where control looks out of reach, Militant may try to smash the branch altogether so as to stop it from falling into the hands of others. A common Militant tactic is to hold LPYS branch meetings as regularly as possible. In this way many of the non-Militant members find that because of other commitments – homework, girl- or boyfriends or families – they are unable to attend every meeting. This only strengthens the position of the disciplined Militant members who, of course, go to every meeting. Once Militant is entrenched in an LPYS branch, non-Militant members will often feel unwelcome and will stop going. LPYS weekend and summer schools are used regularly by Militant as a means of establishing contact with branches they have not yet taken over and for finding and developing new sympathisers.

In 1969 the Labour Party appointed a full-time National Youth Officer, Neil Vann. Vann was an energetic former constituency agent who genuinely wanted the party to have a strong youth section, but he quickly found that he was spending most of his energy battling against Militant, with very little support from his superiors. 'It was a matter all the time of sticking your finger into holes in the dyke,' he recalls.[18] Vann did all he could to encourage non-Militant LPYS members, but it was an uphill task. Many party members of LPYS age ignored the youth section, and many of those who did get involved in the LPYS had other commitments in local Labour parties and student politics which distracted them. Nobody could ever match Militant's dedication. Vann remembers that even before Militant had a majority on the LPYS National Committee, the non-Militant members could never count on out-voting them: 'While all the five Militant supporters would always turn up, it was always in doubt whether the non-Militants would. They often didn't have the time. They'd be local councillors or fully entrenched in other work in the Labour Party.'[19] When Vann started as National Youth Officer, the LPYS National Committee held a three-hour meeting every two months. But once Militant took control the meetings were held monthly and lasted from early on Saturday afternoon to Sunday lunch-time. 'And the annoying thing about it was that they had all met together beforehand any-way,' he remembers.[20]

After 1970, when Militant controlled the National Commit-tee, only one region, the West Midlands, stood out against the tendency, thanks partly to the work of the assistant regional organiser. (The region was to remain outside Militant hands until 1975 and was not totally secure after that.) The 1970 takeover of the LPYS marked a real turning-point in the tendency's fortunes. Thereafter membership climbed rapidly, since the LPYS was an excellent source of recruits, funds and some power. In effect the LPYS became a section not of the Labour Party but of the Militant tendency, and Militant treated the finances almost as if they were integrated. Militant also found the party youth section a good training ground. LPYS National Committees from the early 1970s consisted almost entirely of people who today, a decade later, are full-time workers for Militant. And control of hundreds of LPYS branches gave the tendency a foothold in nearly every constituency. An LPYS branch is entitled to at least two delegates on the General Committee of a constituency Labour party and can also submit resolutions to the committee. The fact that many branches consist of a mere handful of members goes largely unnoticed in the rest of the party. The LPYS manages to carry on with between 5,000 and 10,000 members nationally. Most non-Militant Labour Party members between the ages of fifteen and twenty-five end up ignoring the LPYS and concentrate on the party itself.

In 1972 the party made another concession to the youth section – a place on the NEC for a representative from the LPYS. This move gave Militant an important position within Transport House, and not just a voice and a vote in the party's most important body but ears as well. The left on the NEC was to find the LPYS representative a useful ally. In return for his support in battles against the right, the left would defend the LPYS and Militant. Successive Militant members on the NEC were able to keep the Militant leadership informed of every move inside Labour headquarters, and Peter Taaffe and Ted Grant now had direct access to confidential documents distributed to NEC members. In time journalists too were to find the LPYS NEC member a useful contact.

Almost continuously since 1972 the NEC place has been held by Militant members: Peter Doyle (1972–74), Nick Bradley (1974–78), Tony Saunois (1978–81), Laurence Coates (1981–83), Steve Morgan (1983–84), Frances Curran (1984–86), and from 1986 the first black NEC member, Linda Douglas. Militant regards the position as very useful to its work, and holders are groomed for the job well in advance. Early in 1986 Militant was already planning that after Linda Douglas the LPYS NEC representative should be Paula Hanford, a full-time Militant organiser responsible for youth work in Swansea. The only period when Militant did not hold the position was for six months in 1974, after Peter Doyle was forced to resign. It was suddenly discovered that Doyle was twenty-seven, two years over-age. One of Militant's few opponents within the LPYS had long suspected this and had eventually gone to Somerset House to dig out a copy of Doyle's birth certificate. Doyle's replacement on the NEC was Rose Degiorgio, a non-Militant candidate who had received just seventeen votes at the 1973 LPYS conference (as opposed to 141 for Doyle). Rarely can anybody have found themselves elevated to the NEC with so little support or in such unusual circumstances.

In 1970 Militant bought its own offices in Bethnal Green in east London, and members of the tendency were dragooned into decorating the building and reconstructing the drains. Then Militant bought its own press; until that time the paper had been produced by a friendly printer in a basement in Fulham. As a result *Militant* quickly changed from a 'skimpy monthly' into a 'lively weekly'[21] and extended from four pages to eight. And it started to sport a colour logo too, though it has always been more orange than red. Many of the organisational advances within the tendency were the work of Dave Galashan, Militant's business manager, who had known Peter Taaffe since his days in Liverpool. Galashan masterminded Militant's finances, ran the business side of the newspaper and organised Militant's printing work. He eventually left Militant in about 1980, exhausted by his work, and got a job as a BBC audio engineer. The jobs Galashan did are now carried out by several different people.

During the period of the Heath government, Militant's style of politics – concentrating on economic and industrial issues – began to have more appeal. The Campaign for Nuclear Disarmament and Vietnam protesters who had marched down Whitehall in the 1950s and 1960s gave way to demonstrators angry about the Industrial Relations Act, the Pentonville Five, Upper Clyde Shipbuilders, the Shrewsbury Pickets and the Clay Cross councillors. It was a period of great industrial unrest. On five occasions in less than four years the Heath government had to proclaim a state of emergency. More days were lost through industrial disputes than in any comparable period since records began, and in 1972 and 1974 Britain saw the first national miners' strikes since 1926. The tendency exploited these conflicts and disputes to the full. *Militant*-sellers began to be a common feature of the picket lines, and the newspaper expanded its coverage of industrial affairs. By 1974 the tendency had around 500 members,[22] compared with just over 100 four years before.

Soon Militant began to make an impact on the wider Labour Party. At the 1972 conference in Blackpool, Pat Wall, the delegate from Shipley, and Ray Apps, from Brighton Kemptown, proposed a composite motion calling for 'an enabling Bill to secure the public ownership of major monopolies', a watered-down version of Militant's main policy. The conference, largely unaware that both delegates were members of the Militant National Committee or probably even what Militant was, passed it by 3,501,000 votes to 2,497,000.[23] It was quite an achievement. The fact that Wall and Apps were able to make sure that it was they who were chosen to propose the composite resolution, which amalgamated several constituency motions, showed that there had been considerable planning by Militant beforehand. The following year similar co-ordination was less successful. A Militant motion proposed by Brighton Kemptown and Liverpool Walton, calling for the nation-alisation of 250 monopolies, was defeated overwhelmingly.[24] This period also saw the first attempts by Militant to secure election to the NEC. The early results were promising: 31,000 votes for Ray Apps in 1971; 51,000 for Militant's business manager, Pat Craven, in 1972; and in 1973 81,000 for Apps and 144,000 for David Skinner (brother of the MP, Dennis Skinner),[25] whose vote was boosted because he was one of the Clay Cross councillors who had been disqualified from council office for defying the Housing Finance Act. Although Skinner denies he was ever a member of Militant, he spoke regularly on Militant platforms and was promoted by the tendency as one of its candidates. For the first time Militant mem-bers secured more votes than any other candidate who was not an MP. Even though Militant candidates were less successful in many subsequent years, they have nearly always done better than any other non-parliamentary candidates (see Appendix 1).

It would be wrong, however, to deduce that these rising votes automatically represented growing support for Militant in the con-stituencies. Each local party has 1,000 votes in the constituency ballot (more in the rare case of a party with over 1,000 members) and can vote for seven candidates. But the 81,000 votes for Ray Apps in 1973 did not necessarily mean that eighty-one constituency parties then supported Militant. At that time the mandating of conference delegates on who to vote for was less common than today. The choice was often left to the delegate, and in many parties Militant supporters found it easy to get chosen as delegates (in some cases nobody else volunteered). Where delegates were mandated there was nothing to stop them from breaking the mandates, as the ballot was secret until 1983. Since the introduction of recorded voting it is no surprise that Militant has stopped contesting NEC elections. Above all, in the early 1970s Militant did not suffer the kind of counter-reaction it meets today. Pat Wall could never get his 1972 motion through conference now, simply because he and several of his colleagues are publicly identified as members of Militant.

An internal Militant document published in June 1974 boasted that the tendency had 'extended and given a new dimension to Trotsky's conception of entry'.[26] But for the first decade of its entrism Militant had worked largely unobserved within the Labour Party, swiftly taking over the Young Socialists and establishing a foothold in the wider party. Militant had briefly made a minor attempt at entrism within the Communist Party as well in the early 1970s but, not surprisingly, Communist leaders were more aware, and less tolerant, of Militant than were those of the Labour Party. As Peter Taaffe and Ted Grant celebrated *Militant*'s tenth birthday in October 1974, they did have much to be proud of, but they had also been fortunate. Now they would have to use the gains made in the LPYS as a basis for advances elsewhere: 'The Constituency Parties are assuming more and more importance for our work,' the document stated.[27] 'We must dig roots in the wards and constituencies as we have in the YS. Many are still shells dominated by politically dead old men and women.'[28]

5

POLICIES AND
PERSPECTIVES

For most people in politics 'slogan' is a pejorative term, often used to condemn the propaganda of opponents. Militant, however, happily admits that slogans are an important part of its political strategy. According to Andrew Glyn, formerly one of Militant's leading economic thinkers: 'Militant campaigns for a socialist programme summarised in the slogan: "Nationalise the 200 monopolies and the banks under workers' control and management, and with compensation according to proven need."'[1]

The 'Nationalise the 200 monopolies' demand is the most important of several simple slogans used by the tendency. Others include '£120-a-week minimum wage' and 'Thirty-five-hour week without loss in pay'. These demands can be found throughout Militant's public literature, and indeed Militant resolutions to local Labour parties or party conference can usually be identified by them. Most of the important Militant slogans are among the organisation's basic list of public demands, set out at the start of the pamphlet 'Militant: What We Stand For', written by Peter Taaffe in 1981, and updated in 1986 (the numbering is mine):

JOBS

1. The immediate introduction of a 35-hour week without loss in pay as a step towards the elimination of unemployment.
2. Reversal of all Tory cuts and a massive programme of public works on housing, education, the health service, etc.
3. A minimum wage of £120 a week for all workers, male and female and also for the pensioners, the sick and disabled.
4. Opening of the books of the monopolies to inspection by committees of shop stewards, housewives and small business-men and women.
5. Nationalisation under workers' control and management of all firms threatening redundancies.

YOUTH

6. A choice at sixteen: either a grant of at least £35 a week to stay on at school or college, or training on union rates of pay (at least £55 at sixteen), or a job with a guaranteed minimum wage.
7. A guaranteed job after education or training.

RACISM, FASCISM AND POLICE HARASSMENT

8. Opposition to all discrimination on the basis of race.

9. The immediate repeal of the racist Nationality and Immigration Acts. Abolition of immigration controls.

10. No platform for fascists. Labour authorities to refuse facilities for holding meetings, etc.

11. Full support for black workers who face racial violence. Defence of black communities to be organised by the Labour movement, black organisations, tenants' associations and local groups.

12. Control of the police to be placed under the auspices of democratically elected local authority police committees. For a genuinely independent complaints procedure.

13. Unity of black and white workers in the struggle for socialist change, to eliminate the roots of racism.

FIGHT SEX DISCRIMINATION

14. Opposition to discrimination on the basis of sex and opposition to sexual harassment.

15. Equal pay for work of equal value.

16. A crash building programme to provide nursery and crèche facilities for all who want them.

17. Opposition to the harassment of lesbians and gay men and to all forms of discrimination on grounds of homosexuality.

LABOUR MOVEMENT DEMOCRACY

18. Defence of mandatory re-selection of MPs.

19. Election of a Labour Cabinet/shadow Cabinet by the electoral college.

20. NEC control of the election Manifesto, based on party conference decisions.

21. All trade union officials to be subjected to regular election and to receive the average wage of the members they represent.

22. All Labour MPs to receive the average wage of a skilled worker plus expenses; the surplus to be given to the Labour movement.

23. Representatives of the Labour movement to take jobs outside the movement only with the full agreement of the organisation they represent and all such income to be returned to the Labour movement.

FOR A SOCIALIST SOCIETY

24. Opposition to the Tory government's anti-union laws and reversal of all attacks on the trade unions. For their immediate repeal by a Labour government.

25. Total opposition to the dictatorship of the Fleet Street press who pour out their poison daily against the Labour movement. We propose that a Labour government should nationalise the newspaper printing plant facilities, radio and TV. Access to these facilities should be given to political parties, in proportion to their votes at elections.

26. Massive cuts in arms spending, now running at £18,000 million a year. Transfer the resources to socially useful production.

27. Support for unilateral nuclear disarmament, but with the recognition that only a socialist change of society in Britain and internationally can eliminate the danger of a nuclear holocaust.

28. Renationalisation of all public industries privatised by the Tories, with compensation only on the basis of proven need.

29. Workers' management of the nationalised industries on the basis of one third of the places on the management board elected from the unions in the industry, one third elected from the TUC representing the working class as a whole and one third nominated from the government.

30. National industrial action to harness the maximum possible strength of the trade unions in defence of jobs, living standards, services and against privatisation. For a mass campaign to force the Tories out.

31. Abolition of the monarchy and the House of Lords.

32. Nationalisation of the top 200 monopolies including the banks and insurance companies which control the 'commanding heights' of the economy through an Enabling Bill in Parliament with minimum compensation on the basis of proven need. This would then allow a socialist plan of production to be democratically drawn up and implemented by committees involving the trade unions, shop stewards, housewives and small businessmen and women.

33. Opposition to the capitalist Common Market. For a Socialist United States of Europe as a step towards a World Socialist Federation.[2]

What might surprise some readers is how remarkably unradical most of Militant's shopping list is. Many of the proposals are hardly different from the kind of reforms carried out by past Labour governments. Neil Kinnock would not find too much to worry about in most of the demands, and even Mrs Thatcher would have no difficulty in agreeing with some items, such as the regular election of trade union officials. Only the abolition of the monarchy (item 31) and the proposals on nationalisation and 'monopolies' (items 4, 5, 25, 28 and 32) differ *radically* from existing Labour Party policy as agreed by the party conference, though many of the details in other proposals are at odds with Labour policy.

In recent years this basic list of Militant's public demands has been expanded, partly to allow for mounting criticisms that Militant had no concern for the rights of women, gays and blacks. Hence new sections have been devoted to racism and sex discrimination. The committees which Militant wants to open the books of the 'monopolies' used to include 'businessmen' but now have 'businesswomen' too, although 'househusbands' have yet to win a place alongside housewives. Militant has also expanded its youth proposals. All these additions have been made to increase Militant's appeal among potential recruits, but apart from these alterations, Militant's main economic programme has remained remarkably unchanged over the years.

To understand the origin of Militant's public programme we have to go back to the *Transitional Programme* drawn up by Trotsky for the founding conference of the Fourth International in 1938. Trotsky wrote:

It is necessary to help the masses in the process of the daily struggle to find the bridge between present demands and the socialist programme of the revolution. The bridge should include a system of transitional demands, stemming from today's conditions and from today's consciousness of wide layers of the working class and unalterably leading to one final conclusion: the conquest of power by the proletariat.[3]

For many years one of Militant's main economic theorists was Andrew Glyn, a tutor at Corpus Christi College, Oxford, and member of the William and Glyn's banking family. Recently Glyn left Militant, but in a pamphlet he once wrote for the tendency, he explained how the interests of the working class can be safeguarded only by campaigns around slogans: 'The struggle for these demands by the organisations of the Labour movement immediately raises the question of whether workers' basic requirements can be guaranteed under capitalism, and the corresponding need to generalise these struggles around a programme to transform society.'[4] Militant's public demands are simple policies, which are easily memorable and designed to appeal to working-class people. They are deliberately meant to appear reasonable, and yet unattainable under the existing capitalist system, so that in striving for them workers will see the need for a complete transformation of society.

Militant's public programme can be seen simply as a list of modern-day 'transitional demands', which have been updated since Trotsky's 1938 list – transitional demands must always have a contemporary appeal. Peter Taaffe's 'What We Stand For' can be viewed as an up-to-date version of the *Transitional Programme*. Indeed, several of Militant's public demands, such as opening the books of the 'monopolies' and the programme of public works, have remained almost unaltered from Trotsky's original list.

It is vital to understand, however, that the implementation of these demands is totally irrelevant to Militant's idea of a future socialist society. Militant is a revolutionary organisation, and the list of proposals, though in total more radical than any programme previously implemented by any Labour government, would not in itself amount to the kind of Marxist revolution Militant wants. But Militant recognises that, at the present time, it would be pointless to demand full-blooded revolution in Britain: 'In non-revolutionary periods demands for the arming of the working class and the dismantling of the state will not be sufficient. These presuppose that the workers are arriving at or have reached revolutionary conclusions. Soviets can only be demanded or established when objective conditions are ripe.'[5]

So, in the meantime, it is Militant's task to prepare itself for when the 'conditions are ripe'. As an internal document explained in 1985: 'Before revolutionary activity can even be considered except theoretically, it is necessary to assemble the cadres of Marxism.'[6] Militant's list of public demands must be seen, therefore, as simply a tool for Militant's much more immediate objective – the recruitment of the vanguard, all in preparation for the day when revolution does arrive.

Everything that Militant does has the purpose of preparing its forces and raising the political consciousness of what Militant calls 'the advanced elements of the working class'. The transitional demands are a sort of attractive bait, designed to make Militant appeal to workers and left-wing trade unionists who may have become disillusioned with traditional Labour policies, and, as Militant would see it, are now 'reaching out for the ideas of revolutionary Marxism'. Like loss leaders in a supermarket, the transitional demands are designed to bring people in. Only once the new potential recruit or 'contact member' has been drawn into the tendency is the real nature of the organisation and its purpose revealed.

Ideally, Militant aims to give each new member a careful programme of education to raise further his or her consciousness. Among the basic texts he or she is given to read are the *Transitional Programme, Where is Britain Going?* and the *History of the Russian Revolution*, all by Trotsky, and a collection of Trotsky's works on entrism; Marx's *Communist Manifesto*; and two of Lenin's works, *Imperialism, the Highest Stage of Capitalism* and *State and Revolution*. These are the main works upon which Militant's true organisation, policy and programme are based. Ideally every new member must read and understand them; in practice nowadays this requirement is often ignored. For Militant, which is a revolutionary organisation, parliamentary democracy is not important. True, Militant has two of its members in the House of Commons, but again their parliamentary work is only another part of the consciousness-raising which is so important to the tendency in its progress towards the revolution.

In the late 1930s Trotsky believed that capitalism was going through its 'death agony'. Whether Trotsky would have continued to believe that in the years since then some people would dispute, but Militant has certainly stuck with Trotsky's outlook. 'Capitalism is condemned. Nothing will save it from collapse,' Trotsky wrote then – words that might easily have been written by Ted Grant or Peter Taaffe at any time since. After the war Grant faithfully carried on in the belief that capitalism's collapse was near, even during the post-war boom and in the face of economic indicators that suggested that the Western economy was thriving far more than in Trotsky's day, with unprecedented rates of growth. Militant often criticises other Trotskyist groups for insisting that capitalism's collapse will happen almost immediately, and argues instead that the 'pre-revolutionary situation' will be evident in the 'coming period'. The critical moment is always predicted as being ten to fifteen years away, and as time passes of course, the ten to fifteen year period is extended into the future. Moreover, like most Trotskyist groups, Militant optimism about capitalism's collapse never falters; and that optimism naturally increases with every difficulty suffered by the British and world economies. In the early 1960s Militant asked 'Will there be a slump?', but in recent times the question has become 'Will there be a boom?' Militant sees the world depression of the last decade as a complete vindication of its arguments and predictions in the 1950s and 1960s.

Alongside Militant's conviction that world capitalism is in decline, is the claim that in Western Europe, and particularly in Britain, the capitalist crisis is more severe than anywhere. 'The whole of British society is heading for a gigantic explosion,' Grant wrote in 1973;[7] twelve years later British capitalism was still 'inching forward recklessly towards disaster'.[8] Every article or speech Grant writes will contain an impressive collection of economic statistics and quotations, mainly culled from capitalist publications such as the *Financial Times*, *The Banker* and *Management Today*: Britain's declining share of world trade and output, its low growth rate since the war compared with that of other countries, the decreasing numbers employed in manufacturing industry, the failure of British companies to invest, and the falling value of the pound against foreign currencies. Every possible indication of decline is added to the gloomy (or rosy) picture of 'the terminal and irreversible decline of British capitalism'. And the inevitable conclusion? 'On the basis of capitalism there is absolutely no way out for the working class and the mass of the population. The British capitalist class, in the words of Trotsky, is tobogganing towards disaster with its eyes closed.'[9]

Publicly Militant argues that only its economic programme can avert catastrophe. The centrepiece of this programme is the nationalisation of the 'commanding heights of the economy', the top 200 'monopolies', the banks and insurance companies. This, the tendency says, would be done by means of an Enabling Bill pushed quickly through Parliament, and in answer to critics who argue that this is an undemocratic method, Militant often points to Attlee's support for an Enabling Bill in the 1930s. Militant's proposed nationalisation measures would, they argue, be very different from past nationalised industries, which Militant regards merely as 'state capitalism'. The industries would be run by elected boards consisting of representatives from the workforce, the TUC and the government, and with each board member subject to recall.

That is Militant's public position. Privately it knows that such a programme is unlikely ever to be carried out by a Labour government. But, nevertheless, whatever any Labour administration does instead to tackle Britain's economic problems, Militant believes it will be able to capitalise upon. The constant betrayal of the leadership of the Labour and trade union movement is an important theme in Militant's politics. Past 'betrayals' by MacDonald, Wilson, Callaghan and Foot, and predicted future treachery by the potential next Labour government under Neil Kinnock are constant fuel in Militant's consciousness-raising. Militant wants a Labour government not so that it can perhaps carry out some measure of socialist reform, but so that it can fail and expose the weakness of reforms. Militant depends upon being able to accuse the existing leadership of betrayal in order to put itself forward as the only alternative. The miners' strike, Militant believes, means that a Labour government is now the most likely result at the next election, but Ted Grant predicts it will be a 'government of crisis', with 'a programme which will be more right wing than Labour has put forward for seventy years'.[10]

Militant dismisses Labour's economic policies as unworkable, and argues that a Kinnock government will suffer worse economic difficulties than other recent west European 'reformist' governments in France, Spain and Greece. It predicts that Kinnock's initial reforms will soon, under the pressure of international capitalism, give way to counter reforms.

The tendency often seems remarkably conservative and orthodox in its attitude towards financial matters, and rejects expansionist Keynesian economics as fervently as any Thatcherite monetarist: 'Increased state expenditure in one form or another will be but an additional burden on industry and on inflation. The resort to the printing press, preparatory to a new devaluation, will undermine the stability of the pound and the stability of British society.'[11]

Militant is particularly hostile to the idea of import controls, a major part of the economic strategies put forward by the Labour left in recent years, and part of Labour's economic programme in 1983. It regards these as nationalistic. The tendency says a programme based upon import controls is an even more utopian solution to the problems of the British economy than existing Thatcherite policies: 'It is impossible because 30 per cent of British production is exported, more than any other of the great powers. Consequently Britain is more vulnerable to retaliation than any other country. Under capitalism there cannot be a solution.'[12] Similarly Militant rejects other economic measures usually put forward by the Labour left: industrial democracy, planning agreements, a wealth tax and a limited amount of nationalisation. For Militant such measures would merely be an 'attempt to implant in a partial fashion aspects of a full-blooded socialist plan in what would remain fundamentally a capitalist organism.'[13]

So Militant hopes that the failures and crises of a future Labour government will strengthen its own position, and that a Kinnock administration will show the workers the futility of reformism in a capitalist system: 'Through experience and through the arguments of the Marxists the working class will more and more begin to realise, in spite of all tricks, concessions, repressions, that in the crisis of capitalism it no longer is possible for capitalism to afford reforms except for very temporary periods.'[14]

Militant believes that Britain's capitalist crisis will eventually worsen to the extent that there will be food riots and increasing industrial unrest, armed police and soldiers on the picket lines, the collapse of law and order, and generally deteriorating conditions for working people. All this, of course, will occur against the background of the worsening 'crisis of international capitalism'. Militant expects that in such conditions the government in Whitehall, be it Conservative, reformist Labour or any other type of administration, would become increasingly ineffective. By this stage Militant believes that the existing working-class leadership – Labour Party and trade union leaders – will have become so discredited (partly by unsuccessful periods in government) that the working class will consider itself leaderless. At that point Militant predicts it will be able to step in with its vanguard of steeled cadres, all of whom have patiently been preparing for this moment.

On taking up that vacant leadership Militant would try to form 'workers' councils', or soviets. In Britain, soviets would probably be based on local trades' councils, in which Militant members are often active. In time workers' militias too would probably be necessary, replacing the army and police. The model for this scenario is, of course, the Russian Revolution of 1917, which Militant often says is the most important event in world history.

In Militant's politics there are important lessons to be learned from the Allende government in Chile in the early 1970s which was overthrown by the Chilean military, backed by the CIA. For Militant, Chile shows how there can be no half-measures: 'Chile confirms the analysis of Marxism. It is not possible to carry out half a revolution. In a revolutionary situation gains which are not consolidated through the taking of economic and state power out of the hands of the capitalists will be lost. Marxism explains the need for the replacement of the old state by a state based upon the working class, for a workers' militia, for the ruling of society by workers' councils, etc.'[15]

To what extent will Militant's revolution be a violent one? This question is usually fudged. Publicly Militant always argues that when the time comes for the final transition from capitalism to socialism, the power of the Labour and trade union movement will be such as to ensure that it happens without bloodshed. But privately Militant expects violence, and constantly refers to the example of the Allende government to stress the likelihood of violent resistance to change on the part of the 'capitalist class' in defence of what it sees as its right to rule. Militant believes that Allende could have prevented his fall by arming the workers in Chile, and argues that if similar circumstances arose in Britain, armed workers' militias should be established to prevent the military, the capitalist classes, or the bureaucracy, from overthrowing a Labour government. In an article in an internal document in 1980, Peter Taaffe quoted Trotsky himself: 'It depends entirely on the bureaucracy. If the bureaucracy are inclined to concede to the politically organised expression of the masses, everything will be satisfactory. If they oppose the masses, the masses will use violence. It is legitimate.'[16] So in theory the workers' militias would be solely for defensive purposes: violence would be invoked only to counter-attack. In reality their role would be more coercive. In the circumstances it might become difficult to determine who had used violence first and to define what was meant by violence. In any case who would judge? In a revolutionary situation there would be no neutral arbitrators or judiciary.

That 'taking of economic and state power out of the hands of the capitalists' would, in Pat Wall's words, 'mean the abolition of the monarchy, the House of Lords, the sacking of the generals, the admirals, the air marshals, the senior civil servants, the police chiefs and, in particular, the judges and people of that character.'[17] With the country now under the rule of workers' councils, there would be no need for bourgeois institutions such as Parliament. Political parties shown to be giving support to the 'forces of capitalism' would be outlawed, including possibly the Labour Party. (By this stage Militant would probably have ended its long period of entrism inside the Labour Party, though in a revolution such questions are likely to be fairly academic.) Even the trade unions might not survive: 'We must never forget to train our cadres to the theoretical possibility of the unions as organisations being thrust aside, in a period of revolution or prior to an insurrection, and that workers committees or soviets could take their place.'[18]

Little of Militant's revolutionary plans are ever stated explicitly. You won't find references to workers' militias or soviets in the tendency's public documents. It is only in Militant's internal literature that the strategy is clearer. It is, of course, completely in line with the teachings of Marx, Engels, Lenin and Trotsky, and Peter Taaffe probably sees himself as the modern British Lenin, who will emerge at the moment of crisis and lead us to socialism.

Since Militant's public programme, as outlined at the start of this chapter, is 'transitional' and designed solely as a method of increasing workers' political consciousness, any attempt to argue against Militant about it becomes a fairly pointless exercise, since this public programme disguises the organisation's fundamental strategy. People on the left frequently assert that Militant should be countered by political argument, but it is not as simple as that. Militant's true programme and policies are never openly stated. The tendency denies any link with its internal documents. The items in Militant's public programme have not been designed for implementation, at least not by a Militant government.

Militant is often accused by its critics, especially on the left, of economism, of reducing all issues to economics. It regards all activity on single issues, such as peace and women's rights, as futile unless linked to an 'overall socialist programme'. Over the years Militant has generally refused to join many of the important left-wing single-issue campaigns, and does so only when the issues are of such importance within the Labour movement that they become another means of recruiting people to the tendency and of raising workers' consciousness.

In the late 1970s the tendency shunned the Anti-Nazi League because it was run by the Socialist Workers' Party, and in spite of the fact that most people agreed that the Anti-Nazi League had been quite successful in the fight against the National Front. Often Militant prefers to set up its own front organisations rather than join other pressure groups working in the same field. The tendency formed its own Youth Campaign Against Unemployment rather than join the wider Campaign Against Youth Unemployment, founded by the Young Communist League. Later the Right to Work Campaign was rejected in favour of the Youth Opportunities Programme Trade Union Rights Campaign, set up by the LPYS (now simply the Youth Trade Union Rights Campaign (YTURC)). Militant effectively controls YTURC and finds it a good source of recruits. Within the Labour Party, for many years Militant preferred to campaign on its own for changes in party democracy, and participated in the Campaign for Labour Party Democracy only in the early 1980s, with some reluctance. More recently in Liverpool the existing Black Caucus was vehemently opposed and Militant set up its own Merseyside Action Group to represent black people in the city.

The rule is that Militant will get involved in single-issue organisations, or set up its own single-issue campaigns, only if it sees benefit in terms of recruits to its own organisation. Simple progress on the single issue concerned will do nothing to speed up the British revolution, Militant believes.

For this reason Militant has always adopted a very supercilious attitude to the Campaign for Nuclear Disarmament (CND), which it regards as a bunch of 'vicars and liberals'. The word 'pacifist' is a term of abuse. Militant distrusts the 'middle-class trendies' it sees in CND and reject CND's view that nuclear disarmament is possible without the achievement of socialism. At one point Ted Grant and his colleagues even believed in the idea of the 'workers' bomb' – that the Soviet Union should be allowed to retain nuclear weapons to defend the workers of the world against capitalism. Even today Militant does not seem to worry much about the possibility of nuclear war:

> The capitalists do not wage war for the sake of waging war but in order to extend their power, income and profit ... To destroy the working class, which nuclear war would mean, would be to destroy the goose that lays the golden eggs ... Consequently it is only totalitarian fascist regimes, completely desperate and unbalanced, which would take this road.[19]

Peter Taaffe argued in 1978 that 'a war between Russia and the capitalist West is completely ruled out in the foreseeable future'.[20]

With the growth of the peace movement in recent years Militant has been forced to modify its attitude. It had to join the peace movement, at least nominally, simply so as not to become discredited within the Labour Party and among potential members of the Young Socialists. While officially Militant has always believed in unilateral nuclear disarmament and in withdrawal from NATO, neither has ever been anything like as important as the 'struggle for socialism'.

As a Trotskyist organisation Militant is naturally very critical of the countries of Eastern Europe, which it regards as 'Stalinist' and 'degenerated workers' states'. The tendency does believe, however, that the Soviet Union illustrates the benefits of a planned economy: 'The Stalinist regime in Russia has nothing in common with a healthy workers' state, except for the foundations of state ownership of the means of production.'[21] Militant accuses the East European states of 'waste, chaos, incompetence, corruption and bureaucracy'.[22]

Militant gave strong support to the banned trade union Solidarity in Poland, and sees members of Solidarity as genuine socialists, wanting workers' control in Poland, not a return to a capitalism – the accusation made by some of the left. However, Militant has been fiercely criticised by other Trotskyist groups for its attitude towards the Soviet invasion and occupation of Afghanistan. While Militant condemned the original occupation in 1979, it does not now call for a Soviet withdrawal. In Militant's view this would mean only a return to the previous 'feudal' society in Afghanistan and would leave the country open to American influence.

Similarly, in 1982 Militant took a very unusual line on the Falklands War. Though the tendency initially opposed the war, it did not urge the recall of the Task Force, as had other groups on the left: 'Instead of putting the position in class terms, some lefts and the pacifist wing of the Labour Party put forward the demand "Bring back the Fleet". Such a demand is completely unrealistic and futile.'[23] Ted Grant argued that the Falklands conflict could be used to force a general election which could lead to the return of a Labour government and the formation of a 'socialist federation of Britain, Argentina and the Falklands [which] could then bring enormous benefits to the people of both countries'.[24]

On most of the issues of importance for other groups on the far left Militant takes its own very individual line. On Ireland Militant has often come in for bitter criticism from other Trotskyists for its opposition to violence and its refusal to give its full backing to the 'troops out' policy. The tendency has been calling for the withdrawal of British troops since they went to Ireland, but emphasises that the troops must be replaced by militias based on the Northern Ireland trade unions: 'This mass force, mobilised in action against sectarianism through a defence force based on trade unions, could do what the army could never do: protect the working class from the bigots of all sides.'[25] So strongly does Militant believe in its trade union defence force that in the past the tendency has abstained on resolutions which demand troop withdrawal without offering this alternative: 'We cannot separate the call for withdrawal of British troops from the demand for the trade union defence force.'[26] Although Militant does ultimately want a united Ireland, it is concerned it should be a socialist Ireland. Furthermore, unlike most groups on the left, Militant is very critical of what it calls 'the monstrous crimes of the Provisionals',[27] and other sectarian groups: 'It is complete lunacy to imagine that it is possible to bomb and assassinate the Protestants into unity with a capitalist Southern Ireland.'[28] Militant believes that acts of 'individual terrorism' only worsen the situation in Ireland by strengthening the state and disorientating the working class: 'Individual terrorism does not raise the consciousness of workers. It lowers it. It allows no role to the masses except to sit, watch and applaud as a small, self-appointed band try, and ultimately fail, to change society on their behalf.'[29]

Militant's policies on Ireland, based on the idea that 'class unity' can bridge religious, sectarian and national divisions, are broadly applied to many of the world's trouble spots. In the Middle East conflict, for instance:

> The solution lies in a Socialist Federation of the Middle East, with autonomy for the Kurds, Lebanese Christians, the blacks of Southern Sudan, the Saharans, and also for Israel within the framework of the federation ... The population of the West Bank and Jordan would be re-united as an autonomous state of the federation, with the other Palestinians in Jordan, economically and socially linked through fraternal agreement with Israel.[30]

Similarly in Cyprus the only solution is 'a united front of Turkish and Greek workers' aiming for 'the establishment of a socialist Cyprus linked in the socialist federation of Greece, Turkey and Cyprus.'[31]

The feminist movement is regarded by Militant as 'petty-bourgeois-dominated' and subject to 'hysteria',[32] although political considerations do not stop Militant presses from printing feminist literature or lesbian newspapers for outside groups. Militant is often quite sexist. An internal document once condemned the old guard type of Labour right-wingers as 'old ladies of both sexes'.[33] In the pages of *Militant* cartoons portray women in an inferior role to men, and workers are always boiler-suited, tough-looking men. Within its own ranks there are very few women in important positions and only about 10 per cent of the tendency's full-timers are female, though recently Militant has come to recognise that its shortage of women is a problem.

In the Labour Party Militant has always been lukewarm about the idea of separate women's sections:

> The solution to the problem lies not in the separation of women, or of arousing antagonism against their class brothers, but in unity with the youth and adult workers in the fight to transform the unions, the Labour Party and society ... these struggles must be linked to the idea of a transformation of society and the perspectives and the theory of Marxism.[34]

Nevertheless this view does not stop Militant participating very actively in Labour Party women's sections. Moreover, in recent years, Militant has bowed to the growing mood among its members and taken more notice of women's issues. There is now a Militant women's group.

The tendency regards all social issues essentially as problems of capitalism. Homosexuality is a problem that will disappear under socialism, Militant believes. Gay rights are a 'petty-bourgeois diversion' and Militant is often very hostile to gays, though recently the tendency has made some recognition of gay rights. If there are any gay members of Militant, they keep quiet about it.

Militant has a very puritanical outlook, and requires a strict lifestyle from its members. Short hair and ties are common. At Militant and LPYS summer camps and conferences Militant members are expected to go to bed early, and comrades sleeping together are frowned upon. Indulging in drugs is one of the worst crimes in Militant's eyes, since these are liable to 'corrupt' working-class people and to 'numb their consciousness'. In the past Militant members have even been expelled for smoking cannabis. At the 1983 LPYS summer camp the National Committee immediately informed new recruits who supported Militant that there were some bad 'petty-bourgeois' elements at the camp who might be smoking 'substances which could distract them from the real task of transforming society'. In Swansea, Militant full-timers have warned members not to go to a particular pub which is known locally as the 'druggie' pub.

Issues such as Ireland, gay rights and women's rights illustrate the main differences between Militant and other Trotskyist groups. Militant calls other Trotskyist organisations 'sects', accuses them of being predominantly middle class, and argues that 'all the sects without exception have a contempt for the working class'.[35] One of Militant's Trotskyist rivals inside the Labour Party, the group around the newspaper *Socialist Action*, formerly the International Marxist Group, once Militant's partners, are 'a piddling little sect which constantly splits, then unifies and then splits again, much like the amoeba. It has been mainly student orientated in outlook, membership and in policy.'[36] The tendency's hostility towards such groups is often as great as any feelings it has towards Tories. For Militant other Trotskyist groups 'have no basis in Marxist theory, no mass support and … are utterly incapable of developing a viable tendency. Most of the elements that they have grafted together are human rubbish.'[37]

Equally Militant rejects the ideas of both factions within the British Communist Party – the Stalinist group for their adherence to Moscow and Eastern Europe, and the Euro-Communists for their advocacy of alliances and coalitions between the Labour Party and the Alliance parties (the Liberal Party and the SDP).

The only two Labour Party figures Militant has any praise for are Tony Benn and Arthur Scargill. Benn is spoken of by Militant full-timers as 'probably the best leader of the left in Europe'. Arthur Scargill, in spite of what many regard as his sympathies towards the Stalinist wing of the Communist Party, is praised by Militant for his 'unbending will to struggle in the face of appalling personal abuse'[38] during the coal dispute: 'Unfortunately at the same time he revealed his lack of understanding of strategy and of tactics.'[39] As many of the left have commented since the strike, Militant has argued that the launching of mass pickets into Nottinghamshire was disastrous, and argued when the strike was still in progress that Scargill was wrong not to hold a national strike ballot: 'One of the greatest deficiencies was an initial incapacity to take the campaign to the masses of the miners and explain the issues involved.'[40] Both Militant and Scargill are Marxist, and share similar goals, but until recently Scargill seemed to have little time for Militant. As the miners' leader has found himself increasingly isolated, however, he seems to have become more friendly towards the tendency.

It is important to understand that Militant's policies and programme are not just a more radical version of the views of others on the Labour left such as Tony Benn and Eric Heffer. The demand to nationalise 200 monopolies is more than a more radical form of the long-standing Tribunite demand to take the top twenty-five companies into public ownership. *Militant* is not a more fervent version of *Tribune*; the tendency is committed to revolutionary change and believes this cannot occur through parliamentary democracy.

At its mass rallies held in London every autumn. Militant displays two huge banners behind the platform. On one are Engels and Marx; on the other, Lenin and Trotsky. At no point has Militant repudiated these thinkers on any issue. Militant believes in the kind of revolution carried out by Lenin and Trotsky in the Soviet Union, but without the Stalinist stage that followed. And it believes that revolution in Britain would inevitably lead to revolution throughout the world.

Tony Benn defends Militant by arguing that Marxism has always been a 'legitimate strand of thought' within the Labour Party. But Militant is not just Marxist, but also Leninist and Trotskyist; as a result it has a style of secretive and disciplined politics that is wholly alien to the democratic traditions of the Labour Party.

What Militant's eventual socialist society would actually entail is not entirely clear. According to Marx's *Communist Manifesto*, private property would be abolished and society would be administered by the workers through their workers' councils. There would be no role for political parties, for Parliament as we know it, the media in its present form, or even for trade unions. Ultimately the state, too, would go: 'In a future socialist society the state will ultimately disappear. No separate apparatus for administration or coercion would be necessary. On the basis of a superabundance of goods, and the abolition of want, the economic basis of the state, shortages, queues and a privileged group to keep those queues in order, would naturally disappear.'[41] In this land of undreamed-of plenty, according to Ted Grant and Alan Woods:

> The nightmare of Stalinism and capitalism will become bad memories of the past, and the blossoming of the productive forces of the planet, integrated under a system of democratic control and planning, will enable art, culture and science to rise to unheard of levels. For the first time, Man will be able to draw himself up to his true stature in a world freed from wars, poverty and oppression.[42]

6

OPERATION ICEPICK

Five days before Christmas 1976, a 52-seater coach sped south down the M6 on its way from Scotland to Lancaster. Most people travelling north along the motorway that afternoon probably would not have noticed it: the vehicle was just one of hundreds of coaches you pass on any long motorway journey. But more observant drivers, glancing across the central reservation at the oncoming traffic, might just have spotted that on the front of this particular vehicle, tied by wire to the radiator grille, was a brand-new icepick.

The 'Icepick Express' was not carrying a party of mountaineers back from a climbing weekend in the Cairngorms. On board, in fact, were nearly fifty Scottish students on their way to the 1976 conference of the National Organisation of Labour Students (NOLS) at Lancaster University, all of them sworn enemies of Trotskyism and of Militant in particular. They were going to Lancaster determined to stop Militant from regaining power in NOLS. When the coach left Glasgow the party on board had included a rather lonely band of Militant supporters. But when the party stopped at a café on the A74 just north of Carlisle, by special arrangement with the driver this group was accidentally left behind. As they chased after the coach on its way out of the car park, nearly a hundred fingers could be seen waving furiously in their direction.

That at least is how the story is told today, no doubt embellished somewhat by the passage of time but essentially true. Apparently it was a noisy journey – noisy enough to rival the coaches which every two years take tens of thousands of Scottish football supporters to the England match at Wembley. This coach of Militant-haters contained just as much venom as any contingent of the 'Tartan Army' of football fans and just as much singing. But, unlike most of their soccer predecessors, these Scotsmen were to return victorious.

Until the mid-1970s Militant had never really encountered any serious or concerted opposition in the Labour Party. The LPYS had been taken over in 1970 with hardly any argument; the granting of a place on the NEC to the LPYS in 1972, and the abolition of the famous Proscribed List a year later, almost gave official sanction to the tendency's activities. As the tendency grew more confident that it was secure in the party, *Militant* was sold more openly at party meetings. By the mid-1970s it seemed most unlikely that Militant could be toppled in the party's youth section. However, Militant's second major victory, the taking over of the Labour students' body, NOLS, in January 1974, prompted an immediate reaction. This was matched by a growing feeling among many party officials that something had to be done about Militant, but a combination of bad organisation, lack of willpower and political alliances ensured that Militant survived this opposition virtually unharmed.

The opposition to Militant in the Labour Party youth sections was symbolised by the icepick, the weapon used by a Stalinist agent to kill Trotsky in 1940 – though the students on the coach had mistakenly used a mountaineering icepick. 'Operation Icepick', a serious attempt to out-manoeuvre Militant, was to make future Labour Party sectarianism look mild by comparison.

During the January 1974 NOLS conference in Manchester (at which Militant took control), several non-Militant delegates marched out of the conference hall after the platform had accepted the credentials of a number of Militant delegates which the non-Militant group believed to be false. The protesters gathered in the lounge on the eighteenth floor of the Owen's Park tower block and agreed to form a group specifically to oppose Militant. At first they could not think of a title, so initially their bank account went under the name of OIP – Operation Icepick. Later the group adopted the name Clause 4 after the famous section in the Labour Party constitution which calls for common ownership.

Clause 4 decided that it had to employ much the same kind of discipline and tactics as those used so successfully by Militant over the years. And in NOLS at least it was to be rewarded within two years. Clause 4 candidates won back NOLS in December 1975, and at the December 1976 Lancaster conference – the destination of the Icepick Express – the battle between the two factions reached its peak. First a Clause 4 chairperson was elected by ninety-four votes to seventy-eight. Then Clause 4 candidates were elected to nearly all the other positions by precisely the same margin: ninety-four to seventy-eight.[1] Both sides at the conference had been almost perfectly disciplined; every delegate could be counted on to vote one way or the other. For once Militant had been beaten at its own game. As one prominent Clause 4 member put it later, 'We out-Militanted Militant.'

Like Militant, the Clause 4 organisation officially centred on a journal, a bulletin called *Clause Four*, and the group was run by the journal's Editorial Board. Organisers were appointed to look after each region of the country and to co-ordinate LPYS and student work. There was also an annual Clause 4 conference. Unlike Militant, Clause 4 had no full-time staff – the members did not have sufficient commitment to cough up enough money for them – but Clause 4 did benefit from the work and resources of supporters who held sabbatical posts in student unions. Caucus meetings were arranged before every meeting of the NOLS National Committee; resolutions were sent out to Clause 4 members in Labour clubs and LPYS branches to be put forward for the national conferences of NOLS or the LPYS. At those conferences Clause 4 would hire a hotel for all its delegates and observers and would hold caucus meetings late into the evening to decide on tactics for the following day. By breakfast time 'whips' would have been issued to remind all Clause 4 delegates how to vote. But there was no 'democratic centralism': Clause 4 delegates were not obliged to toe the line: it was just a matter of political convenience.

Politically Clause 4 described itself as 'Tribunite'. Its outlook was broadly similar to that of the Tribune Group of MPs and the *Tribune* newspaper at that time – what would today be called 'soft left', roughly the position of Neil Kinnock. Clause 4 members sold copies of *Tribune* at Labour Party gatherings as if it were a rival paper to *Militant*, but they received little encouragement from either the *Tribune* newspaper or the parliamentary group. The then editor of *Tribune*, Dick Clements, did not wish to become involved in battles between different groups on the left of the party. Many former Clause 4 members feel today that had Clements and the leaders of the Tribune Group been more enthusiastic at that time, Clause 4 might have met with more success.

Clause 4 received great encouragement from Labour Party officials, though at that time they had to be careful not to be seen as partisan. The then National Youth Officer, Barrie Clarke, can admit today, now that Militant is officially outlawed, that he worked 'totally in league' with the Clause 4 organisation. Clarke had succeeded Neil Vann as National Youth Officer in 1974 and served in this position for more than two years. He took on the job determined to do all he could to beat Militant. He kept in close touch with the Clause 4 leadership and spent much of his time investigating Militant. The records of the Militant companies at Companies House in the City of London were scrutinised, and a photographer was posted outside Militant's offices to take pictures of all comings and goings. At every LPYS or NOLS conference Clarke would carefully examine the credentials of Militant delegates to see that they were in order and did not hesitate to disqualify any that were not: 'Much of my job as National Youth Officer was "disorganising" as much as organising. I was acting like a fire brigade, going round the country saying, "No, they can't do that."'[2]

The battle between the two sides was very bitter; there seemed to be no limit to the kinds of tactics that people would employ. Militant was becoming increasingly frustrated by its failure in NOLS: it began sending to its members lists of the universities to which it wanted them to apply, those where Militant votes were most needed. On one occasion in 1977 it was discovered that some of the NOLS delegates from Handsworth College were not actually members of the college. Barrie Clarke believes that somebody even tried to electrocute him at one conference, by wiring up the Labour Party duplicator incorrectly. It was not Clarke who was hurt, however, but his secretary, when she came down early the next morning to print that day's agenda.

Clause 4 was to keep its hold on NOLS for the rest of the 1970s, but its record in the LPYS was disastrous. This was partly the result of a deliberate decision: Clarke believed that by concentrating on the student body Clause 4 could make reasonable progress and could perhaps show the Labour NEC what could be done, whereas the LPYS was regarded as beyond redemption. But its failure in the LPYS was partly also to do with the nature of Clause 4 itself. Because of its origins in NOLS, it was very much a student organisation: university-orientated and middle class. Many working-class people who sympathised with Clause 4's aims were put off by the atmosphere this created. The result was that it rested on its laurels in NOLS and ignored the LPYS almost completely, which meant that Clause 4 candidates at LPYS conferences got derisory results. Over the years Militant's grip on the LPYS has tightened, and the tendency has never been in any danger of losing control. Today Militant is so strong in the LPYS that it cannot only guarantee to win all elections but even puts up second candidates just in case any winning nominees should be disqualified or should fall under the wheels of a bus and runners-up be required to take their places.[3]

The other problem with Clause 4 was that it was not politically positive. The group knew what it disliked more than what it liked. Though professing to be left wing, in reality it was no more than an alliance of people who detested Militant, especially in the early days. It did produce some material on policy matters and it published pamphlets, usually as a result of individual efforts, but Clause 4's time, energy and resources were spent largely in attacking Trotskyism rather than in proposing a coherent alternative. And the sectarianism was as marked as anything generated by Militant itself. Clause 4 produced badges and plastic pens with icepicks on them. At the end of one Christmas conference members performed a pantomime, dancing around the hall waving icepicks in the air. There was even a Clause 4 songbook.

Clause 4 took a far more serious approach to the National Union of Students (NUS) than Militant had done when it ran NOLS, and by the 1980s NOLS candidates were being elected to the NUS Executive. But the importance of Clause 4, and of its success in NOLS and the NUS, can easily be over-emphasised:

in Britain student politics are of little importance to anyone but students and amount, on the whole, merely to practise in the ways of politicians.

For several Clause 4 leaders, however, that practice was invaluable in the careers they pursued later. Nigel Stanley, the Clause 4 NOLS chairman in 1978, became Organising Secretary of the Labour Co-ordinating Committee and a leading member of the Rank and File Mobilising Committee, which in 1980 introduced two important changes to the party constitution: reselection of MPs, and the introduction of a wider franchise to elect the leadership.[4] Stanley used many of the skills he had developed in combating Militant to fight for these changes. (He is now political adviser to Neil Kinnock's right-hand man, Robin Cook.) Mike Gapes, NOLS chairman in 1976, later became Labour Party student organiser and now works in the International Department. Gapes and several of his former colleagues stood as Labour candidates in the 1983 election and, perhaps significantly for the future, some were active in the campaign to get Neil Kinnock elected as leader.

In the meantime Militant has had no further success in NOLS, but nowadays organised opposition to the tendency comes from a wider 'democratic left' grouping.

While plots against Militant were being hatched late at night over coffee in student digs, concern about Trotskyists was also growing at the highest levels of the Labour Party – in the office of the then national agent, Reg (now Lord) Underhill. Underhill had long been an opponent of far-left elements in the party. As far back as the 1939 conference, when he was a delegate from Leyton, he had spoken in a debate on the League of Youth and had referred to 'silly people talking of Trotsky, attacking the party and leaving the rest of the youth stone cold'.[5] After the war, in his position as assistant to the national agent and then as West Midlands regional organiser, Underhill had tried to tackle Communist infiltration in the Labour League of Youth. By the early 1960s, when he was assistant national agent, the problem was again Trotskyists, mainly from the Socialist Labour League.

Ever since Militant's takeover of the LPYS in 1970 Underhill had been gathering evidence against the tendency. Most of it came from his team of regional organisers dotted around the country – a pretty right-wing group, many of whom had been appointed in the Gaitskellite days of the 1950s and early 1960s. Over the years several of Militant's internal documents had been passed on to Underhill from the regional offices. He had discovered infiltration before, but what he read now about Militant came as a genuine shock. 'The first edition of "British Perspectives and Tasks" [a Militant internal document] I saw horrified me. Here was a group of members of the Labour Party setting out on paper how they would work inside the party.'[6]

In September 1975 Underhill got the NEC's consent to prepare a report on entrism based upon the documents he had received from regional organisers and on conversations with local party officials about Militant's activities. But Underhill's aim at that point was not to expel Militant from the party: 'I just wanted to bring it to the party's attention. At that time I thought we could handle it.'[7]

Underhill's report of November 1975 on 'Entryist Activities' was a short, nine-page document.[8] One section of it covered other Trotskyist groups who had previously operated in the Labour Party, such as the Socialist Labour League (now the Workers' Revolutionary Party) and the International Socialists (now the Socialist Workers' Party). Another part dealt with the International Marxist Group, the body which in 1965 had taken over from Militant as the official British section of the Fourth International and which, Underhill reported, was now starting to mole its way into the Labour Party. But most of the report was devoted to Militant and contained extensive quotations from internal Militant documents, 'British Perspectives and Tasks 1974' and the pamphlet 'Entrism', a copy of which fell into Underhill's hands just before his report was presented.

The Underhill report gave an accurate picture of Militant's structure and strategy. It detailed the strength of the tendency, the extent of its organisation and staff, its international links, the ways in which members were recruited and its long-term plans, which included establishing a group of about six Militant MPs. Yet the document made little impact on the NEC. On the day on which it came before the NEC's Organisation Sub-Committee (known as the 'Org-Sub') very few members of the committee bothered to turn up. Eric Heffer successfully proposed that because of the low turnout the committee should let the report 'lie on the table' – in other words, they should do nothing. 'There have been Trotskyists in the Labour Party for thirty years,' Heffer remarked, with the benefit of personal experience (his own constituency, Liverpool Walton, had been a Trotskyist stronghold almost since the war). He argued that the 'threat' should be met with 'political arguments'. The motion was seconded by the Militant Young Socialist member, Nick Bradley, who said Militant was just like the *Tribune* newspaper and had no organisation.[9] 'Reg, you've been conned,' he told Underhill.

When the Org-Sub's report came to the full Executive, the railwaymen's union member, Russell Tuck, and Shirley Williams tried to reverse the decision. But in spite of a long statement from Harold Wilson about the dangers of extremists on both sides of the party, the NEC accepted the Organisation Sub-Committee's decision by sixteen votes to twelve.[10]

In 1975 the National Executive was dominated by the left, and the left–right split was more clear-cut than it is today: the left group were united against the right, not divided between 'soft' and 'hard', as they have been recently. Many members of the Executive, such as Barbara Castle and, in particular, Michael Foot, thought they were seeing the start of another purge;[11] among those on the left Underhill had a long-standing reputation as a witch-hunter who had been involved in the discipline of the 1950s.

Some trade union NEC members knew very little about Militant beyond the Underhill report itself. When Nick Bradley claimed that Underhill's documents were forgeries, some Executive members may have been sufficiently out of touch to believe him.

The decision effectively to ignore Militant was yet another in a long series of embarrassments for Wilson caused by the Labour NEC. Underhill himself was extremely 'upset'. Others in his position would have had no qualms about leaking the report, but Underhill saw himself as a loyal servant of the party. He would never have dreamed of doing such a thing. As it turned out, others did it for him.

The Underhill report 'provided a lot of fuel for the press'.[12] *The Times* published two whole columns of extracts,[13] and the report received wide coverage in every other paper. Some journalists had carried out their own investigations, notably Nora Beloff of *The Observer*, who wrote a long front-page lead article entitled '"Trot" Conspirators inside the Labour Party – Revolutionary Plot is Exposed', which for the first time told the story of Ted Grant and the RSL.[14] (Grant replied with a solicitor's letter denying any link with the RSL.)[15] But the NEC's refusal to publish the Underhill report only intensified the speculation and the press coverage. The general reaction was: why not publish the report? What was there to hide? The story was a source of considerable discomfort for the party and seemed to confirm public feeling that extremists were taking over local constituency parties.

That impression had been stimulated partly by the publicity over Reg Prentice, who in July 1975 had been dropped as a candidate by his constituency party in Newham North-East. Within days the Prime Minister, Harold Wilson, reacted by condemning what he termed 'small and certainly not necessarily representative groups' and 'infiltration from outside the constituency, sometimes by change of residence'.[16] The Prentice affair was to drag on for almost two years.

Every move in the Prentice story was covered extensively by the media. Here, apparently, was a 'moderate' Cabinet minister being ousted by extremists. The Newham North-East constituency party was presented as a typical inner-city local party, a decrepit organisation in a safe seat, ripe for takeover by bed-sit infiltrators. The party had very few members. Local officials had never really bothered with recruitment, simply because at that point Labour was never in any danger of losing at election time.[17] Harold Wilson's outburst had fuelled the popular belief that large numbers of left-wing activists spent their lives deliberately moving from constituency to constituency causing trouble. In the end the more notable bed-sit infiltrators proved to be Paul McCormick and Julian Lewis, two students who had come to Prentice's defence.

Certainly it was true that many members of the Newham General Management Committee had lived in the constituency for only a few months, but that can be said of most London constituencies. Young people tend to live in different places for short periods of time. Militant was strong in Newham North-East, but it did not have a majority: when a new candidate was eventually selected the Militant nominee, Nick Bradley, got just over one-third of the votes.[18] Prentice was quick to point his finger at Militant, and in an internal document Militant claimed to have acted as the 'catalyst' in the constituency.[19] A key figure was Andy Bevan, a leading Militant member and National Chairman of the LPYS who had moved to the constituency with his wife a few months before Prentice was dropped. Bevan helped to set up a LPYS branch and became vice-chairman of the party, but the fact was that many of Prentice's other critics were not Militant supporters. The man who was regarded as the leader of the anti-Prentice group, Tony Kelly, for instance, was not a Militant member, although he did call himself a revolutionary Marxist. Prentice's opponents included a wide range of left-wingers and people who thought that his politics were wrong and that he was not a good MP. Militant itself was delighted to take the blame (or glory) for getting rid of Prentice, especially when the MP later joined the Conservatives. Most important for our story, however, are not the facts of the Prentice affair or whether Militant played an important role in Newham, but rather the impression these events gave that the Labour Party was being taken over by extremists.

Andy Bevan was at the centre of another major controversy over Militant, which began a year later, in the autumn of 1976. This issue probably did more than anything else to intensify concern about Militant. After little more than two years as National Youth Officer, Barrie Clarke was somewhat relieved to be promoted to Political Education Officer. Around twenty people applied for the vacant post, but the final choice was between Terry Ashton, a young constituency agent, and Bevan, who was still chairman of the LPYS. The selection panel consisted of three people: Bryan Stanley of the Post Office Engineering Union in the chair; Ron Hayward, the Labour Party's general secretary; and Herbert Hickling of the General and Municipal Workers' Union. Bevan was impressive at the interview, coming across as able, charming and energetic. Ashton, regarded as the favourite for the job, had arrived late. Somehow he had been told to turn up at the wrong time and was hot and flustered. Hickling, a blunt trade unionist on the right of the party, was much struck by Bevan and, to everybody's surprise, said that there was no other choice. Ron Hayward, believing perhaps that a former poacher might make a good gamekeeper, seconded this. Ashton got the support of Stanley, but the job went to Bevan by two votes to one. No one was more surprised than Bevan himself, who had thought that for political reasons he did not stand a chance. Although Underhill had briefed the panel about Bevan's links with Militant, it seems that Bert Hickling did not really appreciate what Militant was. Bevan had got the job almost by accident. And since it was traditional for party appointments to be ratified automatically by the NEC, it now looked as though it was too late to reverse it.

Political considerations aside, Bevan probably deserved to be appointed. Even his critics conceded he had considerable ability; right-wing NEC member John Cartwright (now an SDP MP) said that Bevan was 'probably the most effective National Chairman of the Young Socialists there has been'.[20] Brought up in Swansea, Bevan was active in the National Union of School Students and later turned down a place at New College, Oxford, in favour of Bristol University because he thought Oxford 'petty bourgeois'. As a student Bevan had pursued what could be described as a typical Trotskyist career, making rousing speeches in the students' union but never standing for positions that would involve a lot of bureaucratic work. In the LPYS he quickly rose to be National Chairman and was extremely popular. Like many leading Militant figures, Bevan gets on with people and always has time to stop and chat, even to political opponents.

The appointment caused uproar and was naturally seized on by the press. It did not take long for the tabloids to call Bevan 'Red Andy'.[21] The *Daily Telegraph* said that the Labour Party's appointment of a Trotskyist was the equivalent of the Conservatives employing a Nazi.[22] When the matter came before the full NEC in November the new leader Jim Callaghan managed to get the approval delayed because a number of Cabinet colleagues had not been able to turn up. At the December meeting Callaghan argued fervently against Bevan's appointment, and Hayward now seemed to be having second thoughts; but the NEC maintained tradition and accepted Bevan by fifteen votes to twelve. The meeting also rejected what it called 'a further descent into McCarthyism'.[23] It was nearly a straight left–right split. This time, though, the right was joined by Michael Foot, who had been alarmed by a speech of Bevan's a few days before, in which he had advocated the withdrawal of Britain's 'imperialist' troops from Ireland and had called the Irish Prime Minister a 'gangster' and the Northern Ireland peace campaigners 'bigots'.[24] Leading the supporters of Andy Bevan was Tony Benn, who opposed Callaghan publicly by publishing in *The Guardian* an article which Transport House had refused to circulate to the NEC.[25] Benn's defence of Bevan's appointment occupied a whole page, and it argued that Marxism was 'one of the many sources of inspiration within our movement'.

Benn said that he knew Bevan personally: the two had worked closely in Benn's Bristol constituency in the 1974 elections. Bevan had been effective in the local party: Benn said his speeches had impressed other party members, who had recognised in them 'the authentic voice of a political faith they have not heard advocated with such moral force since their own youth'.[26] The December 1976 NEC meeting was the first occasion on which Bevan was to find Benn a useful ally.

At first the party's agents refused to work with Bevan, and the dispute was resolved only when the NEC agreed that an inquiry should now examine the Underhill documents. They also agreed to give some of his tasks to a new student organiser.

Bevan's appointment had again stimulated wide press coverage of Militant. *The Times* ran a long series on the tendency the week before the December meeting.[27] These articles 'revealed' that twelve MPs felt threatened by Militant. Apart from Prentice, two other right-wing MPs, Neville Sandelson in Hayes and Harlington and Frank Tomney in Hammersmith North, were both at war with their parties. There was even speculation that Jim Callaghan was in danger in Cardiff South-East. This press attention, fuelled by right-wingers such as Sandelson, had played an important part in forcing the Labour Party to hold its inquiry.

The inquiry team consisted of two union members, John Chalmers and Tom Bradley, together with two MPs, Eric Heffer and Michael Foot, and general secretary Ron Hayward. Eric Heffer was initially against any action. Michael Foot, though he did not like the idea of a 'party within a party', did not care for witch-hunts either. When the inquiry team reported four months later, in May 1977, it had managed to hammer out a typical Labour Party compromise, avoiding disciplinary action but accepting that Militant was in breach of the rules. The report's recommendations, drawn up by Eric Heffer, were largely cosmetic. Local parties were urged to recruit new members and to make meetings more interesting. The report said that the Young Socialists should not be 'an organisation with only limited membership and a narrow appeal' and called on local parties to 'intensify the development of political education' and to hold discussions, lectures and day schools to explain the Labour Party's belief in democratic socialism. But the report urged tolerance, arguing that 'Trotskyist views cannot be beaten by disciplinary action.'[28]

Militant had escaped again. Nothing came of the Heffer recommendations. The LPYS remained small in numbers and lacking in appeal; no local party is known to have carried out the education suggested. For the next two years the Militant issue was dormant. It was becoming increasingly difficult to rock the boat when Labour's precarious position in Parliament made an election possible at any moment. Meanwhile Militant took advantage of the greater access it had to the Labour headquarters. For example, young people who wrote in to join the party were frequently visited by members of Militant before they had been contacted by local Labour officials.

By the late 1970s, Militant had been brought out into the open, but it had little to fear while the NEC was held by the left. Most left-wingers on the NEC were firmly opposed to expulsions, remembering well the atmosphere in the Labour Party in the 1950s and the time when Bevan had almost been expelled from the party. At the same time the left wanted Militant's support against the right in impending internal battles, such as those over party democracy. (That support was not always forthcoming: in 1977 Militant wrecked an early attempt to introduce mandatory reselection by proposing its own more radical motion to conference.) Some NEC members felt that an attack on Militant was also an attack on the Young Socialists, who were traditionally given extra leeway for their youthful excesses. 'Don't you think we're being a bit hard on the youth?' the Youth Committee chairman, Frank Allaun, used to say whenever Barrie Clarke produced another controversial report. Joan Maynard frequently complained about people attacking 'the lads and lasses'.[29] It was only in later years that many of Militant's defenders on the left, in private at least, were to become more critical of the tendency.

7
THE ORGANISATION

The busy East London Motorway, the A102(M), runs north from the Blackwall Tunnel through Hackney, and, at the point where it divides Victoria Park on the western side from Hackney Wick to the east, a footbridge crosses the six-lane highway. Stand on the bridge shortly after midday and you're quite likely to encounter a dozen or so men dressed in football kit, Militant full-timers from the organisation's headquarters, rushing to their daily lunchtime soccer match in the park.

Hackney Wick is in an area dominated by the six tall 1960s council tower blocks of the Trowbridge Estate. There used to be a seventh block: Hackney Council knocked it down in 1985, amid great publicity, though at first, readers may recall, the building would fall down only half way. Running east to west through this area are the tracks of the newly extended North London Line, with its recently opened Hackney Wick station. The motorway and the railway are joined by two other local carriageways – the

River Lea, which has just left Hackney Marshes half a mile to the north, and the Hertford Union Canal which joins up with the Lea at this point.

The rectangle bounded by the motorway, railway, canal and river is no more than a quarter of a mile square, filled with the kind of businesses one expects in this part of the East End – scrap metal and tyres for instance. Before reaching the River Lea the canal, with its swans and ducks but few barges, passes a timber yard on one side, and a high wall on the other. Behind the wall, wedged between a furniture factory and the local British Telecom service centre is a yellow-brick building, three storeys high, guarded by security cameras perched high on each corner, and electrically operated gates.

This is the Centre. Militant moved here, to Hepscott Road, in late 1984, after the previous Centre at Mentmore Terrace, a mile and a quarter to the west, had become too small to cope with the organisation's rapid expansion. They bought the building and its acre site for a bargain £175,000, from a chemical company who wanted a quick sale, and had no idea who the purchasers, Cambridge Heath Press Limited, really were. 'We thought we were dealing with an ordinary, rather successful, printing firm,' they said later. 'They struck us as very confident businessmen.'[1] Tower Hamlets Council, told that the new owners would be creating fifty local jobs, rushed through planning permission for a printing works. The council's predominantly right-wing Labour members also had no idea that Militant was buying the site. And, on advice from the council, the tendency was able to benefit from a number of development grants.

The Centre is occupied at all hours of the day and night. So worried is Militant about intruders and politically motivated attacks that London members have to guard the premises overnight on a rota basis, and even on Christmas Day. The reception area houses potted plants, as if it was any normal business. The member assigned to reception duties signs visitors in and out, noting the time of arrival and departure. In between times he or she monitors the TV screens linked to the cameras around the building, and it is also the receptionist's job to answer the phone.

Inside the building are directed Militant's operations both in Britain and across the globe. Militant boasts that the Centre is almost as large as the Labour Party HQ at Walworth Road, and the tendency has applied for planning permission for further expansion. The Centre does not just contain the editorial area and printing presses for the *Militant* newspaper, but all the departments one would expect in any major political party. There is even a bookshop, and a small canteen, where workers can eat beneath large posters of Marx, Engels, Lenin and Trotsky.

In addition to the Centre in London, Militant has more than a dozen regional offices around the country. The London region's HQ is at 375 Cambridge Heath Road, Bethnal Green, a three-storey terraced building which Militant bought from the local Boy Scouts in 1970. It served as the national Centre until 1976. Other offices are situated in Brighton, Bristol, Birmingham, Cardiff, Edinburgh, Glasgow, Harlow, Hull, Leeds, Liverpool, Manchester, Newcastle and Swansea. Many of these offices are houses bought on mortgages by members on behalf of Militant, such as in the case of the Page Street office in Swansea. In Newcastle the Militant office is above the Star Inn in Westgate Street, and rented from Bass Breweries. In Cardiff, Militant has a room in an office block, the APEX building, while in some cases, such as Harlow, the regional headquarters are simply rooms in the homes of full-timers. Most of the regional headquarters are equipped with libraries and simple printing presses.

At the very top of the Militant hierarchy is the Executive Committee (referred to publicly as the Editorial Board) which, Militant asserts, consists of five people: Peter Taaffe, the editor of *Militant*; Ted Grant, the political editor; Lynn Walsh, the assistant editor; Clare Doyle, the business manager; and Keith Dickinson, in charge of administration and security. These were the five who were expelled from the Labour Party in February 1983. Three of them, Taaffe, Grant and Dickinson, have been at the centre of Militant since the very beginning of its newspaper in 1964, though only Grant has been in the RSL since the start. Walsh and Doyle are both from the group once based at Sussex University and joined the organisation in the mid-1960s but did not become key figures until later.

Peter Taaffe was born into a family of five children in Birkenhead during the war. His father, a sheet-metal worker, died when he was a child, and the family lived in what Taaffe describes as 'atrocious housing':[2] he still has a scar on the bridge of his nose which is a legacy from the time when the ceiling fell down on him while he was asleep in bed. Taaffe mixes well. He gets on with working people and understands them; he will have a drink with the lads, talk about television or football and his favourite team, Everton. At lunchtime you will often find him playing soccer in Victoria Park with other Militant staff (Taaffe is always allowed to pick the best side). He is married with two daughters. His wife Linda sometimes writes for *Militant*, usually on women's issues, and has been active in the Labour Party in Islington. Before his expulsion Taaffe himself had not been seen at his local ward party for several years.

The eccentric Ted Grant is a more private character than Taaffe, and he enjoys the air of mystery that surrounds him. His whole life has been devoted to revolutionary politics. He has few hobbies; one of them is table tennis, at which he always beats Taaffe, much to the editor's annoyance. Beethoven and Bach are another diversion. Grant very rarely drinks and is obsessed with keeping fit and healthy, eating health foods and doing exercises every morning. His only known vices are Jelly Babies and gobstoppers. Militant's other leaders are resigned to the fact that even though Grant is now over seventy, he will be around for the next twenty years. He often teases Taaffe that he will outlive him. Certainly Grant appears to be ten years younger than his real age. Even so, Militant colleagues sometimes refer to Grant as the 'Old Man' (the nickname given to Trotsky himself in the 1930s). On public occasions he is often seen in smart, expensive clothes, but he never wears them well: it is said in Militant that Grant is paid so badly by the organisation that his clothes have been passed on to him by his sister's husband, a wealthy businessman in France. Grant did not become a full-timer with Militant until 1969; Taaffe and Dickinson were employed by the tendency before him.

Until then he carried on working as a night-time telephone operator. Grant's office at the Centre contains hundreds of books by and about Marx, Lenin, Engels, Trotsky and Plekhanov. The walls are piled with back issues of *The Banker*, *The Economist*, *Investors Chronicle* and the *Financial Times*: he even has copies of the *FT* going back to the 1930s. One can always recognise articles written by Grant: they are sprinkled with quotations from these journals, using 'capitalist' quotations against capitalism.

The relationship between Taaffe and Grant is an interesting one. Officially Taaffe is editor of *Militant*; in reality he does little work on the paper. His real job is general secretary. Nominally he occupies a position superior to Grant's, but it was Grant who helped to appoint Taaffe in the first place, and Grant has assumed the role of keeping Militant's ideology 'pure'. Broadly speaking, Taaffe is responsible for organisation and Grant for political and economic analysis. As we have seen, Grant played a similar role with Jock Haston in the RCP in the 1940s and, less successfully, with Jimmy Deane in the RSL in the 1950s. In the unlikely event that Militant ever came to power, one could speculate that Grant would be president (once the monarchy had been abolished) and Taaffe would continue as general secretary of the party and probably Prime Minister as well. Grant is the theoretician; Taaffe masterminds the strategy, putting the theories into practice. This is only a rough guide to their comparative functions: the two men would have difficulty explaining their relationship themselves. Taaffe does have an important policy role too, and he writes a great deal. Their respective roles also seem to be changing:

with time Taaffe has gradually been taking on even more responsibility and power. Grant appears to be on the decline.

Peter Taaffe often finds Grant difficult to cope with in public.
On one occasion when Militant's leaders met the Labour Party
NEC, the general secretary Jim Mortimer complained that certain Militant supporters had been causing trouble. 'Then give
us the names', shot back Grant, 'and we'll discipline them.' Peter
Taaffe was clearly embarrassed by his colleague's indiscretion.
Once, during a television interview, he took out his handkerchief
and energetically wiped his nose. Grant is famous throughout the
Labour movement for his mannerisms and violent hand movements while speaking: these are frequently imitated by Militant's
younger members, sometimes in admiration but often in jest.

The assistant editor of *Militant*, Lynn Walsh, is one of the
younger generation of Militant leaders bred politically at Sussex
University in the mid-1960s. After university he lectured in a college
of technology and then became a Militant full-timer. During the
early 1970s he became a specialist on Spain and Portugal, spending
a lot of time in both countries, where Militant had high expectations after the fall of the two dictatorships. Walsh is obviously
middle class and does not feel the need to conceal it by adopting a
Liverpool or East End accent, as do some of his more self-conscious
middle-class colleagues. He avoids many of the stock phrases and
clichés and, presumably because of his more natural manner, often
chairs Militant press conferences and does television interviews.
In practice it is Walsh, not Taaffe, who edits the paper. He writes
many of the editorials: Taaffe casts an eye over them later.

The only woman in the Militant leadership, Clare Doyle, is publicly the organisation's business manager and internally treasurer of the tendency. Like Walsh, she joined the Labour Party in Brighton in 1964. The daughter of a vicar from Sussex, she was once married to another prominent Militant character, Peter Doyle, chairman of the LPYS in the early 1970s and the first LPYS representative on the NEC before it was discovered he was too old. They met through Militant when Clare was working on Tyneside as a nursery-school teacher. She hit the national headlines during the Toxteth riots in 1981, when she went to Liverpool to distribute leaflets and to explain to the Liverpool comrades what could be learned from Brixton, where she lives.

Keith Dickinson is responsible for Militant administration and for running the offices. He is also in charge of security, which means not only protecting Militant's properties but also vetting all Militant documents, internal and public, for slips which might give something away. Nicknamed 'the Nag', Dickinson was for eight years (until 1983) caretaker of the committee rooms of the Hammersmith Labour Party and lived in a flat above them. Of the five expelled in 1983 Dickinson is probably the most active in the Labour Party: he has served on the Hammersmith party's General Committee for several years and has stood unsuccessfully in several council elections. He first joined the Labour Party in Liverpool Walton in 1957 and in 1960 spoke in the famous conference debate on defence, in which Hugh Gaitskell made his 'Fight, fight and fight again' speech. One of the founders of the *Militant* newspaper, he had previously been on the editorial boards of *Rally* and *Socialist Fight* as well as business manager of *Young Guard*, which was eventually taken over by the Cliff group (later the Socialist Workers' Party). Dickinson is a shy person – you will more often see him sitting at the back of the hall than on the platform at the front – but he is very popular within the tendency.

These five ostensibly form Militant's Editorial Board. In reality, though, the Executive usually contains about ten to twelve people. The five well-known names were simply listed for public consumption when the Labour Party was about to expel people. Other members of the Executive are Roger Silverman (International secretary), Alan Woods (the editor of *Militant International Review*), Brian Ingham, John Pickard and Peter Jarvis (Industrial organiser and his deputies) and Rob Sewell (Organisation Department). Bob Labi may also attend Executive meetings on behalf of the International Department during Roger Silverman's frequent trips abroad.

Militant's organisation is based on the principles of a Marxist–Leninist revolutionary party. Its style of administration is that of most democratic centralist parties – the system devised by Lenin for the Bolsheviks in Russia, which later came to be adopted by all Communist organisations.

The Militant Executive Committee has a function similar to that of the Politburo in most Communist parties. Every Friday it meets to make the day-to-day decisions for the tendency. The larger Central Committee (until 1974 called the National Committee) consists of about forty-five people and includes representatives from each of the regions and the tendency's bureaux.

It meets monthly over a weekend at the Centre to sort out broader, longer-term policy and organisational matters. Apart from the elected members, other regular attenders at Central Committee meetings are some of the full-timers and Militant members on the LPYS National Committee. At one time Militant went even further in the tradition of democratic centralist parties and had 'alternate members' of its Central Committee; these were expected to attend the committee's meetings and could speak but were allowed to vote only if any full members were absent. A few years ago alternate membership of the committee was abolished, though, and the committee itself was enlarged.

At the new Hepscott Road headquarters a special room has been set aside on the top floor for the Central Committee. A large table and chairs are permanently laid out, and, rather like the Cabinet Room at No. 10, each member of the committee has a set place.

At the 1981 conference Militant changed its rules so that only full-time workers for the tendency could sit on the Central Committee. This meant that several long-serving Central Committee members, who wanted to carry on doing normal jobs, had to step down. Among them were Pat Wall, Tony Mulhearn, Peter Doyle, Bob McKee, Jim Brookshaw and Bill Mullins. (Mullins was subsequently sacked from his job at Rover Solihull and is now back on the committee.) The change was made because Central Committee meetings often drag on for several days and members in full-time employment could not always attend throughout, but the change was bitterly opposed and some believe it may have had an important political effect on the organisation. It is argued that the committee lost the benefit of several people with practical experience of working inside the Labour movement, and who were active trade unionists. Their replacements, younger full-time workers with less practical experience, were appointed by the Militant leadership. The independent voice of men like Wall and Mulhearn had led to robust debates in the past, whereas their successors are much more likely to agree with what the Executive proposes. Some recent defectors argue that this change has led to some very unwise decisions by the committee, and has led to it losing touch with the wider Labour movement.

At the next level down in the hierarchy, below the Central Committee, are the full-timers. 'Full-timer' is a political rank in Militant rather than an indication that one is a paid employee. Full-timers do not apply for the positions; they are simply appointed by the Executive Committee, and once a Militant member gets the call he or she is expected to give up existing employment. In most cases full-timers go through a training period beforehand, but even after this they may not necessarily be paid by the organisation: many full-timers claim state benefits, especially those who were unemployed before working for Militant. Sometimes these dole payments will be topped up by extra money from Militant – for instance, in the form of over-generous expenses. Other full-timers are so badly paid that they have to live off the earnings of their spouses, who will nearly always be members of the tendency. At the time of writing, Militant has over 300 people in the 'full-timer' position, many more than the figure it has acknowledged publicly for the past few years (sixty-four). This compares well with established political parties. The Labour Party has about 200 full-time staff in all, adding together those in London, its regional offices and the constituencies. The Social Democrats now have more than fifty (following redundancies the SDP had to make after the 1983 election) and the Liberals have about seventy employees in total. The former Liberal Party Secretary-General, Sir Hugh Jones, often complained of having fewer staff than Militant.

About half the full-timers work in Militant's three offices in London: as journalists on the paper, as print workers or in Militant's bureaux: Political, Organisation, Education, Finance, Industrial, Youth, Black and Asian, Student, and International. The rest of the full-timers are scattered around the country. Outside London the more senior of these have overall responsibility for a region; others concentrate on regional youth or industrial work, or work in a particular district within the region.

The Militant full-time workers are part of a much larger grouping, more than 1,000-strong Militant 'cadres'. Cadres are those members perfectly 'steeled' in the ideas of the organisation, with long experience both in Militant and the Labour movement. Many cadres, Tony Mulhearn and Pat Wall for instance, carry more weight within the organisation than many full-timers, and will have extremely important roles when the revolution comes. Their activity within the trade union movement is seen as just as important for Militant as the work of the official full-timers. At one time the idea was that every Militant member should pick up sufficient experience and understanding to become a cadre.

But recently Militant has seemed to believe that its cadre force is now sufficiently strong, and is concentrating its efforts on supplementing the cadre force with a mass membership built up from raw recruits.

Ever since the beginning of the RSL there has been an annual conference or 'congress', as it was called in the very early days. Since 1979 these have always been held at the Spa Royal Hall, Bridlington. The gathering is held with the utmost secrecy: security is impressive. Only members bearing special tickets ('V' for visitor and 'D' for delegate) are allowed in. Administrative reports are individually marked and numbered before being handed out and have to be returned at the end of each session. On one occasion cleaners were not even permitted to replace the towels in the lavatories, and the conference hall bar staff were not allowed to watch what was going on in spite of protestations that they were sympathetic. In 1980 several journalists tried to wheedle their way in, and one reporter was even found hiding in the lavatories. No journalist has ever succeeded in seeing what goes on, but the publicity given to the secret events has done Militant a lot of harm. In 1982, at the height of the Labour Party campaign against Militant, at the last minute it was thought best to cancel that year's conference. To placate the Labour NEC the tendency said that in future it would open the occasion to outsiders, but after the expulsion of the Militant Editorial Board this offer was withdrawn and Militant returned to Bridlington in November 1983 and February 1985. The conference scheduled for January 1986 was also cancelled for tactical reasons during the Liverpool inquiry.

Publicly the conference is always referred to as an annual *Militant* sellers' rally, for people who sell the paper regularly. In reality it is a full-scale party conference.

Each Militant branch sends delegates, one for every five members, but other members are encouraged to go too. (When the membership was small all members were strongly urged to attend.) The conference sessions are chaired by members of the Central Committee in rotation. Most of the two or three days is taken up with discussion of the latest copies of 'British Perspectives and Tasks' and 'World Perspectives', the discussion documents written collectively by the Militant leadership every year. Before being presented to the conference, the 'Perspectives' will have been approved by the Executive and Central Committee and sent out to members in advance. All the conference is expected to do is to debate the documents and pass them unanimously. It always does. Amendments are rare.

The rest of the conference time is taken up with administrative matters. The general secretary and the treasurer of the Militant organisation, Peter Taaffe and Clare Doyle, give reports on organisation and finance. There will also be accounts of the tendency's progress in other areas from the head of each bureau: Youth, International, Industrial and so on. At the end of the assembly comes a rallying speech from Ted Grant, which serves just the same purpose as the leader's speech at the end of a Conservative conference. Then all the delegates return to their branches to give reports on the conference to the ordinary members and to outline the 'perspectives and tasks' for the year ahead.

Every year the conference also has the task of re-electing the Central Committee. In the true traditions of democratic centralism it usually does just that. As in most Marxist-Leninist parties, the outgoing committee will propose to the conference its recommendations for the new Central Committee. Delegates can pass or reject the list of names only en bloc. They can propose other candidates for election, but only by putting forward an amendment to the official list, which also means proposing who should be replaced. Not surprisingly, challenges to the official list rarely occur, which explains the remarkable continuity of the Militant leadership over the years.

This is not to say there are never any disagreements at Militant conferences. There have been several over the years. The general pattern is for the minority group to propose alternative 'Perspectives' to the Militant conference, for it to be defeated, and for the minority then to leave the organisation.

The 1973 gathering at Sheffield University saw the most serious division when a group of twenty-one members, led by the Militant treasurer, Ted Coxhead, proposed an alternative document calling for more involvement in single-issue campaigns and co-operation with other left-wing pressure groups. The group had in fact been holding discussions with the International Marxist Group beforehand, and the IMG Political Committee had actually helped to draw up their document. The dissidents were allowed to address the conference, and their document was circulated in advance by the Central Committee; but with support from only one branch, Nottingham, these 'petty-bourgeois' rebels were defeated overwhelmingly. Nevertheless the Militant leadership was seriously worried by the challenge and tried to conciliate the dissidents, in vain. After the defeat they left and joined the IMG.

The subject of devolution caused another serious split two years later. The Militant leadership wanted to change the tendency's position from anti- to pro-devolution. Most of the Scottish delegates to the conference, led by an alternate Central Committee member, Alex Wood, argued vehemently against this change of policy. The leadership won the battle, and Wood eventually left the tendency.

The exclusion of members who weren't full-timers from the Central Committee in 1981 provoked a serious discussion. Later, in 1985, economic theorist Andrew Glyn proposed an alternative document to the conference, but not surprisingly was defeated by the arguments put forward by Ted Grant.

There have been two other divisions of note, both in the early years. In 1966, a group of four members in the north, led by Sean Matgamna and his wife Rachel Lever, proposed an alternative document called 'What We Are and What We Must Become'. The group accused Militant of 'quietism' and argued that Militant's fear of disciplinary action meant it was making too little impact, and not taking enough advantage of the political situation and events such as the seamen's strike to develop its organisation. After a national aggregate in London refused to circulate their document, the four walked out. Matgamna and Lever eventually went on to play leading roles in another Trotskyist entrist group, based around the newspaper *Socialist Organiser*.

A year or two later Chris Knight was expelled by the National Committee for putting forward an alternative programme, entitled 'All Power to the Labour Government', which argued that Militant should be less sectarian and more willing to join with other groups. He appealed against his expulsion to the conference, but the appeal was turned down, and Knight went off with a handful of other Militant members to help found *The Chartist* newspaper. For several years in the early 1970s the Chartist group was the main Trotskyist opposition to Militant in the LPYS. Later Knight was a leading member of the Labour Briefing group which became so influential in London Labour politics in the early 1980s. *Labour Briefing* even adopted Knight's slogan, 'Labour to Power'.

Geographically the Militant organisation is divided into regions, districts and branches. There are twelve regions in all: London, southern, West Midlands, East Midlands, eastern, south-west, Yorkshire and Humberside, Manchester and Lancashire, Merseyside, northern, Wales, and Scotland. Though the names are broadly similar to those of the Labour Party regions, the boundaries have deliberately been drawn differently, perhaps to cause confusion to Labour officials. Within each region are several districts, each of which generally covers a conurbation or county. In turn each district is made up of a number of branches. The branch is the lowest organisational unit: it may cover a small town or part of a city, often the same area as a single parliamentary constituency. But it should be stressed that the system of districts and branches is only the ideal model. In some parts of the country, particularly in rural areas, Militant may not be strong enough to sustain branches or even districts, and in such cases the region forms the basic administrative unit. As the Militant organisation has expanded, more and more districts and branches have been established: as soon as anyone unit is big enough – more than about a dozen people – it will be split into two. At the start of 1986 Militant had around 400 branches.

Each region, district and branch is administered by a committee, often referred to in public as a regional, district or local 'editorial board'. Nominally these committees are elected by all the members in the area they cover; in reality they are self-perpetuating groups nominated by themselves, just as the Central Committee is.

Branches meet weekly and are the ordinary members' main contact with the Militant organisation. But even where branches are strong, regions and districts remain important levels in the Militant structure: the higher levels are given targets for new members and paper sales, and they look after Militant's financial contributions. In addition, all communications from the Centre come down to the branches via the regional and district full-timers. As well as weekly branch meetings, members will go to district 'aggregate' meetings – attended by all the members in the district – at least once a quarter. There is also an aggregate meeting for each region at least once a year. Then there are regular weekend 'cadre schools', organised by districts and regions, whose aim is to educate members in Marxist theory and to train them in political skills such as public speaking and selling papers.

Apart from its hierarchical structure covering the country, Militant organises a number of caucuses for its work in particular trade unions and now has groups operating in nearly twenty different unions. Union work is becoming an increasingly important area for Militant because of the attention the tendency has received within the Labour Party. There is also a Black and Asian Militant caucus and a women's group. In addition Militant organises a number of front organisations, which to outsiders have no obvious connection with the tendency. Among these are PNP Youth, a British youth section of the Jamaican National Party, which has tried, fairly unsuccessfully, to recruit young West Indians and even Asians to the tendency.

Apart from its newspaper, Militant produces a wide range of other publications, some public and some strictly internal. Among the former is the quarterly *Militant International Review*, a theoretical magazine which was started in 1969. Alan Woods recently took over as editor – a sign that he may assume part of Ted Grant's theoretical role in the future. There are also sporadic Militant publications for distribution in certain unions, such as *Militant Teacher*, *CPSA Militant*, *Militant Miner*, *NALGO Militant* and *Beacon*, the Militant journal for the electricians' union. On top of that are regular pamphlets and books on a wide range of subjects, from Marxist theory and ideological issues to the situation in particular countries and even CIA infiltration of the Labour Party.

Secret internal documents are far less common than they once were. It seems that since the early 1980s Militant has cut down on the number of internal documents, presumably because too many of them were leaking out. Perhaps the most famous of the 'internals' is 'Entrism', Ted Grant's pamphlet, republished several times, which sets out for new members the basis of Militant's operations inside the Labour Party. Then, since 1957, there have been the annual 'British Perspectives' and 'World Perspectives' documents, prepared before each Militant conference, setting out the Militant view of Britain or the world, and its future. In 1985, however, Militant took the decision to publish its British Perspectives document openly for the first time, as 'Capitalism at an Impasse – Marxist Perspectives for Britain', and a supplement came out later in the year. Both these pamphlets were printed in exactly the same style as the old 'Perspectives' internals, although the contents were rather less revealing. Until 1981 there were also regular internal magazines – *Bulletin*, *Industrial Bulletin*, *Student Bulletin*, and the *International Bulletin*, which mainly dealt with organisational matters. A decision was made to stop publication of these, but since 1984 Militant has again been publishing an internal *Bulletin of Marxist Studies*. This comes out about twice a year and is partly theoretical and partly organisational.

All the secret documents are carefully written so as not to give away any details about who publishes or prints them. Militant is never referred to by name, only by phrases such as 'our tendency'. Once or twice, though, the man in charge of security, Keith Dickinson, has slipped up. The 1973 edition of 'Entrism', for instance, accidentally carried the Cambridge Heath Press imprint.[3] Articles are signed with pseudonyms (Tom Pearce is Peter Taaffe) or with reversed initials (so TP is Peter Taaffe, GE Ted Grant, WP Pat Wall, DC Clare Doyle and so on), but often, especially on political matters, it is difficult to see the need for a secret internal document anyway. Sometimes there is little difference between what is published internally and what is distributed in public. 'British Perspectives 1981', for instance, is the same, almost word for word, as a pamphlet by Ted Grant entitled 'Britain in Crisis'. The only difference was that the private version had paragraph numbers, while the public one did not, and an unfavourable reference to Michael Foot was deleted from the public edition.

This, then, is the Militant organisation. It is the organisation of a political party – and one operating secretly within the Labour Party – that practises entrism. It is this extensive organisation, rather than political differences, that has provided the main argument for the recent action against Militant. In that debate the party establishment has turned to its own rule book to uphold its case. Clause II, Section 3, of the Labour Party constitution states:

> Political organisations not affiliated to or associated under a National Agreement with the Party on 1 January 1946, having their own Programme, Principles and Policy for distinctive and separate propaganda, or possessing Branches in the Constituencies or engaged in the promotion of Parliamentary or Local Government Candidates or owing allegiance to any political organisation situated abroad, shall be ineligible for affiliation to the Party.[4]

That Militant is in breach of this part of the Labour Party constitution must be beyond doubt. It does have its 'own Programme, Principles and Policy for distinctive and separate propaganda'. It does possess 'Branches in the Constituencies'. We shall also see in the next chapter how Militant owes allegiance to its own international organisation. On three points of Section 3 Militant is guilty.

Only on the fourth count (promoting 'Parliamentary or Local Government Candidates') is Militant not breaching the constitution. Nevertheless, when five Militant supporters stood as Labour candidates in the 1983 election they stood on a Militant programme rather than on Labour's manifesto, and Militant treated them almost as if they were standing for its organisation, not for Labour.

If Militant is breaking the Labour Party's rules, so, strictly speaking, are many other Labour Party pressure groups. Labour Solidarity, the Labour Co-ordinating Committee and the Campaign for Labour Party Democracy, to name only three of the most prominent bodies, all have their own distinctive propaganda and policies. The Labour Co-ordinating Committee and several other groups have branches in the constituencies. Other bodies, such as Labour Friends of Israel and the Labour Committee for Europe, clearly have allegiance to 'political organisations situated abroad'; furthermore, they openly receive funds from abroad. The Labour Party constitution is so strict that dozens of pressure groups within the party ranks are in breach of it; but it has always been a tradition within the party to take the constitution with a pinch of salt, and Clause II, Section 3, has always been taken by all pressure groups, on the left and on the right, with a particularly large pinch. In just the same way many on the right have long ignored the famous Clause IV, Part 4, which calls for common ownership. Dislike of Militant has grown not simply because its organisation has been in breach of the Labour Party's constitution – that is a widespread offence – but because it has breached the constitution so blatantly and, perhaps more important, so effectively.

8

MILITANT'S MONEY

The financial year 1976–77 was a disaster in the eyes of Her Majesty's Treasury. The pound hit an all-time low against the dollar; twice the Chancellor had to announce cuts in public expenditure, on the second occasion after humiliating negotiations with the International Monetary Fund. The Public Sector Borrowing Requirement, the difference between government income and expenditure, was at its highest level ever. And the Labour Chancellor, Denis Healey, was not getting much help from British industry. That year thirteen of Britain's top twenty firms, including BP, Esso, Dunlop and Ford, managed to avoid paying any 'mainstream' Corporation Tax.[1] But if Healey received little support from the commanding heights of the economy, the Exchequer was at least benefiting from the efforts of one tiny company in Hackney, which was less than three years old but had great ambitions for international expansion. From No. 1 Mentmore Terrace, London E8, came a cheque for £546, the Corporation Tax payment on the profits of WIR Publications Limited, one of the two companies then owned by Militant.[2]

For a left-wing organisation to do well enough to pay tax on its profits, as WIR Publications has frequently done, is unusual. But then Militant has had an unusual financial history. Ever since the first issue of its newspaper in October 1964 it has enjoyed remarkable success. During two decades which have seen print, paper and labour costs rise faster than inflation *Militant* has not just survived as a newspaper but has vastly expanded. It was a four-page monthly when it began on the eve of Labour's return to power in 1964. According to one of the founders, Terry Harrison, the starting funds were scraped together by the people involved, some of whom 'sold off family heirlooms'.[3] Most left-wing newspapers count themselves lucky if they survive beyond a few issues: it is rare for radical politicians to possess sufficient entrepreneurial flair, or simply enough money, to keep a paper going after the initial enthusiasm and funds have run out. But *Militant* has not just remained on its feet financially: it has prospered. Today it is a sixteen-page weekly, a substantial read, and since 1983 Militant has been talking of making the paper twice-weekly in the near future and then daily. Indeed, the move to new premises in 1984 was carried out with this in mind. Although the plans for a more frequent paper seem to have fallen well behind schedule (1987 is the latest target for a twice-weekly paper), if they do work out it will be an interesting indication of the tendency's organisation, strength and determination, at a time when the Labour Party's and the TUC's dream of a daily paper still seems some way off.

While *Militant*'s claimed circulation of 40,000 is almost certainly an exaggeration – 20,000 would be more accurate – after the *New Statesman* the paper is probably the most popular left-wing weekly in Britain. But it would be wrong to spend too much time comparing the *Militant* newspaper with other journals. As we have seen, Militant is much more than just a newspaper: it is a large-scale political organisation with more full-time paid staff than either the Liberal Party or the Social Democrats, and probably more full-time workers, although not full-time *paid* workers, than the Labour Party itself. So where does the money come from?

One source is obvious. Every week *Militant* carries a 'Fighting Fund' column in its pages, urging readers to send in money to help the paper. In the early days the Fund's target was to raise a modest £500 as soon as possible; today it aims to raise £70,000 every three months, though it has never been successful. £47,000 was received by the Fighting Fund in 1977, £66,000 in 1978, £80,000 in 1979, £94,000 in 1980, £103,000 in 1981, £148,000 in 1982, £152,000 in 1983, £159,000 in 1984 and £194,000 in 1985. In addition, since October 1983 Militant has raised £262,000 through its Daily Building Fund set up to raise money to buy its new premises and eventually launch *Militant* on a daily basis.[4] Each week *Militant* carries news of the latest generous contributions, from 50p given by an old-age pensioner to thousands of pounds raised at one public meeting. A table shows how well each area is doing with respect to the target set for it. Any area which achieves its target in one quarter will get a higher one next time; areas that fail get the same target again. The Fund has in the past included donations from several

Labour MPs, including Eddie Loyden (a Militant sympathiser in Liverpool)[5] and, in October 1974, Manchester MP Paul Rose, who sent £3 to thank Militant supporters for their help in his election campaign.[6] Rose described his Militant election workers in 1974 as 'a breath of fresh air'.[7] Seven years later he joined the SDP.

But even with revenue of nearly £200,000 a year, the Fighting Fund alone could not possibly support an organisation the size of Militant, whose electricity and phone bills are tens of thousands of pounds each for the London headquarters alone. There must be some other, more substantial, source of money.

It has frequently been suggested by Militant's critics that the tendency receives a foreign subsidy – the 'Moscow Gold' theory. How else could it keep going on sales and donations alone? it is asked. Examples of other left-wing papers that depend on foreign support are often quoted. The *Morning Star*, for instance, now down to a daily circulation of under 30,000, sells half its copies to Eastern Europe, and by all accounts Moscow news agents do not sell out halfway through the morning rush-hour. The *Morning Star*'s reliance on the Soviet bloc has long been public knowledge. Less well known until recently have been the links between Libya and certain left-wing papers in Britain. It is difficult to imagine what foreign power would want to subsidise *Militant*, though. Neither the Soviet Union nor Colonel Gaddafi's Libya would find it an attractive proposition, since the paper is highly critical of both these regimes.

During the period that the RSL was a member of the Fourth International, until 1965, the League seems to have received *some* modest financial assistance from the International Secretariat and from the American Socialist Workers' Party to help publish pamphlets, but this obviously ended when Militant left the Fourth International in 1965. The only other financial benefit Militant seems to have gained from any international links was the printing of some of its pamphlets and books by comrades in Sri Lanka in the early 1970s. In return for arranging the cheap printing, the Sri Lankans were allowed a few pages at the back of one pamphlet for an article by one of their members.[8]

The leaders of Militant vehemently deny any foreign source of funds, and I have found no evidence whatsoever that the tendency receives money from abroad. To understand where most of its money does *come* from one needs first to look at the tendency's formal financial organisation.

Militant owns three limited companies: WIR Publications Limited, Cambridge Heath Press Limited and Eastway Offset Limited. WIR Publications Limited was an 'off-the-shelf £100 company incorporated in June 1973 with an ambitious object: 'to aid and further the interests of the international working class' and 'to render aid, pecuniary or otherwise, to Labour or socialist candidates in parliamentary, municipal or other elections'.[9] This firm is clearly a continuation of previous RSL and Militant trading names dating back to the foundation of the *Workers' International Review* in 1956. The Revolutionary Socialist League ran a business (as opposed to a company) called Workers' International Review (publishers), which in 1963 seems to have become WIR Publications (again not a company), the predecessor of the present firm.

Cambridge Heath Press Limited, the earliest of the companies, was incorporated in August 1971. Presumably it was named after Cambridge Heath Road in Bethnal Green, where Militant had bought premises and installed their new printing press only a few months before. Cambridge Heath Press has the aims of a printing and publishing company.[10]

The tendency's third limited company, Eastway Offset Limited, was set up only in May 1985. One of its stated objects is to do printing work for the Labour movement.

As limited companies, such firms are legally obliged to lodge up-to-date lists of directors and shareholders with Companies House in the City and to submit annual accounts.

Journalists and Militant's enemies have spent hours hunched over the microfilm projectors in the Public Search Room at Companies House, trying to make something out of the records of these companies. They do make interesting reading. WIR Publications Limited, for instance, has twenty-five people listed as its original shareholders: Robert Reeves, Raymond Apps, Robert Faulkes, Robert Edwards, Robert McKee, Terence Harrison, Michael Newman, Edward Mooney, Anthony Mulhearn, Thomas Ward, Lynn Walsh, Robin Jamieson, Peter Doyle, Alan Woods, Muriel Browning, Pat Wall, Bryan Beckingham, William Webster, Peter Hadden, Alex Wood, Terence Wilson, Pat Craven, Clare Doyle, Ted Grant and Keith Dickinson. Patrick Craven was the first company secretary.[11] The list corresponds exactly to Militant's Central (National) Committee when the company was set up in 1973, when Patrick Craven was treasurer of the RSL.

In 1982 it was being suggested that these names should provide the list of those to be expelled from the Labour Party. That would have been rather unfair, since at least one of those named, Alex Wood, was no longer involved in Militant. In 1980, three years after Wood had left the tendency, Clare Doyle wrote to ask him to send his one share back. Wood duly obliged, unaware perhaps that the certificate might have fetched a good price in some circles. Later it seems that Michael Newman and Robin Jamieson left the organisation, while Peter Doyle resigned in 1985.

What of the accounts themselves? Can these provide the answer to the Militant riches? The first person to analyse them in any detail was a solicitor and Labour Party member, Charles James. The result of James's work was a series of reports, each entitled 'The Companies We Keep', the first of which came out in 1977. Each was passed on to officials in Labour's regional and head offices, and at least one edition reached the then leader, Jim Callaghan. Several journalists were also given copies, and the information was used in newspaper and television reports. All Charles James's discoveries were based on public information produced by Militant itself, either in returns to Companies House or in the pages of the *Militant* newspaper. His work eventually helped to lead to the simple (and, to some people, disappointing) answer to the question of where Militant gets most of its money.

Charles James discovered that one of the Militant companies, WIR Publications Limited, seemed to be making regular loans to another, Cambridge Heath Press Limited: in the year 1976 £50,000 was lent, in 1977, £48,500; in 1978, £50,000; in 1979,

£66,966; in 1980, £89,236; in 1981, £119,000; in 1982, £173,000; in 1983, £173,000 again; in 1984, £287,000 and in 1985, an estimated £300,000.[12] At first they were simple loans due for repayment in 1986, but now they have been converted into mortgage debentures. The companies' accountants, Maurice A. Braganza & Co., have said in the annual accounts that they consider the money 'may be irrecoverable'.[13] By 1985 the total amount loaned by WIR Publications Limited to its sister company was around £1,400,000. In short, WIR Publications acts as a collecting box for Cambridge Heath Press. This arrangement was made 'on advice from lawyers and accountants':[14] if the *Militant* newspaper got into libel difficulties, only the official publisher, Cambridge Heath Press, could be sued (along with certain individuals), and any money in WIR Publications would remain untouchable. That sum is considerable. According to its accounts, WIR Publications received £18,000 income in the year 1974, £30,000 in 1975, £42,000 in 1976, £61,000 in 1977, £77,000 in 1978, £92,000 in 1979, £114,000 in 1980 and £147,000 in 1981. Since 1982 the company returns have been shorter, not stating the level of donations, but it is possible to deduce these on the basis of previous years' accounts. In 1982 about £181,000 was probably received, in 1983 around £205,000, in 1984 about £260,000 and in 1985 around £365,000.[15]

But until 1980 it was not certain where these donations to WIR Publications were coming from in the first place. The answer was suddenly provided by Militant itself, perhaps to dampen the mounting speculation prompted by the work of Charles James and others. In April 1980, in reply to a questionnaire from the

NEC of the Labour Party, Peter Taaffe said that WIR Publications Limited's income was 'derived solely from the donations of active members of the Labour Party and trade unions who, in addition to occasional donations to the *Militant* Fighting Fund, are prepared to make regular contributions to develop the support for Marxist policies within the Labour movement'.[16] In other words, WIR's income was coming simply from Militant members and supporters. In saying this Taaffe was admitting for the first time that the *Militant* Fighting Fund was not the only source of donations from individuals. It was a remarkable statement, since anybody reading the exhortations every week in the Fighting Fund column in *Militant* would quite naturally have assumed that the paper's survival depended entirely on the fund. Close examination shows, however, that names in the column are usually 'unknowns' in Militant terms. They are almost exclusively those of people who are regular readers but not yet heavily involved in the tendency: the 'contacts' and 'contact members'. The column in *Militant* is used to encourage them; names are included not according to the size of donations but on the recommendation of local full-timers who want to entice potential recruits. When names appear in print the full-timers will make a big thing of it and make the 'contacts' feel important.

The case of one Militant ex-member from the early 1970s illustrates this. Richard Hart's name appeared in the Fighting Fund column on a number of occasions in early 1973.[17] At that point, Hart now admits, he was undergoing the 'contact' process. Later in the year, when Hart had become a full Militant member, his name no longer appeared in the column. As his bank statements show, he was by then making a regular £5 monthly banker's order payment to WIR Publications instead. This was his subscription.

All Militant defectors confirm that they had to pay regular and large subscriptions, though, unlike Hart, many paid weekly and in cash. There are no set subscription rates, only minimum levels: in general people are obliged to pay between 10 and 15 per cent of their income. 'I never knew how much anybody else paid,' remembers one defector. 'It was always a thing between you and the treasurer.'[18] Today a member on a typical weekly wage of about £130 might have to pay about £15 a week: one member says that he paid £55 a month when he was earning £100 a week at Ford.[19] The higher-paid members pay astonishing sums – as much as £60 a week for those earning more than £10,000 a year. Students can expect to have to pay about £4 a week nowadays, with an extra £10 lump sum when grant cheques come through at the start of term. People still at school are asked for a large share of their pocket money – 25p out of his weekly £1, one ex-member told me. Even the unemployed are asked to pay a minimum of £4 a week. It all makes the Labour Party's 1986 subscription of £8.60 a year look minute.

Large though Militant's subscriptions are, they are not the only sums that members have to fork out: they are constantly being badgered for extra money. As one ex-member put it:

You know when you're at a Militant 'social': you pay to get in, you pay for food, booze, raffle tickets, even pamphlets and books; then there's a Fighting Fund collection; and if your pockets aren't empty by then, somebody's bound to tip you upside-down to make sure your coffers are bare when you leave. I know people who used to hide their last 30p so they could get home on the bus.[20]

Members are always expected to be the first to contribute to Fighting Fund collections at Young Socialist and public meetings. In many cases Militant branch treasurers will go round and arrange beforehand exactly who will make large contributions to encourage the rest. IOUs are discouraged because they cause branch treasurers so much trouble in following people up, but in the end a pledge is regarded as better than nothing. At the LPYS conference in 1984, £8,000 was raised at the Militant fringe meeting (although the target had been £10,000).[21] Sometimes when the organisation is in deficit extra money will be collected from each member in a nationwide branch levy. For instance, in December 1982 each member was asked to pay a sum corresponding to twice his weekly subscription, and people were warned this might be done again in future.[22] Members who get tax rebates are always expected to donate all of them to the cause, and the organisation occasionally receives bequests in wills, though because the membership is mainly young the benefits of this have yet to be fully realised.

Activity in trade unions is another important source of funds from Militant members. Members of the tendency who serve on union conference delegations often receive generous overnight allowances for the time that they are away from home, as do full-time union officials. The civil service union, the CPSA, in which Militant has been strong for some time, pays an allowance of £32 a night when members are away on union business. Recently the union has had in important positions several Militant members, many of whom live outside London but frequently have to visit the capital for union matters. Militant's finances have thus benefited from the several thousands of pounds contributed by CPSA officials and union delegates who choose to take cheap accommodation and donate most of their allowances to Militant. (It should be stressed that there is nothing illegal or irregular about this.)

Only 75 per cent of members' subscriptions goes to London or appears in the accounts of WIR Publications Limited. A quarter of Militant's subscription income is retained at the local level to pay for full-timers and other expenses. Each region, district and branch has its own budget and bank account. In Lancashire, for example, Militant had a bank account in Blackburn under the name of the Lancashire Book Club; in Brixton its account was called the 'Lambeth Political Education Society'; in Swansea there have been at least two bank accounts, one called MELTOK (standing for 'Marx, Engels, Lenin, Trotsky OK!') and the other in the name of the South Wales Trade Union Group; nationally one of the accounts is entitled 'MSC No. 1'. Militant also has various bankers, including the Co-op Bank and the National Westminster Bank.[23] The rest of each subscription is sent on to the Militant financial office run by Clare Doyle in London. Presumably accountants have advised Militant that diverse national and regional bank accounts will help to avoid any unnecessary tax payments. They also mislead people doing investigations based on the returns at Companies House.

Apart from the Fighting Fund, members' subscriptions and other donations, there are several other important sources of income for the tendency.

First, there are sales of the *Militant* newspaper. Around 20,000 copies are sold per week – including twelve subscriptions to the Metropolitan Police and one to the US Embassy. Paper sales should theoretically bring in about £5,000 a week in all, or £250,000 a year, but Militant suffers from quite a severe leakage among sellers who genuinely forget to hand the money in. In some cases members will pay money in without having sold their quota of papers, so as to avoid criticism or the trouble of having to stand on a street corner selling them. Sometimes the paper will be given away to 'good types' if they cannot afford to buy it. The organisation does not count paper sales as a particularly important or reliable source of income. The paper is regarded more as a means of spreading the gospel.

Second, the bookshop at Hepscott Road brings in money. Under the business name of World Socialist Books (formerly World Books), it sells a wide range of books and pamphlets – not just Militant or Marxist literature – and its titles include books from many leading publishers. Militant even sold the first edition of this book, even though they denounced it publicly as a 'hatchet job'. The thinking was that members were going to buy it anyway, so Militant might as well take the sellers' mark-up rather than capitalist booksellers. And after the 1985 Liverpool budget crisis they cheekily sold copies of Liverpool City Council's famous redundancy notices. All Militant members are expected to buy their set

149

texts and books from the shop, and members even have to pay 30p for internal documents such as the regular 'Bulletin of Marxist Studies'. Militant never misses an opportunity to raise extra cash. But since World Socialist Books is not a limited company, it is difficult to assess its turnover.

The third source of income is commercial printing. Over the last few years income from this has greatly increased. In February 1983, when Peter Tatchell got into trouble with Walworth Road for using Cambridge Heath Press to print his election leaflets, it was revealed that sixty local Labour parties in London alone had used Cambridge Heath Press as a printer at one time or another. As Tatchell explained: 'We did this not out of political sympathy with Militant but because they were fast, cheap and knew what we wanted. More important, they were a trade union shop, and all the workers were Labour Party members.'[24]

Militant tries to ensure that the Labour Party bodies it controls always place their printing orders with Cambridge Heath Press. Added together, the value of these orders can be considerable. For instance, in 1977–78 the London region of NOLS, controlled by Militant, had a total expenditure of £269.71. Of this £178.90 was spent on printing with Cambridge Heath Press and a further £8 went on advertising in *Militant* – a total of £186.90.[25] In other words, nearly 70 per cent of the NOLS region's spending went to the tendency. The sums may have been small in that case, but the same thing was going on in many other LPYS and NOLS bodies. It is all part of a strategy by Militant effectively to integrate the finances of the tendency with those of the Labour Party bodies that it controls, allowing the former to be subsidised by the latter. In recent years party officials have tried to stop some of these bodies from using Militant for Labour Party printing jobs, and most LPYS and NOLS print work now goes elsewhere. Instead Militant is doing an increasing amount of work for left-wing pressure groups, many of which have no association with the Labour Party, and for unions. Militant prints several of the CPSA's sectional magazines, for instance. And it is not just socialists who find Militant's printing rates competitive: in 1983 a local Conservative association even used Cambridge Heath Press, unaware of the company's identity.

Militant's new printing company, Eastway Offset Limited, was probably set up in 1985 to attract potential customers who might have been reluctant to use Cambridge Heath Press Limited because of its increasingly well-known associations with Militant.

In the 1960s the tendency's internal motto was 'The Three Ps – Premises, Press and Professionals', Militant's three organisational ambitions. It is a measure of Militant's growth since then that each aim has been achieved several times over. But of the three the press is perhaps the most important because of its financial advantages. Militant bought its first press in 1971, helped partly by donations from two members of the then Militant Executive, Roger and Julian Silverman. They had just inherited a large sum from their father, Sydney Silverman, the left-wing MP for Nelson and Colne, who died in 1968, leaving £63,548. Within fifteen months of acquiring that first press the paper had progressed from being a four-page monthly to an eight-page weekly and had adopted a colour logo. The paper has expanded rapidly since then, along with the organisation, and today Militant has at least three big presses in its London offices.

Now that it has its own printing facilities Militant no longer has to rely on outsiders and can make money from doing commercial printing for others. But, most important, it has cut the costs of printing its own literature. Other printers' rates not only include a profit margin for themselves but also allow for labour paid at union rates. Although its print workers are members of the relevant print unions, the NGA and SOGAT '82, and their journalists belong to the National Union of Journalists (NUJ), Militant does not, in effect, pay them at union rates. Of course, when asked, Militant always *says* that its staff gets standard rates of pay; what it forgets to add is that every member of the newspaper and printing staff chooses not to take his or her full wages – the amount they forego is a donation to Militant. Though Militant itself campaigns publicly for the introduction of a £120-a-week minimum wage, all Militant's staff – print workers, journalists and organisers – receive much less than this. But if Militant employees choose to give back some of their nominal income, there is nothing that the NUJ or the print unions can do about it.

Wages for full-time staff vary according to rank and needs. Those who are single may get as little as £40 a week; those with a spouse and children, up to £80. The partners of Militant employees are always encouraged to take well-paid jobs elsewhere to support their spouses' meagre earnings. And probably only about a quarter of the current full-time staff of more than 300 people are paid in any case: as I have noted, the rest rely on state benefits, though in some cases Militant adds to these.

Since 1984, there have been many signs that Militant is having increasing financial difficulties, particularly in raising money from its newest recruits. At the September 1984 Militant National Council meeting in London it was reported that 40 per cent of Militant members were not paying their subscriptions, that 50 per cent were not selling the newspaper, and that 60 per cent were not raising money for the Fighting Fund. Three-quarters of comrades were failing to buy *Militant International Review,* and many were spending hardly any money at all on books. The council complained how the average amount of money paid in by each 'comrade' per week over the previous year had actually fallen, and said that paper sales had 'stagnated'.[26] So bad was Militant's financial state that certain internal bulletins could not be published, or had to be delayed. In March 1986 an internal document spoke of 'our weekly shortfall which has held our work back for some time', though it claimed this had now been nearly eradicated.[27] These internal statements all need to be taken with a pinch of salt, since they were clearly designed to get members working harder to raise money, but Militant's rapid growth does seem to have brought money problems. Many of the new members seem far less prepared to make financial sacrifices than the existing membership. In an effort to discipline members' money-raising work, in 1984 members were issued with pink collectors' cards to record paper sales and Fighting Fund donations week by week. In one branch, members who forgot to bring their pink cards to branch meetings were fined 10p.

It is not easy to put a figure to Militant's total annual turnover from both members and other sources, particularly in the light of the above difficulties. Although Militant defectors know about their own contributions during their time in the organisation, even those formerly in important positions know very little about overall figures. This is for reasons of security: there is no cause for ordinary members to be told.

The total income raised simply from members' subscriptions can only be estimated, but is probably at least £750,000 a year. Eight thousand one hundred members paying a minimum of £4 a week works out at more than £1.6 million a year, but people at school and on state benefits do not even pay the minimum, and it seems that large numbers are paying nothing at all; on the other hand many pay more than the minimum. Sales of *Militant* and other publications bring in probably about £150,000 a year, the Fighting and Building Funds about £250,000 a year, and commercial printing perhaps £100,000. A total estimate for Militant's annual income of between £1 million and £1.25 million seems to be borne out by leaks from inside the organisation. Indeed, *Militant*'s assistant editor has admitted that Militant's income is at least £1 million.[28]

With financial resources on this scale, the question one has to ask is: where does all the money go? First, salaries and National Insurance must account for £300,000 or £400,000 a year. Second, the *Militant* newspaper is not commercially viable and has to be subsidised – the cost of printing and distribution are by no means balanced by sales and the small amount of advertising revenue. Militant's internal documents must be costly too. On top of that there are rents and rates on Militant's properties, telephone, electricity and gas bills and day-to-day administrative expenses. A very large amount of money goes towards subsidising Militant's operations abroad.

How does Militant's turnover compare with those of other political parties and pressure groups? Calculating annual income or expenditure figures for political parties can be difficult, as the Houghton Inquiry found out in 1976.[29] While records are kept of national income and expenditure, no party keeps central records of the finances of each constituency. There is also the danger of double-counting money that passes from the local level to the centre. For the calendar year 1984, not an election year, a very rough estimate of total Labour Party income was about £6 million.[30] An approximate figure for the Liberal Party's total income for 1985 was £2 million.[31] The Social Democrats' annual income is about £1 million. So the income of Militant is almost as high as that of the Liberal Party and about the same as the SDP's, although the comparison is not entirely appropriate, since these parties do not make money from commercial printing and publishing operations. Perhaps Militant has something to teach them.

By comparison simply with internal Labour Party pressure groups, Militant is in a totally different league. The Fabian Society's income for the year ending June 1985 was £86,552.[32] *Tribune* has an annual income of about £180,000,[33] while the influential pressure group the Labour Co-ordinating Committee had an income of £11,800 in the twelve months to September 1985. Militant may try to argue that it is merely another Labour Party pressure group, but its finances are at the level of those of a major political party.

9
MILITANT
ABROAD

f Militant's perspectives are eventually proved correct, and there is the kind of world socialist revolution that the tendency predicts, then Sunday 21 April 1974 should prove to be a historic date. On that day, the furniture workers' union premises, NUFTO Hall in Jockey's Fields, Holborn, had the honour of hosting the founding conference of what Militant described as 'a great landmark in the history of the international working class'.[1] Only a few hundred yards from the British Museum, where Karl Marx had done so much of his work, forty-six comrades from twelve different countries, but most of them from Britain, met to found a body called the Committee for the Workers' International (CWI). They believed it was 'the germ of the mighty workers' International which will within the next decade become the decisive force on the planet'.[2]

As a Trotskyist group Militant, of course, believes in the importance of international socialism; that a transformation of society in Britain should and will lead to revolutions in other countries. The dispute over Stalin's policy of 'socialism in one country' was one of Trotsky's main differences with the Soviet dictator.

For the first ten years of its existence the RSL had held the British franchise of the Fourth International. Indeed, it was the acquisition of the franchise in 1955 which really got the RSL underway. But they had never been very enthusiastic members, and in 1965 the League and the International parted company. The RSL was told it had 'a poorly functioning organisation',[3] and the British franchise was given instead to Militant's former allies the International Marxist Group, who have held it ever since. (The IMG have since become the Socialist League, publishing *Socialist Action*, and have resumed entrism within the Labour Party.) For nine years after 1965 Militant functioned alone, without any formal international affiliations.

Twelve years on from the meeting in Holborn, the CWI seems to be somewhat behind schedule, but it lives on, co-ordinating national sections – in effect sister Militant tendencies – across western Europe and beyond. Militant now has groups operating in more than twenty countries, including France, West Germany, Sweden, Denmark, Ireland, Belgium, the Netherlands, Greece, Cyprus, Spain, Portugal, Chile, Sri Lanka, India, Pakistan and South Africa. All of them produce their own versions of the *Militant* newspaper; all have the same tight democratic centralist organisations operating secretly inside socialist or social democratic parties, and all subscribe to Militant's brand of revolutionary Bolshevism.

The international comrades that Sunday in spring 1974 included representatives from four full-fledged national Militant sections: Britain, Ireland, Sweden and West Germany, and, it was reported, individual representatives from Belgium, Sri Lanka, Greece, Portugal, Spain and Austria. The conference listened to speeches from Ted Grant and from Roger Silverman, who for two years had been working on international contacts at Militant's headquarters in London. They agreed on a founding resolution and on a constitution for a body they called the Committee for the Workers' International. That they only founded a committee rather than proclaimed the Workers' International itself was a modest recognition that at that stage the group was too small to represent the workers of the world. The Workers' International would come later.

Militant's new international organisation was a direct spin-off from the RSL's domination of the Labour Party Young Socialists. The Labour Party youth section maintained good contacts with young members of other socialist and social democratic parties in the Socialist International. In particular this involved attending the annual conferences of these youth sections along with the regular conferences and summer camps of the International Union of Socialist Youth. For Militant, as with virtually any political event, these conferences were seen as an important opportunity for recruitment. So, in the early 1970s, leading members of the LPYS National Committee, such as Andy Bevan, Peter Doyle, Tony Aitman, Brian Monaghan and Alex Wood, were only too happy to go to young socialist conferences across Europe as fraternal delegates.

They would spend the conference sessions carefully observing, noticing which of the host delegates appeared to be on the left, and under attack from the right. At the end of each session they would chat to promising contacts, sounding them out. Before the conference was over an informal meeting would have been arranged, and the nucleus of a sister Militant organisation would have been formed.

The fraternal delegates from Great Britain found it all surprisingly easy, and inexpensive – after all, the Labour Party was paying all their expenses.

By the time of the CWI founding conference in April 1974, Militant's expansion abroad was progressing well. The May Day edition of *Militant* that year carried advertisements for a newspaper called *Offensiv*, the 'Marxist newspaper within the Swedish Labour movement'; for *Voran*, the 'German Marxist paper'; and for *Militant Irish Monthly*.[4] These, together with subsequent advertisements for other newspapers over the years, and occasional mentions in *Militant* articles, are the only real public indication of Militant's extensive organisation abroad.

Other newspapers that emerged in other countries in the mid-1970s were *Vonk* in Belgium, *Xekinima* in Greece, *Voorwarts* in the Netherlands, *Nuevo Claridad* in Spain, and much later, in 1983, came *L'Avance Socialiste* in France, and *Socialisten* in Denmark. The only major western European country where Militant failed to make progress was Italy. In addition Militant supporters in Benazir Bhutto's Pakistan People's Party publish a paper called *The Struggle* and the Marxist Workers' Tendency in the African

National Congress have a paper called *Inqaba Ya Basebenzi*. The links these papers have with Militant are not hard to spot. Often articles are reproduced in several different editions of the papers, the work of *Militant's* cartoonist, Alan Hardman, appears in nearly all of them, with their English captions suitably translated and modified to suit local circumstances. Some papers even carry their own fighting fund charts designed in exactly the same way as Militant's. And the papers frequently advertise each other. But so far none of the newspapers has equalled *Militant* in achieving weekly publication. Some are monthly; others appear less frequently and rather sporadically.

Nevertheless, Militant is even more secretive about the work of the CWI than it is about its own British organisation. One reason is that foreign groups are often operating in difficult circumstances. The comrades in South Africa, Sri Lanka and Pakistan, for instance, risk arrest and punishment. In South Africa some have even been killed. The second, less important reason is that Militant's international activities are probably its most blatant breach of the Labour Party rules, which forbid affiliation to international organisations other than the Socialist International.

Militant's Irish section is the oldest affiliate after Britain. Comrades on both sides of the Irish border have been publishing *Militant Irish Monthly* since 1972, though a formal Irish section was not established until July 1974. In appearance the newspaper is very similar to *Militant* itself. The typesetting and layout are done in Dublin, but it is actually printed at Militant's headquarters in London, then shipped to Belfast, where copies are distributed by train throughout Ireland. Though Militant is keen to treat Ireland as one country, most issues of *Militant Irish Monthly* have separate outside pages for north and south of the border, with common inside pages. Militant operates in Ireland either as two separate bodies or as one, depending on the circumstances, and in the border areas certain individuals are politically active in both countries.

Much of the initial work in Northern Ireland was carried out by Alex Wood while he was a student at the university of Coleraine from 1969 to 1972. In its early years in the province Militant carried out entrist work within the very weak Northern Ireland Labour Party (NILP). It was also the dominant force within the Derry Labour and Trade Union Party. When the NILP collapsed in the mid-1970s, entrism there had to be abandoned. So instead, in 1978, Militant set up its own open organisation, the Labour and Trade Union Group (LTUG), which incorporated the Derry Labour and Trade Union Party. Today the group claims about 600 members and campaigns for the establishment of a non-sectarian trade union party in Northern Ireland. Not all its members are Militant members, but Militant is by far the dominant force. By keeping membership open in this way new members can more easily be drawn into the tendency's ranks. It is almost as if Militant, having no other socialist party in Northern Ireland to enter, set up its own party to continue the practice of entrism.

The group operates from offices in Waring Street in the centre of Belfast, though recently it has been searching for new premises. The LTUG has branches across the province and a Young

Socialists section. The secretary is Peter Hadden, the son of a Presbyterian minister, and the LTUG chairman is Bill Webster, a Liverpudlian. Hadden looks after the eastern part of Ulster from Belfast, Webster the western part, based in Derry. Both sit on Militant's British Central Committee.

At the 1979 general election, Webster, who was at that time secretary of the Derry Trades Council, stood for the group in the Londonderry constituency, but received only 1 per cent of the vote. In the 1983 general election an LTUG candidate, Muriel Tang, contested Belfast East, an overwhelmingly Protestant seat. Although she received only 1.5 per cent of the poll, this was more than both the Social Democratic and Labour Party and the Workers' Party, and only 100 votes fewer than Provisional Sinn Féin. Three LTUG candidates fought the 1985 local elections in Belfast, but none contested the January 1986 Westminster by-elections.

As one would expect in view of its belief in the need for a trade union defence force in Northern Ireland, Militant is also very active in the Northern Ireland trade unions. Its greatest influence is probably in the civil service union, the Northern Ireland Public Service Alliance, where it holds several Executive places, and in the shop workers' union, USDAW. It is also quite strong on both the Belfast and Derry Trades Councils.

With the Anglo-Irish Agreement in the autumn of 1985, and increasing tension in Northern Ireland, Militant's supporters in the north feared that they might get nastily squeezed in the event of civil war between the communities, and they drew up plans for all their 300 members in the north to be moved across the

Irish Sea. The plans were so advanced that it had even been worked out the addresses each member would move to in Britain. If they were to move en bloc, 300 new Militant members could make quite an impact on the Labour politics of any city they chose to descend upon.

In the Irish Republic Militant operates from quite extensive offices in Middle Abbey Street, Dublin, where activities are looked after by Joe Higgins. As in Britain, Militant's Irish section runs a company, Middle Abbey Publications Limited, set up in 1984, which often does small commercial typesetting and layout work. The other important figure in the Republic is John Throne, Militant's first full-timer in Ireland in the early 1970s, who later spent some time working for Militant in the United States, before returning to Ireland. Throne sits on the International Executive.

When Militant began its work in the Irish Republic the Irish Labour Party had no young socialists to work on. 'The lack of a youth section is hindering us,' the Irish comrades complained in 1974. 'We are fighting the bureaucracy to get one established.'[5] In 1978 one was set up, and Militant soon assumed almost complete control of Labour Youth, the Irish equivalent of the LPYS. Militant now has four people on the 39-strong Administrative Council of the Irish Labour Party itself, including Joe Higgins, but so far has made no progress in getting councillors elected or members into the Dáil. There are probably about 300 or 400 Militant supporters in the Republic, many of them in the Dublin constituencies where the tendency is strongest. The tendency is also quite strong in Galway and Limerick.

In 1983, the Irish Labour Party set up an inquiry into the affairs of *Militant Irish Monthly* and its tendency. But shortly afterwards Militant's Dublin offices were raided by armed Special Branch officers, and the inquiry was suspended so as to avoid accusations that the raid had been set up by the party. In 1986, the Executive of the party set up a working party to examine ways in which the organisation of Labour Youth could be modified, and Militant's influence looked likely to be one of the areas under examination. But in Ireland, unlike Britain, many areas of the local Labour Party have deliberately hindered Militant's work by choosing not to have branches of Labour Youth, or have even closed them down.

In Ireland as a whole, Militant has an organisation modelled on the British group, with branches, a Central Committee, national conferences and so on. Overall, Militant probably has only about 700 or 800 Irish members. As a proportion of the Irish population that makes it stronger than in Britain, particularly if one takes into account the relative unpopularity of socialist parties in both north and south. The tendency now has several dozen full-time organisers in Ireland, but there are no signs of rapid growth. In April 1986, it was announced that *Militant Irish Monthly* would go fortnightly later in the year, and that the Irish comrades were planning to buy new printing equipment.

Militant's Spanish section, based around the newspaper, *Nuevo Claridad* ('New Clarity'), was first cultivated during the last years of the Franco dictatorship, when activities had to be carried out in secrecy as all political parties were officially banned. In the early 1970s the present assistant editor of *Militant*, or, more accurately, assistant general secretary, Lynn Walsh, spent a lot of time in both Spain and Portugal. Julian Silverman (Roger's brother), Pat Wall and Tony Aitman also visited Spain, while Militant members from the Spanish Young Socialists went on tours organised through official young socialist organisations of the other European sections. By means of the LPYS's Spanish Young Socialists Defence Campaign thousands of pounds were raised, nominally to help the Spanish Young Socialists who were having to operate under cover. Because the funds could be taken to Spain only clandestinely, Militant was able to ensure that the funds went largely to a certain faction in the Spanish YS, a sympathetic group they were trying to win over to their cause.

Today Militant still regards Spain as one of its most important sections, and in recent years two leading Militant Executive members, Alan Woods, the editor of *Militant International Review*, and Tony Saunois, once the LPYS member on Labour's National Executive, have both spent long periods in Madrid.

Militant suffered severe setbacks in Spain almost from the beginning. In 1975, Militant realised that its plans to win over an existing faction in the Spanish YS were failing, and so they were abandoned. Several years' hard work had been wasted. As Spain moved towards democracy in the late 1970s, Militant stepped up its efforts. Partly through the LPYS, Militant sent money, organisers and even a printing press to Spain to help the tendency's group and its paper in the hope of quick dividends: 'In the short run, international aid will remain vital,' the Spanish comrades wrote in 1976. 'But every penny that is invested in this work will pay off a thousand-fold in the medium term – i.e. within a year to eighteen months or even less.'[6] But this was not to be, as the Socialist Party (PSOE) youth section was purged of Militant members in 1977 and 1978.

In response to this and subsequent disciplinary action, in recent years the Nuevo Claridad group has operated a modified form of entrism. Those who have been expelled operate quite openly as a separate group outside the party, while many Militant members still operate inside the PSOE.

The Nuevo Claridad group has been particularly strong in the province of Alava in the Basque country, just south of Bilbao, and recently this has led to them contesting public elections and actually standing against the PSOE. Recently several Nuevo Claridad members have been expelled from the PSOE in the area, while the Spanish socialist trade union organisation, the UGT, has spent years trying to tackle Nuevo Claridad supporters in its organisation in Alava. At one point the UGT national leadership tried to take the Alava UGT headquarters by force, and eventually, in 1983, the national union expelled the entire Alava UGT Executive Committee. These expulsions gave Militant's Spanish organisation the opportunity and excuse for its Alava group to contest the February 1984 Basque elections, under the party name of Left Socialist Candidature.

Left Socialist Candidature candidates campaigned under the main slogan of 'A worker's MP on a worker's wage', which just happens to be exactly the same slogan used by Militant MPs Terry Fields and David Nellist, and other Militant candidates, in the 1983 general election. Though backed by the Alava UGT, and aided by Nuevo Claridad members from the rest of Spain, the candidates polled only 2 per cent of the vote, well short of the 5 per cent needed under the proportional representation system to secure any MPs in the Alava assembly. But the Left Socialist Candidature had been formed only a month before the elections, and the assassination of a PSOE senator three days before polling day cannot have helped their campaign. For anybody considering whether Militant might stand its own candidates in the event of large numbers of expulsions from the Labour Party in Britain, it is interesting to note that a Militant internal document commented after this election that the 'analysis of this experience provides a wealth of lessons for Marxists in Britain and other countries'.[7] Militant now publishes a second Spanish newspaper, for the Basque region, called *Ezkerra Marxista* ('Basque Marxist').

In Greece, Militant also had high hopes after the return to democracy in the 1970s. Contact was made with two separate existing Trotskyist groups – one largely industrial workers, the other mainly students who had been expelled from Gerry Healy's International. In 1974 Militant persuaded the groups to merge, join the CWI, and pursue a policy of entrism inside PASOK, the Greek Socialist Party. But these Greek comrades, who have been publishing *Xekinima* for more than a decade, first suffered expulsions from PASOK in 1975. By 1981 they had a mere forty-five members, half inside PASOK, the rest expelled and operating outside. Then in 1985, with an election approaching, the PASOK leadership suddenly took a more tolerant attitude towards the Xekinima group, and even helped publish the newspaper as part of the party's propaganda effort.

The Cypriot group publishes a newspaper called *Socialistiki Ekfrasi* and works inside the youth section of the socialist party, EDEK, but again has suffered from expulsions.

Militant's sister group in Sweden has probably endured the most severe disciplinary action. The Swedish comrades, based around the newspaper *Offensiv* (meaning 'Offensive' or 'Attack'), call themselves internally the Socialist Union, or Socialist Federation. Their paper was started in September 1973, after contacts between members of the Social Democratic/Labour Party's youth section, the SSU, and LPYS delegates at the 1972 SSU conference. Offensiv's SSU work during the 1970s gave them only a few hundred members in an organisation 45,000 strong – the largest youth section in the Socialist International. Even so, in 1976, after revelations from two defectors, the leadership of the youth section took swift action against the organisation, and seven of Offensiv's leaders were expelled. The defectors' evidence indicated that Offensiv had quickly built itself an organisation very similar in structure to Militant in Britain.

In 1981, after further revelations from defectors indicated that Offensiv was carrying on with its work, even stronger action was taken, this time by the Swedish Labour Party authorities, not simply the youth section. About 150 Offensiv members were interviewed by the party; about twenty apparently gave up any allegiance to Offensiv, and the 130 or so who refused were expelled. Ironically perhaps, it was only after hearing about Militant in Britain that the party took any action, well before the British Labour Party had expelled any Militant members: 'We thought that mustn't happen to us, so we collected a great deal of information about Trotskyist groups,' the party's general secretary said later.[8] In the opinion of *Guardian* journalist Martin Linton, the action revealed an important difference between the two parties in their attitude:

> The Swedish Labour Party regards the SSU as central to its political strategy, whereas the British Labour Party regards the LPYS as marginal and dispensable. The British Labour Party has expelled the Editorial Board of Militant but it has left the LPYS under Militant control. This would be unthinkable in the SAP [Swedish Labour Party] because they regard their youth movement as their chief recruiting agent, their training ground for party and trade union activists.[9]

Those expelled from the Swedish Labour Party in the late 1970s are now able to operate openly outside the party, and have devoted much of their energies to non-party-political work in trade unions, particularly those with youth sections. They planned to work in environmental groups and international solidarity campaigns and to become involved in political campaigns on issues such as housing and unemployment. The aim has been to continue mixing with political types, and Swedish Labour Party members, and to carry on trying to win them over to the tendency's ideas.

The Swedish group was used as a base for branching out into the rest of Scandinavia. By October 1981 there were eight comrades in Denmark, and in 1983 they started their own newspaper, *Socialisten* ('Socialist'). The Danish Socialist Party reacted swiftly, however, and in 1984 seven of the Socialisten group in Aarhus were expelled after the authorities had consulted the British Labour Party. The Swedish Militant members also went into Finland, and at one stage even had plans to work in Poland.

In West Germany, the Voran ('Front') group, founded in March 1974, again built up several hundred members and sections both inside the German SPD and outside. There are reports recently that the Voran group has suffered severe internal splits, and even that it may have been expelled from the CWI.

The Vonk ('Spark') group in Belgium publishes editions of its newspaper in both Flemish and French, and is probably no more than 100 strong. It was originally based on an existing Trotskyist group which came into contact with Militant. The L' Avance Socialiste ('Socialist Advance') group in France has been in existence only since 1982 and is still too insignificant to have come to the attention of the Socialist Party leadership. In Holland, the group which originally published *Voorwarts* ('Forward') recently changed the name of the paper to *Offensies* ('Offensive' or 'Attack'). They too are very small. These, like all the European groups, concentrate almost entirely upon work in their young socialist sections and in the unions.

The United States has always been an important country for Trotskyist groups. For many years Militant has had a handful of supporters operating in the US, based in Oakland, California. In January 1986 they published an American version of the 'Perspectives' documents.

Militant's largest foreign section is probably in Sri Lanka, one of the few countries ever to have a mass Trotskyist party.

The Lanka Sama Samaja Party (LSSP), one of the coalition partners in the former governments of Mrs Bandaranaike, split in the mid-1970s. However, Trotskyists in the LSSP sympathetic to Militant had already affiliated to the CWI in 1974, and in December 1976, following large numbers of expulsions by the party leadership, they led a large section of the LSSP away to form their own Nava Sama Samaja Party (NSSP) (New Socialist Party). In 1981 NSSP boasted ninety-three full-time workers – about as many as Militant at that stage – and four different monthly papers. In the presidential election the following year, an NSSP candidate, Vasudeva Nanayakkara, recorded 17,000 votes, in sixth place behind President Jayewardene, who received 3.4 million. In 1985 Nanayakkara was jailed and released on bail after a month, charged, according to *Militant*, with distributing leaflets.

Ted Grant, Roger Silverman and Pat Wall have made frequent visits to Sri Lanka for Militant; the last time Grant visited, in 1981, he was expelled by President Jayewardene's government. Militant supporters have also controlled one of the two Sri Lankan trade unions, the United Federation of Labour, and when they tried to organise a general strike in 1980, several were jailed and the union's offices were seized. In Britain the Federation has an office in Ockenden Road, Islington, only five doors from the house Peter Taaffe lived in until recently. The NSSP, which recently seems to have dropped Militant's traditional non-sectarianism to champion the cause of the minority Tamils, was banned for several months after the violence in 1983, and is now in a weak state. *Militant* has naturally given Sri Lanka's troubles extensive coverage, and Militant MP David Nellist has often raised the problems of Sri Lanka on the floor of the Commons.

In Sri Lanka, Militant forged links with a Trotskyist group that had already been long in existence. A third way of developing international contacts has been through immigrant and exile groups in Britain. The founding CWI conference established an Asian Bureau, a group of Asian comrades whose first meeting, in Bradford in August 1974, was designed to 'discuss our intervention, through Asian comrades living in Britain, in the Asian countries'.[10] A second meeting was arranged to develop work among Asian immigrants in this country.

Since 1980, Pakistani Militant members based in Britain, the Netherlands and Belgium have been responsible for publishing *The Struggle*, the magazine of Militant's faction inside Benazir Bhutto's Pakistan People's Party (PPP). An Urdu edition is published every six weeks; an English edition four times a year. Writers use fictitious names and copies have to be smuggled into Pakistan since the paper has twice been banned by General Zia. *The Struggle* gives its address in London as the Centerprise office, Kingsland High Street, in Dalston, a publishing centre for many different radical groups. The London group has held regular meetings for the Pakistani community in Britain. In October 1982, the *Struggle* offices in Amsterdam were raided by armed police and searched, after it appears the Dutch authorities had received a tip-off from Karachi. Several supporters were charged with 'conspiracy to hijack', but were later released. As elsewhere, a number of *Struggle* supporters have been expelled from the PPP.

Another Militant group working from London are the Marxist Workers' Tendency, which publishes the quarterly journal, *Inqaba Ya Basebenzi* (which means Workers' Fortress) and which operates inside the African National Congress (ANC) and the South African Congress of Trades Unions (SACTU). In South Africa the tendency has to operate under cover, and readers of its journal are urged to photocopy copies and pass them on. As with most of Militant's other entrist operations, the work inside the ANC resulted in four of the tendency's leading comrades being suspended by the London section of the ANC in 1979, because of their activities in SACTU. The ANC said the four had been contacting international solidarity organisations with a mailing list they had allegedly stolen from SACTU, and accused them of wanting 'to create an alternative "workers' army"'.[11] At the ANC consultative conference in Lusaka in June 1985 they were expelled.

As in other countries such disciplinary action has not deterred the South African comrades. In recent months, as South Africa's troubles have worsened, Militant members have been active in the South African National Union of Mineworkers and the Chemical Workers' Union. With the emergence of the United Democratic Front in South Africa in 1985, Militant members started publishing a *Bulletin of UDF Militants*.

In Britain, Militant's South African work has been co-ordinated since 1980 through the South African Labour Education Project (SALEP), from its office in a house in Martello Street, Hackney, only a few yards from Militant's former headquarters in Mentmore Terrace. SALEP claims to provide educational material for trade unionists in southern Africa. It also has a youth-orientated organisation called Socialists Links with South African Youth, SOLSAY. Since 1985 SALEP has been boycotted and condemned by the Labour Party.

During the 1983–84 miners' strike SALEP helped to sponsor a visit by a striking British miner, Roy Jones, to South Africa, much to the 'disquiet' of the British NUM who had not been asked for approval. South African trade union leaders have also been invited to Britain. Militant has been keen on establishing 'direct links' of this kind, between union branches in Britain and South Africa, and bypassing the union hierarchies. But these unapproved 'direct links' have particularly annoyed both the ANC and SACTU.

The Martello Street office in London also houses the Zimbabwe Trade Union Defence Campaign, an organisation founded in March 1985 after fourteen trade unionists were arrested and jailed without charge by the Zimbabwean government. Among the fourteen were three SALEP workers, two South African and one Dutch, who were accused by Prime Minister Robert Mugabe of having been sent to Zimbabwe by the British Labour Party.[12] They were eventually released and the two South Africans were deported.

South Africa is considered to be one of Militant's most important areas of international work at the present time, along with Chile. Militant full-timers have been working in Chile within a faction of the Chilean Socialist Party called the 24th Congress faction, but work in Chile has to be carried out amid great secrecy. In Britain, Militant raises money for its Chilean work through its

Chile Socialist Defence Campaign, an organisation set up by the LPYS in 1980, which seems to have been based on the idea of the Spanish Young Socialists' Defence Campaign in the early 1970s. CSDC has an office in Emma Street, Hackney, and publishes an occasional bulletin. This group should not be confused with the much larger Chile Solidarity Campaign, which has Labour Party backing. In 1985, the Labour Party advised local parties to have nothing to do with the Militant-backed group.

All Militant's international work is co-ordinated from the International Department at Hepscott Road, run by the CWI secretary, Roger Silverman, and his deputy, Bob Labi, who deals with the day-to-day running of the department. Militant regards this work as one of its most important areas, and other leading Militant figures who have been involved in international operations include Alan Woods, who speaks eight languages, Woods's half-brother, Rob Sewell, and Tony Saunois. Between them they often spend long periods abroad, and in recent years seem to have concentrated their efforts and finance on the volatile political situations in the young Spanish and Greek Socialist parties, as well as Chile and South Africa.

Militant's operations abroad have been by no means as successful as in Britain. In nearly every case socialist and social democratic parties overseas have been swifter in taking disciplinary action than the British Labour Party, and these parties have usually found it an easier operation since they often have more centralised organisations and national membership lists. But no socialist party has ever managed totally to rid itself of Militant's foreign comrades. Experience in several countries shows that if Militant are determined to be entrists it is almost impossible to stop them. When people have been expelled they will continue to work openly outside the party, while those members who have escaped expulsion carry on inside.

Militant's foreign experience is a useful guide to its probable tactics in Britain in future. Only in Sri Lanka, Spain, and the exceptional circumstances of Northern Ireland have they formed separate parties. In Sri Lanka, Spain and Northern Ireland, where members of these parties have stood in elections, they have failed to secure more than 2 per cent of the vote. Should Militant ever consider forming its own party and standing candidates in Britain (and this option has been considered in Liverpool), foreign experience is not encouraging.

With the exceptions of Ireland and Sri Lanka, none of Militant's sister organisations has ever made as much political impact as the British comrades. Most of the sections are tiny, insignificant and unknown in the countries where they operate. After twelve years of existence, more than half the CWI's members worldwide live in Britain. That 'decisive force on the planet' the CWI envisaged in 1974 seems a little way off.

10

THE MILITANT LIFE

At the start of the 1970s, Militant still had only between 100 and 200 members. The really big jump in membership occurred during the following five years, after Militant had taken over the LPYS. In 1971, membership was such that the Militant annual conference was held in a pub in London. By January 1975, the tendency had 600 members, and later that year, when the annual gathering was held at a proper conference centre, Owen's Park in Manchester, Ted Grant is reported to have got up and announced proudly that membership had now soared past the 1,000 mark. 'The first thousand is the hard thing,' Grant apparently told the cheering delegates. 'The next thousand will be easier and ten thousand easier still.'[1]

Grant's announcement was probably premature, but Militant's control of the LPYS was clearly paying dividends. From about the mid-1970s, however, there seems to have been a significant fall in the 'quality' of Militant membership. In the early days, when

Militant's membership numbered only a few hundred people, each new recruit had to be properly 'steeled in the ideas'. It usually took at least six months for a 'contact' to go through the recruitment process – sometimes as many as eighteen months, especially for those who were middle class. Peter Taaffe used to say of 'middle-class types': 'They should be dried in the wind, buried in the snow, fried on the grill, then dried in the wind and buried in the snow again, and then, and only then, we might accept them.'[2]

In the very early days, during the 1960s, all new recruits would travel to the Militant headquarters in London to be approved in person by Grant or Taaffe before being accepted as members. By the early 1970s the organisation was becoming so large that this was no longer possible, but even then new members would be visited by Central Committee members. As membership expanded still further and the annual targets became increasingly ambitious, full-timers and branches started cutting corners to bring in new recruits. By 1979, there were 1,800 members; by November 1981, 2,500; by November 1982, 3,500; 4,700 at the end of 1983, 6,000 by the end of 1984 and more than 8,100 by March 1986. People did not have to go through anything like the same process to join, and standards dropped – so much so that nowadays it may be only a matter of weeks before potential recruits became members. The result is that not only are they less well educated in, and less committed to Militant's ideas, but they also feel less privileged to be part of the tendency. Since the mid-1970s Militant has suffered from a constant stream of embarrassing defectors, many of whom have spoken to Labour Party officials and the press. In the thirty years of its existence it seems likely that at least 2,000 people have left the tendency or have been expelled. In researching this book I have managed to talk to twenty-six of those former members, from different periods and from different levels of the organisation. Some were unwilling to be named, but others were happy to be quoted.

David Mason was a member of Militant in Hull for about eighteen months in the mid-1970s. He was not with Militant long enough to become very important, but his case is typical of those of many young people who join the tendency.

Mason joined the Labour Party in October 1974 after working for Labour during that month's election campaign. As a young recruit he quite naturally began going to local LPYS meetings in Hull. Soon he came across Alastair Tice, a Militant member, who sold him copies of the paper and started discussing politics with him. Often after a meeting they would go to the pub and talk, or they would arrange to go out for a drink on a Friday evening. Sometimes Tice would bring along friends from other Young Socialist branches in Hull. He gave Mason Militant pamphlets and books to read; they soon started discussing Marxism, and the meetings became more regular. From the pub they would often go back to Tice's home and carry on talking politics well into the night:

> After about a month of fairly intensive discussion, Alastair broke
> the news to me that there was this organisation, the Revolutionary

Socialist League. He gave me copies of 'British Perspectives and Tasks' and 'World Perspectives' and the pamphlet 'Entrism', all of which I took away and read. Then we discussed them, and after about a month I was accepted into membership.[3]

Reflecting on it now, Mason admits that at the time the arguments put forward by Tice and his friends 'seemed quite reasonable'. And, importantly, Mason got on well with them. He found the rest of the left in the Hull Labour Party 'weak and flabby': Militant and the Young Socialists were the only group to challenge the local party's right-wing leadership.

Mason started attending meetings of the Hull Militant branch, which were held every week in the back room of the Minerva pub, situated at the end of what was then the pier from which the Humber ferries used to leave. The branch had about a dozen members, drawn from the three Hull constituencies and from the university Labour Club. The set-up was very formal, with a chairman, treasurer and secretary and other ad hoc officers; minutes were read at the start of each meeting. Mason himself was later appointed Irish organiser for the branch, which meant that he had to talk about Ireland at local Labour Party and Young Socialist meetings and at private and public meetings of Militant. The officers were elected by the branch itself, but every time it was obvious to Mason who was going to get which job.

Soon Mason himself became involved in the slow recruitment of new members. He was assigned a small paper round of four or five 'contacts'. Every week he had to sell each of them a copy of the paper and discuss politics. The procedure was exactly the same as the one through which he himself had gone only a few weeks before. At the weekly branch meeting each member had to report back on how his or her 'contacts' were progressing: if they looked good, the branch would vote on whether to accept them into membership. Then, after the minutes, the officers' reports and instructions and news on 'contacts', a member of the branch had to lead off a political discussion:

> At only my second or third meeting I had to introduce the discussion. My talk was on Trotsky's 'Transitional Programme'. Everybody who had just joined got the 'Transitional Programme' because it was easy, but slowly you got harder and harder things to speak on. Nothing beyond you, though – every subject was chosen to stretch you a little bit more. You did a lot of preparation for them.[4]

Mason lasted about a year and a half in Militant, but in the end he left because of policy disagreements. He could not accept the tendency's policy on Ireland, and Stuart Holland's book *The Socialist Challenge* persuaded him that there were other forms of socialism:

> It wasn't a big bust-up. I announced I had disagreements. They said it was politically inept. They tried to keep me in and agreed to let me make a 'Why I Want to Leave' speech. Then at its next meeting the branch voted on whether I should be expelled or not. I was told not to turn up. The decision was that I should remain a nominal member – in effect it was a suspension. Their theory was that when

the 'Perspectives' were one day fulfilled I'd want to come back in. But then I wrote an article in *Labour Weekly* defending import controls, and I was finally expelled for publicly opposing Militant policy. I had to give back my main documents, and they asked if I would go to the press about it. I didn't. Later, when I was elected to NOLS National Committee, Andy Bevan revealed that I'd been a Militant supporter just to cause trouble for me on the National Committee.[5]

Today, ten years later, David Mason remembers that on the whole his life in Militant was 'unending tedium':

> A lot of it boiled down to selling papers. The pace didn't bother me, but one day I suddenly realised that after a year my social circle had totally drifted. I had only political friends left, simply because of the lack of time. There'd be the Militant branch on Monday evening, the Young Socialists meeting another evening, 'contact' work on Friday night, selling papers on Sunday afternoon, and on top of that, to prove to the local Labour Party we were good party members, we went canvassing for them every week and worked like hell in the local elections.[6]

Terry McDonald was a member of Militant in the tendency's home patch, Liverpool. Like many other defectors, his membership was brief – about eighteen months. After leaving Militant he soon left the Labour Party and joined the Social Democrats. In the circumstances this is perhaps understandable. It can't be particularly easy to be an ex-member of Militant and carry on as a Labour Party activist on Merseyside.

McDonald worked for Knowsley Borough Council and became involved with the tendency through his union, NALGO. Although NALGO is not affiliated to the Labour Party, the Knowsley NALGO branch contained a number of Militant members, thanks to the work of a young community development officer who had recently come to Knowsley from Sheffield. His name – Derek Hatton. 'He was a nobody at first,' McDonald recalls. With Hatton, McDonald started going to NALGO *Militant* readers meetings and later to his ward Labour Party in the then Kirkdale constituency of Liverpool. There followed the usual series of chats in local pubs until McDonald was told: 'We have this group which meets and has discussions about party matters.' McDonald says:

> It didn't surprise me. I knew there was some sort of caucus. They invited me to the next meeting, so I went along to this house in Anfield. When I got there I was shocked. There was a table set up at the top of the room with a chairman, secretary, minutes secretary and treasurer – it was just like a Labour Party meeting.[7]

Militant always advises members not to take on positions in the Labour Party which require a lot of donkey work. In most cases, members are advised simply to go for party positions with political influence, such as Youth Officer and Political Education Officer. Because of Militant's strength in his local party in Kirkdale, McDonald quickly found that after joining Militant there were no problems about a career in the Kirkdale Labour Party or his union: 'I fought the council elections three times. I was made ward chairman, constituency party chairman, district Labour Party delegate and I was treasurer of my union branch. The higher tier of Militant had obviously decided that I was suitable for these posts, and so I got them.'[8]

And McDonald soon got over his initial shock: 'I was told at the start that we didn't ever mention this group had ever met. You weren't supposed to ask questions. It was frowned upon. But I was flattered. You were one of the chosen few. A lot of those who joined were just looking for a cause.'[9]

Like all Militant members, McDonald became involved in the search for others looking for a cause:

> We were always being told to look out for 'good types'. Part of the business at branch meetings was 'Any good types?' You'd say so-and-so spoke well at a union meeting. 'Really?' they'd say. 'See if he'll second this motion.' The next week I'd go back and tell them he had seconded it. 'That's interesting.' So then one of the officers would make contact with him, and it went from there.[10]

McDonald remembers life in Militant as a 'series of tests'. Members were given a quota of papers to sell each week but often ended up paying for them with their own money instead. He also recalls the political education: 'One week you'd get the latest "Perspectives" document. Next week the members were tested on it. "You didn't read page four," they'd accuse you.'[11]

In the end McDonald left Militant in anger at its attitude towards other Labour Party members who were not in the tendency:

Several new people joined my ward. They were true socialists but were treated shabbily by Militant and were verbally abused. Just because their motions were deemed to be 'unacceptable', they weren't getting through. I started to question this. These people had worked hard for me in the council elections. In the end it came to a meeting in a pub in Huyton with Derek Hatton. I told him they were too doctrinaire and that I was unhappy about these people who were 'real socialists'. I was told I'd lose all my positions, that I'd be a 'non-person' as far as the Labour Party was concerned.[12]

And that's exactly what happened. In the months that followed his departure from Militant, McDonald failed to get re-elected to the posts that Militant had once secured for him. The only position he did retain – thanks to some clever footwork – was the chairmanship of the Kirkdale constituency party. But when McDonald started speaking to the press about his time in Militant and giving television interviews, he says that the Militant supporters in his party made his position unbearable. In the end he gave up and left the Labour Party altogether.

Richard Hart joined Militant in March 1973, seven years after joining the Labour Party, and was a member of a branch in south London. There he shared a house at 13 Elsiemaud Road in Deptford, which became a sort of Militant household, with several leading Militant people as tenants. The building was also used for Marxist discussion meetings and for putting people up when they came to London: 'Keith Dickinson used to say you should give up your bed for members of the National Committee, because they were working hard all week.'[13] At one point the Labour Party was so suspicious about the fact that several Militant supporters were living in the same building that it carried out an inquiry into 13 Elsiemaud Road, but investigations revealed nothing more sinister than several like-minded friends sharing the same house.

Hart left Militant in the end for several reasons. One was that he got married; another was the conflict between his work for Militant and his job as a librarian:

> I told them I couldn't help out on Saturdays because of my job. They felt I was using my job as an excuse not to do more work for the tendency and they held it up to ridicule. I was told that my job wasn't really all that important, and that the tendency is. They didn't regard it as a useful job in the community. I was told to fake migraine, but I thought this was dishonest and so I didn't. Then that summer I found I was addressing a meeting and coming out with all their phrases. I no longer felt an independent person. I felt sucked into them and started feeling the tendency could take over my whole life.[14]

Mike Barnes was a member of Militant in the mid-1970s, first in Edinburgh, when he was at school, and later in York, when he was at university. He is now a film director with the BBC in Scotland.

Barnes was recruited in exactly the same way as everybody else. When he was a member of the Young Socialists in Edinburgh the local Militant branch had allocated members to talk to him about politics and to report on progress:

Eventually the great day came when the Organisation was revealed to me, followed by an invitation to internal meetings. I was sworn to secrecy and, with a feeling of being involved in something very important, agreed to attend.[15]

It was a secret spy-like world. There was tremendous excitement about it all and tremendous attraction at first.[16]

Barnes agrees with many ex-defectors that, as well as helping prevent expulsion from the Labour Party, this secrecy contributes to the 'cohesion, sense of self-importance and siege mentality'.[17]

The most abiding memories of life in Militant are filled with the sheer strain of it all. If you were even moderately active, you would be asked to attend up to six or seven boring meetings in one week.[18]

You built up an alternative set of social contacts as much as political activity. It can easily take over people's lives. It became obsessive. They were almost inventing meetings to attend. There was a ridiculous number of meetings held to discuss such a small amount of work. Even if you didn't have a meeting one evening, you'd end up drinking with them.[19]

The kind of commitment that Militant required was bundled together in the form of highly alienating personal relationships. You had to make sure your subscriptions were paid and your papers sold so as not to feel guilty when you chatted to other members. The only way out seemed to be 'family commitments' and the unspoken truth that as soon as a young Militant member got a girlfriend he either recruited her or left.[20]

Barnes particularly remembers how difficult it was to be a member of Militant and a student:

> When I was at York University there was this attitude that students weren't really proper members – which only added to our guilt feelings. The important thing, we were told, was to get workers involved – people from the town. So you had all these students trying to do their bit by chatting up railway workers and buying them drinks in the hope they would buy a copy of the paper. Then you had the horrible thing of going round a council estate on a Sunday afternoon trying to sell papers. We all hated it, but nobody dared admit it.[21]

Mike Barnes eventually left because of policy differences. He soon tired of reading Militant's set texts – Marx, Lenin and Grant ('easily the most boring writer in the entire far left') – and began to explore other Marxist literature. Soon the inconsistencies he saw in Militant's thinking became just too great.

> I sent them a long letter to say why I was resigning. So they brought in the full-timers and I was persuaded into having a chat in the university bar. It went on all night and we ended up in someone's room. It really turned into a theological argument and one full-timer turned to me and said, 'You've lost your faith in the working class.' This was after an evening during which I'd been saying it was all religious and they'd been denying it.[22]

The similarities between Militant and religion are obvious from the lifestyle of the members. One has only to attend a large public Militant rally to notice the parallels with a Billy Graham meeting. Militant's set texts are treated like the Bible, and quotations from Trotsky and Marx are used in the same way as biblical extracts. Meetings on political matters are more a matter of teaching the members about Marx, Trotsky and Lenin than of developing any new thought. Members are tested on the set texts as if they were Holy Writ. Militant's simple political philosophy has an appeal to a certain type of person because, like a religion, it answers life's problems. As Mike Barnes points out, there is tremendous faith in the working class and an almost inexplicable optimism about the eventual demise of capitalism. The full-timer plays the role of the priest, interpreting the teachings passed down from on high and dealing with the problems of individual members of his congregation.

What happens to members of Militant when they leave? Most of the ex-members I have met are still involved in Labour politics, but it was far more likely that I would come across ex-members still in politics than those who had given it up. My estimate is that about half leave politics altogether, although they may return later, and most retain left-wing sympathies. Many who stay in the Labour Party go on to pursue orthodox careers – several former members of Militant stood as Labour candidates at the 1983 election (for example, Ian Pearson in Bexhill and Battle, Martin Upham in Harborough, Alex Wood in Edinburgh West and Jake Magee in Uxbridge). There seems to be no real trend in the political direction of ex-members. Mike Barnes says that his political views now probably correspond most closely with those of the

Socialist Workers' Party, and others I have met still call themselves Marxists. Some defectors are still on the left of the Labour Party, while others, such as Mason and McDonald, have moved further to the right.

11

THE SACRIFICIAL
LAMBS

For the Labour leadership, the 'winter of discontent' of 1979 turned into a summer that was far from glorious and an autumn that was a disaster. Labour's defeat at the polls in May that year unleashed all the dissatisfaction that had been building up among party activists over the past five years. Jim Callaghan was not only blamed for getting the date of the election wrong but was also held responsible for the confrontation with the unions during the previous winter which had lost Labour millions of votes.

The 1979 conference in Brighton saw a major defeat for the right. Delegate after delegate laid into the party leadership, and the assembly agreed, at least in principle, to two important constitutional changes that the left had been demanding for years: mandatory reselection of MPs, and the NEC's sole responsibility for drawing up the election manifesto. Brighton 1979 also marked the start of four years of internal wrangling that eventually helped to deny the Labour Party victory in 1983.

Militant was just one of several important issues that would divide left from right.

Two months after the 1979 election, the national agent, Reg Underhill, retired, having served the party all his working life. His reward was a seat in the Lords. Underhill was looking forward to a rest from party organisational matters; he hoped to concentrate on being an opposition spokesman in the upper chamber. But before long he came under intense pressure from right-wing MPs and journalists to make public the work on Militant, which the Labour NEC had refused to publish when he was a party official. Underhill eventually decided to update his Militant report with new evidence that he had received. In January 1980 he sent his new report to the general secretary, Ron Hayward, and to his successor as national agent, David Hughes. But Hughes was not interested in Militant. He did not even bother to read the report. 'We dealt with it and that was the end of it,' he is reported to have remarked. 'I have a lot of other things to do. This job carries a heavy work load. We *have* just lost an election, you know.'[1]

Not surprisingly, the revival of the Militant issue rekindled press interest and several insecure right-wing Labour MPs were only too happy to keep journalists informed. The *Daily Mirror* managed to get hold of a copy of Underhill's report and made a front-page story of it.[2] The *Sunday Times* printed an article on Militant's finances, asking where a loan of £148,000 had come from.[3] Both *New Society*[4] and the *New Statesman*[5] published long and well-researched articles on Militant, and the new BBC 2 programme *Newsnight* showed a film report that was based partly on

Charles James's work on Militant's finances.[6] This also included a dramatic interview with a Militant defector called 'Jane', filmed in the back of a car travelling through the streets of London.

When the NEC met in February it decided that the best thing to do was to send a questionnaire to all the pressure groups operating within the party, including Militant, asking for details about their organisation, finances and democratic procedures. But the NEC decided not to set up what it called an 'inquisition' or to publish Underhill's work. Its resolution concluded: 'The National Executive Committee invites Lord Underhill to publish any documents he wishes to publish.'[7] So he did.

> I said to my wife, 'How much can we afford?' [Underhill recalls] and then we printed 750 copies at our own expense. I had built up a list of addresses of constituency secretaries, and my daughter typed out the labels and filled the envelopes. We sent a copy to each NEC member, each constituency party and every affiliated trade union.[8]

The left, which was still in control of the NEC, had no wish to attack Militant, and it increasingly needed the tendency's support in the important battles over democratising the party. Tony Benn told a television interviewer: 'I remember the Zinoviev letter was a forgery,' and he dismissed the Underhill documents. 'As far as I can make out [they] came in plain envelopes from the Intelligence Service or wherever.' Eric Heffer compared the new campaign against Militant with Goebbels's Nazi propaganda.[9]

A few days after the 1980 conference Jim Callaghan resigned

as leader, and Michael Foot was elected to succeed him (under the old system of election by MPs – the exact composition of the new electoral college had not yet been decided). Foot is reported to have been shocked by his victory. The cause was partly surprise that he had won (Denis Healey was the favourite) but probably more a sudden realisation of the responsibilities thrust upon him. As the 'unity' candidate, Foot was now expected to hold together a party in which civil war had been waging for several months.

Michael Foot's first year as leader must have turned out to be a bigger nightmare than even he had feared. Within weeks of his election came the special conference at Wembley to agree the precise make-up of the electoral college. Contrary to expectations, this gave the unions the biggest share – 40 per cent of the votes, against 30 per cent each for the MPs and the constituencies. A right-wing union, USDAW, had unexpectedly put forward the 40–30–30 formula after Militant supporters had lobbied several members of the union's delegation. The day after Wembley, a Sunday, came the Limehouse Declaration and, a few weeks later, the formation of the Social Democratic Party. Foot had pleaded with the Social Democrats to stay but with no success. Then almost as soon as that problem had subsided there came another. Tony Benn suddenly announced, early one morning in April, that he was going to test the new electoral college by challenging Denis Healey for the deputy leadership.

The deputy leadership of the Labour Party is an odd post. Like the Vice-Presidency of the United States, it confers more prestige than power. But, for some peculiar reason, in the summer of

1981 the post of Labour Party deputy leader suddenly assumed a new significance, especially when, as the conference drew near, it looked as if Benn might win. Arguably, the election received wider media publicity than the leadership battle of 1983.[10]

Party activists thought the contest vitally important too. Those bodies that had campaigned vigorously for constitutional changes now pulled out all the stops for Benn. Militant was among them. But the campaign also marked the beginning of a significant rift on the left: Tribunites Neil Kinnock and Joan Lestor were never forgiven by the Bennites for abstaining. And throughout the six-month campaign Michael Foot made it clear that he was furious with Benn for standing in the first place. In the end Denis Healey held on ('by a whisker' was the common description).

This period also saw the first signs that trade union leaders were becoming worried about Militant. Until the late 1970s, Militant had concentrated its work on the Labour Party and had made little impact on the unions. After the establishment of its Industrial Bureau in the mid-1970s, Militant saw its work in the unions as the natural extension to its work in the Labour Party. It was regarded as another means of raising workers' consciousness and finding new recruits. Where the unions were affiliated to the Labour Party, it could be a new source of voting power at party meetings. By the start of the 1980s, the tendency was having small but increasing success in this field. Progress had often been helped by unsuccessful industrial action. The 1977–78 firemen's strike, for instance, prompted Militant gains in the Fire Brigades' Union, and the 1980 steel strike increased Militant's influence in the Iron and Steel Trades' Confederation. In 1979, after the unsuccessful 1978 bakers' strike, a Militant member, Joe Marino, was elected general secretary of the Bakers' Union. Above all Militant had been gaining ground in the civil service unions, in particular the CPSA, where Militant had been progressing since the mid-1970s. Eventually, in 1982, after the long and unsuccessful civil service strike, the union elected a Militant member, Kevin Roddy, as president, though he was deposed after a year.

In the past, calls for action against Militant had come almost entirely from MPs and party officials, but after the 1979 election right-wing unions became increasingly concerned about the tendency too. The clerical workers' union, APEX, called for action after the 1980 Underhill report, and later in the year the NUR annual conference called on the Labour Party to bring back the Proscribed List. They sent a similar resolution to the 1981 Labour conference, but there was not enough support to secure a debate. The resolution was remitted (passed to the NEC for consideration).

After the 1981 Brighton conference Michael Foot was coming under increasing pressure from the right. The implied threat was that if he did not act against the far left, the ranks of Labour MPs would shrink still further. Throughout the autumn of 1981, a steady flow of MPs trickled from Labour to the Social Democrats. The possibility of further departures, perhaps on a large scale, was a constant worry for Foot, especially at a time when Labour was falling behind the Liberals and the SDP in the polls and in by-elections. In October, the right-wing Manifesto Group of MPs went to see Foot about something else that had been troubling them for some months: the selection of Militant members as Labour parliamentary candidates.

Several years earlier Militant had spoken internally of 'establishing a group of half a dozen or so MPs identified with the tendency',[11] but until now little progress had been made towards this aim. This plan was not part of some long-term scheme eventually to take over the Parliamentary Labour Party: the thinking was simply that candidates and MPs would give Militant a powerful platform from which more people could be won over to the ideas of the tendency. In 1979, three Militant candidates had stood for Labour: Tony Mulhearn in Crosby, David White in Croydon Central and Cathy Wilson on the Isle of Wight. But only White, in a marginal seat, got much publicity. All three candidates lost with slightly larger than average swings against them (see Appendix 2).

But in 1980 and 1981 the tendency began to get more candidates selected and this time in good seats. It almost looked as if a deliberate decision had suddenly been taken by Militant to go for safe seats: in reality the tendency was simply being more successful. By October 1981, five Militant members had been chosen; three of them were in Labour seats (Pat Wall in Bradford North, Tony Mulhearn in Liverpool Toxteth and David Nellist in Coventry South-East). Two more were in former Labour seats that the party could hope to regain in a good year (Terry Harrison in Liverpool Edge Hill and Rod Fitch in Brighton Kemptown). And the word was that a sixth Militant candidate would soon be chosen in another safe seat, Liverpool Kirkdale. And in Scotland a Militant candidate almost stood for Labour in the June 1980 Glasgow

Central by-election. Ronnie Stevenson lost the nomination by only one vote, and since it was a safe Labour seat, he very nearly became Militant's first MP. But the case that worried the right most was Bradford North.

There, in October 1981, one of the founders of Militant, Pat Wall, had defeated the sitting MP, Ben Ford, by thirty-five votes to twenty-eight. Ford was well to the right of the party and had made himself unpopular by visiting countries with right-wing dictatorships. Wall, on the other hand, was a popular figure in the area, having been president of Bradford Trades Council since 1973. At the age of sixteen, in 1950, Wall had been party secretary in Liverpool Garston and was its conference delegate the following year. His work for *Rally*, *Socialist Fight* and *Militant* over the years had accompanied long service to the Labour movement. Wall had been a councillor in both Liverpool and Bingley and had become a familiar figure at Labour conferences, usually managing to speak at least once whenever he was a delegate. Since 1973 he had been a regular candidate for the Labour NEC (see Appendix 1) and had more than once got the highest vote of any non-MP.

Wall has the lifestyle of a man from a working-class background who has done well in life. A hardware buyer with a mail-order firm, he owns a small cottage on the edge of the moors. He is different from most of the other Militant founder members, more of an individual. Though clearly committed to Militant, politics are not the only thing in his life: he likes listening to jazz and goes clay-pigeon shooting. Most Saturdays he travels around the country to support Everton Football Club.

The Bradford North constituency had had a weak party, with only about 150 members, in the mid-1970s. Militant had taken advantage of this weakness and had become a strong force in the constituency, but when Wall was chosen it was by no means in a majority. In other places Militant candidates had been selected simply because the tendency had taken control of a party (as in some of the Liverpool seats), but this was not the case in Bradford North. Wall got the nomination because of two extra ingredients – personal popularity and his party record – not simply because he was a member of Militant.

In the autumn of 1981 the pressures on Michael Foot from members of the Parliamentary Labour Party became quite intense. After the victories for the left on both constitutional issues and policy in recent years, the right was looking to make something of a comeback. Militant was a useful issue on which to do it. But the pressure came not just from long-standing right-wingers, and members of the Manifesto Group, but also from people Foot regarded as being on the left. Peter Shore was worried about moves to unseat him in his own constituency. Up-and-coming Tribunites such as Jeff Rooker, Robert Kilroy-Silk, Andrew Bennett and Jack Straw – people who could expect to be ministers in a future Labour government – were worried that unless something was done there might not be a future Labour government. All went to see Michael Foot to ask him to take action.

This period really marks the turning-point in relations between Militant and the party establishment. The key figure was Michael Foot. Until then he had helped to prevent any action against Militant, but afterwards he was to the fore in initiating it.

Foot is reported to have told one NEC meeting that since being elected leader he had received hundreds of letters from 'the people I marched with at Aldermaston' telling him to take action against the far left. At a Parliamentary Labour Party meeting he complained of 'caucusitis' and called Militant a 'pestilential nuisance'. Then, at the NEC Organisation Committee, he supported a call for an inquiry to look into Militant's activities. But Militant was not the only victim of the new Michael Foot. His tough stand was also directed against a young, unknown left-winger called Peter Tatchell, who had just been selected as candidate for Bermondsey but not yet endorsed by the NEC.

Fortunately for Foot, the NEC had swung rightwards at the 1981 conference, but to ensure a majority Foot still needed the support of people who were now being called 'soft-left', notably Neil Kinnock and Joan Lestor. At the December 1981 NEC, with the soft left's support, Foot won the day as far as both Tatchell and Militant were concerned.

The NEC set up a full-scale inquiry to look into Militant. Compared with the investigations in 1977, it looked now as if the inquiry would result in strong action against the tendency, including expulsions.

For the next fifteen months the stories of Militant and Peter Tatchell were to merge, at least in the public mind. Several tabloid papers repeatedly described Tatchell as a member of Militant in spite of his continual denials.[12] Politically Tatchell's views were more in tune with the new left than with Militant, and for its part Militant dislikes not only Tatchell's 'community politics' but also the fact that he is gay. Tatchell has described since how Militant members waged a 'word-of-mouth campaign' against him in Bermondsey and had never wanted him as candidate,[13] but these differences were not always apparent at the time. The confusion may also have had something to do with the fact that Peter Tatchell and Peter Taaffe have similar names.

The two men asked to carry out the Militant investigation were Ron Hayward, the general secretary, who was about to retire, and David Hughes, the national agent. In view of their past attitude to such matters, neither man can have viewed the job with much relish.

Nevertheless, Hayward and Hughes quickly set about their task. Regional organisers were asked to send in reports on Militant activities in their areas. Most complied, though the Scottish organiser, James Allison, refused, saying he had no intention of becoming a 'private investigator'.[14] They also received a large amount of unsolicited material from MPs and ordinary party members. A lot of this 'evidence' was poor, along the lines of: 'And then he tried to sell me a copy of *Militant*...' But there were many useful contributions. Labour Solidarity enlisted the help of Lord Underhill and the evidence of several defectors to compile a seventeen-page report detailing Militant's history, organisation and finances; Roy Hattersley subedited it, adding a few literary touches. Another helpful contribution came from the party's student organiser, John Dennis, who had been approached by

Hughes. Dennis rewrote one of Charles James's reports on the finances, provided an account from David Mason (see Chapter 10) of his experiences in the tendency and gave details himself on how Militant operates within NOLS. One of several MPs to submit evidence was Frank Field, who argued, among other things, that Militant should be asked to hand over its full-time workers, newspaper and printing network to the Labour Party.[15]

Hayward and Hughes also received information from Militant defectors, some of whom they interviewed. Militant too was approached. At the start of the inquiry it was sent a list of questions about the organisation. In reply Peter Taaffe said that the Editorial Board consisted of five people: himself, Lynn Walsh, Ted Grant, Clare Doyle and Keith Dickinson and declared that there were sixty-four full-time staff. This statement was never really challenged. Towards the end of the investigation, in May, Hayward and Hughes interviewed Taaffe, Grant and Walsh at Walworth Road.

Meanwhile, the Pat Wall controversy dragged on. Ben Ford, MP for Bradford North, had made some rather petty allegations of irregularities in the selection procedure, and so a three-man NEC inquiry team had visited Bradford and recommended that a new selection be got under way. But the Organisation Committee rejected the inquiry's recommendation on the grounds that one member of the team, John Golding, had declared beforehand that Pat Wall should not be the candidate. Instead the committee recommended that Wall's candidature be accepted. But the NEC, in turn, rejected the Org-Sub's report and called for a new selection.

Then, the day before the Organisation Committee was due to meet yet again, the *Sunday Times* ran a front-page 'exclusive' story about Pat Wall under the headline 'New Shock for Foot – Labour Man Urges Overthrow of State'.[16]

The paper's political correspondent, Michael Jones, had gone to a meeting in Bradford at which Wall had been debating with the Socialist Workers' Party, and secretly tape-recorded Wall's speech. Wall was recorded as saying the 'issue of Parliament' was a minor one, and that a Marxist Labour government would have to deal with the capitalist state machine immediately on coming to office:

> It would mean the abolition of the monarchy, the House of Lords, the sacking of the generals, the admirals, the air marshals, the senior civil servants, the police chiefs and in particular, the judges and people of that character ... We will face bloodshed. We will face the possibility of civil war and the terrible death and destruction and bloodshed that would mean.[17]

Jones's tape-recording was played on radio and television bulletins that Sunday. The *Daily Mail* and *Daily Telegraph* ran the story as their front-page leads the following day.[18] Newsmen flocked to Pat Wall's home in Bradford, where his wife Pauline retaliated by taking photos of the photographers and posting up a copy of the NUJ Code of Conduct.

The Hayward–Hughes inquiry reported in June, though its recommendations were leaked widely in advance of official publication. The three-page report contained nothing new and no evidence against Militant. It concluded that Militant was 'not a group formed solely to support a newspaper' and that the tendency was in 'conflict with Clause II, Section 3, of the party constitution'. The two officials recommended that the NEC should set up a register of non-affiliated groups of members, which would be allowed to operate within the party. In their opinion, 'the Militant Tendency [*sic*] as presently constituted would not be eligible to be included on the proposed register in the light of our findings.'[19]

It was a solution that satisfied hardly anybody. The right wanted to know why none of the evidence had been published and why Militant had to be dealt with in such a roundabout manner. It wanted definite expulsions, possibly through the reintroduction of the Proscribed List. The register seemed to pose all sorts of problems. It was not clear what would happen to Militant once the register was established. What would the party do if other groups refused to register, in sympathy with Militant? Would they be expelled too? And there was a general feeling that it was unfair to declare Militant excluded from the register before it had had a chance to apply. Peter Taaffe said that the register would inevitably lead to expulsions, though privately Militant believed that the number of names on the hit list was small. 'Hayward doesn't want to go down in history as a witch-hunter-general,' Taaffe said to one journalist on his return from the meeting with Hayward and Hughes. The far left said it was the beginning of a witch-hunt against the whole of the left, and a group called the Unregistered Alliance was formed. As the Labour Party's own paper, *Labour Weekly*, commented on the register: 'It could only work in an atmosphere of co-operation. There is no evidence that such an atmosphere exists.'[20]

The register was a typical Labour Party compromise. Hayward, Hughes and Foot all knew in the summer of 1982 that they would not necessarily win support for outright expulsions, either on the NEC or at the coming conference. Michael Foot said the party would have been within its rights to expel Militant there and then but still argued, 'If there is some other way, we should seek a remedy.'[21] The register would almost certainly lead to some expulsions, of course, but at this stage they could not spell that out. Expulsions would be delayed until the register itself had been agreed by conference and until a more favourable NEC had been elected, as seemed likely. It was also seen as a means of avoiding the revival of the notorious Proscribed List, which had been abolished in 1973. What was not realised at the time was just how much the procedure would delay the matter. It would be another eight months before any expulsions took place, and that period would see another of the long-drawn-out battles in which the Labour Party seems to specialise.

Meanwhile, two days after the Hayward–Hughes report was accepted by the NEC, Pat Wall was selected again by Bradford North. This time his majority over Ben Ford was much larger – forty-nine votes to twelve (compared with thirty-five to twenty-eight before).

'Now what the hell are they going to do?' Wall asked.[22] The same day Ron Hayward retired as general secretary, to be succeeded by Jim Mortimer, former chairman of the conciliation service, ACAS, and once victim of the former Proscribed List.

Mortimer had played no role in the preparation of the Hayward–Hughes report, but it was now his job to make sure that the register worked and to carry out the disciplinary action. Mortimer had a long-standing dislike of Trotskyist groups. In his youth the new general secretary had had strong links with orthodox Communists in the fight against fascism in the 1930s, and he had briefly been a member of the Young Communist League. Even so, Militant had grudgingly voted for Mortimer's appointment.

Over the summer the question of the register became an important issue on the left, almost a symbol of left-wing virility. Some organisations, such as the Tribune Group of MPs and the Labour Co-ordinating Committee, did register. Others, such as the Campaign for Labour Party Democracy and the Labour Abortion Rights Campaign, refused at first. Michael Foot staked his leadership on the register decision, but as unions held their summer conferences and meetings to decide on policy for the forthcoming Labour Party conference in Blackpool, it was increasingly clear that even though most constituencies were against the register, the union block votes would probably save Foot from defeat.

At the beginning of September Militant held what it called a 'Labour Movement Conference' at Wembley. In effect, it was a show of strength against the Labour leadership, as 2,600 Militant members and sympathisers came from all over the country to protest about the 'witch-hunt'. The gathering received wide coverage in the press and on television. Earlier that summer Tony Benn had agreed to sponsor the occasion, but another engagement prevented him from attending and he merely sent a message of support –

a sign perhaps that the leader of the left wished to distance himself from the tendency. In fact, the only MP willing to attend was Les Huckfield, who was at that point in severe danger of losing his place on the Labour NEC and his seat in Parliament (in the end he lost both). This was rather ironic, since Huckfield had a long history of vehement opposition to the tendency. In his youth Huckfield had campaigned against Trotskyists in the LPYS in the West Midlands. Much later, in 1978, when a junior minister, Huckfield had gone to see John Golding at the Department of Employment with a list of people whom he believed to be Militant full-timers. He suggested that Golding might like to investigate whether any of them were also claiming state benefits.

The 1982 Labour Party conference was a low-key affair compared with the three historic conferences that had preceded it. For most people in Blackpool the main interest of the week was whether the right would manage to strengthen its position on the NEC.

The Militant debate took place on the Monday afternoon, the first day of conference. For the television companies and the press this was the big set piece of the week. Sitting in the gallery were the five public members of Militant's Editorial Board, all of whom must have thought that once the register was approved, it would be only a few weeks before they were expelled from the party.

The debate was opened by Jim Mortimer, who formally presented the Hayward–Hughes report on behalf of the NEC. It was his first speech to conference as general secretary. '... Militant is not just a newspaper. The Militant tendency is an organised faction – an organised party – within the Labour Party,' Mortimer argued. 'It has, first, its own long-term programme, principles and policy – quite distinct from those of the Labour Party.'[23] Mortimer spoke of the huge 'trunk' of evidence accumulated at Walworth Road but did not give any details. Yet, perhaps surprisingly, nearly half of his address was devoted to attacking Militant's policies and ideology. He criticised its attitude to trade unionism and its treatment of wider popular groups such as the women's movement and the campaign against nuclear weapons. And he denounced Militant's approach to 'détente and the relaxation of international tension', calling Militant members the 'ideological allies' of the 'right wing of the Conservative Party'.[24]

The clerical union, APEX, and the electricians' union, the EETPU, proposed the main motion against Militant. They were supported from the floor by the former national agent, Lord Underhill, the man who had first raised the Militant issue seven years earlier. Defending the tendency were Alan Sapper of the TV technicians' union and the Tribunite MP Martin Flannery. Two Militant supporters were also allowed to speak – the long-standing candidates for the National Executive, Ray Apps and Pat Wall, who ironically was attending conference in his new capacity as properly endorsed prospective candidate for Bradford North. 'You cannot witch-hunt ideas,' Wall proclaimed.[25]

Michael Foot chose to wind up the debate himself – a sign of how important the issue was to him. The man who had so often been the victim of party discipline in the past refuted Pat Wall's accusations:

What is a witch-hunt? A witch-hunt is to pursue people, to persecute people – in the Labour Party context to expel people for crimes they have not committed or for crimes that are fantasies. I have been opposed to witch-hunts in this party, and I will be opposed to witch-hunts in this party until the day I die. I intend all the time to oppose such witch-hunts, but there is a sharp distinction between witch-hunts and real offences against the constitution.[26]

In three separate votes on the register and Militant, the leadership and the NEC were supported by margins of three to one.

But perhaps more important than the debate on the Monday afternoon were the results of the NEC elections the following morning. Thanks partly to the fact that the railwaymen's leader, Sid Weighell, had failed to vote for the miners' candidate, Eric Clarke, as his union traditionally did, there was a bigger swing to the right than had been expected. For the first time in memory the right had a majority even without the support of Michael Foot or the soft left. Michael Foot would have no trouble now in getting together a majority for whatever action he wished to take. Over the years the man who had emerged as leader of the right-wingers on the NEC was John Golding. By the autumn of 1982, Golding was becoming known publicly as the hatchet man of the right. *Tribune* described him as the 'most powerful man in the Labour Party'.[27]

Golding's opening move after the 1982 conference came at the first meeting of the NEC, the last Wednesday in October. When Jim Mortimer read out his proposals as to who should serve on each of the NEC sub-committees, Golding systematically deleted left-wingers and replaced them with his colleagues. The right's new majority ensured that each time Golding got his way, sometimes by voting margins of sixteen to eleven or, at the closest, fourteen to thirteen. Michael Foot took no part in the voting; he just watched as Golding clinically carried out his task. 'Michael hasn't got any guts left,' Dennis Skinner shouted across the room.[28] It was one of the most acrimonious NEC meetings in memory.

As a result Tony Benn lost his position as chairman of the Home Policy Committee and was replaced by Golding himself. On the Organisation Committee right-winger Russell Tuck of the NUR replaced Eric Heffer in the chair.

At this point it looked only a matter of weeks before a large-scale purge of Militant would be under way. The leaders of Militant were taking careful measures to try to minimise the possible damage. Although in theory the Labour Party now had both the power and the will to take strong action, in practice Militant was still in a good position. For one thing the party could expel only those whom it was sure belonged to Militant. As has been noted, the tendency had told the Hayward–Hughes inquiry that there were five people on its Editorial Board and that it had sixty-four full-time organisers.[29] In reality the Board had about ten members, and there were by this time more than 120 full-timers. Party officials did not know this, though, and the one or two people who suspected it could not prove it.

Jim Mortimer and Michael Foot had no option but to go by the figures and names supplied by Militant itself. They acted on the assumption that the five Editorial Board members they had been told about were the only board members. At the same time neither man wanted a large-scale purge and the shortage of names enabled them to restrict the number of people to be considered for expulsion. While Mortimer supported the action against Militant, he felt there were far more important things he should be spending his time on.

Militant had the upper hand throughout. The tactic that the tendency employed was to focus attention on the five named members of the Editorial Board and thus to deflect inquiries about the parliamentary candidates. The five were almost sacrificial lambs. It hardly mattered if they were expelled – Taaffe and Grant had not been to a local party meeting for years anyway, though the other three were more active. The tactic worked.

Already the eight parliamentary candidates had begun deliberately to distance themselves publicly from Militant. In May 1982 the shares in WIR Publications Limited that were held by Pat Wall, Terry Harrison and Tony Mulhearn were transferred to Ted Grant, Clare Doyle and Keith Dickinson. The Militant candidates denied any formal link with the tendency and claimed merely to be readers of the paper. It was all part of a careful effort by Militant to reduce the damage of any possible disciplinary action and to present a more acceptable public image. An important part of this new approach was improved relations between Militant and the media, which naturally led to more favourable coverage.

Until this point the press and television had played a crucial part in the campaign against Militant. Many of the press 'exposés' and 'revelations' had actually been fuelled by members of the

Labour Party. For instance, Lord Underhill had provided the press with copies of his 1980 report and evidence, in the hope that media coverage would increase pressure on the Labour Party NEC, and Underhill was always willing to help journalists in their work on Militant. Labour MP Frank Field is another who admits to having used the media in his campaign against the tendency.

The media coverage had been useful to Militant's enemies in two ways. First, it had helped to inform Labour Party members at all levels about just how extensive and organised Militant was. Second, it had been used by the right to force moves against Militant. The more Militant's activities in the party were publicly revealed, the more this exposure had pressurised the leadership to act, if only in the interests of preserving Labour votes. But this did not so much mean taking action against Militant as being *seen* to take it. In the end the media coverage of Militant had become so extensive that Michael Foot – who had once come to Militant's defence – was forced into measures against it.

Until 1982, Militant's press relations had been almost non-existent; like many organisations in the Labour movement, the tendency was suspicious of the media. Interviews were given, but journalists never found Militant particularly forthcoming or informative. There was never any question of an off-the-record briefing.

In mid-1982 things changed. In June, Militant appointed a press officer called Pat Edlin. He had no experience of journalism beyond a few articles in *Militant*, but, after reading Denis MacShane's book *Using the Media*, Edlin started building up a series of contacts in Fleet Street and broadcasting. He drank with them and had lunches and dinners, all at their expense. Edlin telephoned his contacts regularly rather than waited for the press to call him. Above all Edlin got to know journalists and quickly learned who was hostile and who was not, who needed exclusive stories to help his or her career and who did not. 'He was the best press officer I've ever come across,' says Richard Evans of *The Times*. 'He made press men in Whitehall or the big companies look like beginners. He ought to give lessons in it.'[30]

Edlin's work began to infuriate Labour Party officials. 'He made them look like idiots,' says one Fleet Street journalist. 'Mortimer and co. would produce these papers marked "private and confidential"; next day they'd be on the front page of *The Times* or *The Guardian* before most of the NEC had even seen them.'[31] Before each meeting of the NEC or the Organisation Committee, Militant's photocopier was working non-stop printing the leaked papers. The street outside began to resemble Silverstone as dispatch riders waited to rush the latest set of confidential documents back to Fleet Street.

Militant's new 'cosiness with the media' (as *The Scotsman* put it) meant that press coverage was less hostile and, in some cases, almost sympathetic to the tendency. And whatever the Labour Party decided to do now had to be seen to be fair. By embarrassing Jim Mortimer in the pages of the quality press and on television, Militant was restricting his room for manoeuvre.

Immediately after Blackpool, Militant made another clever move: it applied to join the register in spite of the fact that the Hayward–Hughes report had said that it would be ineligible for registration. In Militant's application Peter Taaffe confirmed that in future the annual *Militant* readers' rally would be open to Labour Party members and the press. He even offered to provide a list of Militant's full-time workers, provided that it would not be used as a basis for expulsions, and to allow Militant's accounts to be inspected. Taaffe then asked what other changes the NEC wanted Militant to make.

After complaining that Militant was being treated unfairly by comparison with other groups, Peter Taaffe revealed that Militant had taken legal advice, which argued that the NEC's action was 'unconstitutional and could be subject to review in the courts'.[32] It was a sign that Militant was suddenly thinking of legal action. A Labour Party member from Liverpool, who was a lawyer, had written to Taaffe to point out that there was a strong legal case against the party. Settling internal problems in the 'capitalist courts' has always been frowned on within the Labour movement, but Militant was about to have serious action taken against it. Furthermore, looking at it from Militant's point of view, there was an interesting precedent. Three years earlier John Golding had taken legal action against *Militant* when the newspaper had mistakenly alleged that Golding had voted against the policy of the 35-hour week at an NEC meeting. Tony Benn told the NEC in November that if he had been in the same position as Militant, he too would have gone to court.

When the new Organisation Sub-Committee met for the first time early in November, it agreed to a plan of action against Militant proposed by Mortimer. First, the five members of the

Militant Editorial Board would be expelled from the Labour Party. Then those paid 'sales organisers' (again using Militant's phraseology) who were known would be asked if they would stop working for Militant. The eight Militant parliamentary candidates would be asked to undertake to withdraw their support for the tendency; the National Youth Committee and Youth Officer (Andy Bevan) would be asked to give a similar undertaking.[33] No mention was made of what would happen if these people did not give their assurances. The assumption was that they would be expelled. By the time the Organisation Sub-Committee's report reached the full Executive, however, Jim Mortimer had been forced to change his tactics completely.[34] In between the two meetings he had received legal advice, which had been obtained by a shadow Cabinet member, John Smith.

People on the right had long been worried about the possibility that Militant might take legal action. They feared that this would be time-consuming and would delay effective action against the tendency. It would also be costly and extremely embarrassing, especially if the party lost.

Several people associated with the right-wing Labour Solidarity Campaign had thought of this possibility long before the Hayward–Hughes inquiry even reported. Then, after the Blackpool conference, John Smith got together with other Solidarity supporters and decided that independently they would seek legal advice from a sympathetic barrister, Alexander (Derry) Irvine QC. Irvine told them that, given Mortimer's proposals, Militant would have a strong case if the tendency took legal action.

Quickly Mortimer had to revise his proposals so that they would be watertight in any court of law.

The register was shelved as a means of expulsion, though not discarded altogether. The target was narrowed down to the five declared members of Militant's Editorial Board. The parliamentary candidates and full-time workers seemed to be out of danger, at least for the time being. This, of course, was exactly what Militant wanted, although the last thing it could do was admit this in public. At the November NEC meeting Mortimer proposed that Militant should first be deemed ineligible for affiliation to the Labour Party – the same argument that had been used in the old days to justify the Proscribed List under which Mortimer himself had once been expelled; only then would Editorial Board members be thrown out. After the NEC meeting, however, Mortimer acknowledged that because of the legal difficulties it was 'impossible to answer' whether the party would ever be able to expel anybody.

Between November 1982 and February 1983 successive meetings of the NEC and its Organisation Sub-Committee had to steer a careful course through what they saw as a legal minefield.

In December 1982, on the day that the NEC was due to declare that Militant was ineligible for affiliation, the tendency applied for a High Court injunction to prevent any action from proceeding. The Editorial Board argued that it had not been given a chance to see any of the evidence against it. (In reality, of course, Militant had a pretty good idea of nearly everything in the famous trunk at Walworth Road.) Though sympathetic to its case, Mr Justice Nourse decided against the Editorial Board. He argued that Militant should have made its legal move three months earlier, before the party conference had reached its decision.[35]

The five Editorial Board members turned up at Walworth Road to appear before the NEC – the Executive was by this time concerned to be seen to be according them natural justice – but their appearance was limited to brief statements by the five; for legal reasons NEC members were told not to ask questions. Dennis Skinner stomped out of the meeting, calling it both a 'kangaroo court' and an 'example of Star Chamber procedures'.[36] The committee then agreed that the tendency was ineligible for affiliation to the party, but expulsions could be made only once the NEC had agreed on a definition of Militant membership. The final decision had been delayed again.

Deciding who was a member of the Militant organisation was not easy. The leaders of Militant denied that there was even an organisation. It had been much simpler in the days of the Proscribed List, as one NEC paper commented: 'Proscribed organisations did not normally deny their existence. They had formal membership.'[37]

As the tale dragged on, it looked increasingly as if the NEC would never manage to expel anybody. The final decision was constantly delayed from one meeting to the next. At one point Jim Mortimer considered the option of avoiding expulsions altogether and trying instead to persuade Militant to dissolve the organisation.[38] The general secretary was becoming more and more frustrated by the legal problems and was particularly annoyed that every move he made was being leaked to Militant and, furthermore, covered extensively in the pages of the newspapers and on TV. And it was taking up substantial amounts of his time when the party should have been preparing for a general election.

On 23 February 1983, five months after the Blackpool conference, fourteen months after the Hayward–Hughes inquiry had been set up and thirty-three years after Ted Grant had rejoined the Labour Party, it finally happened. The five Editorial Board members were called in front of the NEC for a second time and expelled. Again, no questions were asked.

The following day saw the famous Bermondsey by-election – the worst by-election result for Labour during the 1979 parliament. A Labour majority of 38.7 per cent over the Conservatives was converted into a 31.7 per cent majority for the Liberals over Labour. After the election Tatchell complained that he had lost support during the campaign through being wrongly associated with Militant. But, inconsistently, he refused to accept that Militant was electorally damaging to Labour. The left argued that the Militant expulsions the day before polling had also lost votes. Even if this were so, by the time of the NEC meeting Tatchell had effectively already lost.

Immediately after the expulsion meeting the five held a press conference to announce the start of a campaign to secure reinstatement. Posters had even been printed in advance. Later that day, when the five returned to Militant's headquarters at Mentmore Terrace, they were almost euphoric, partly because they were relieved that the fight was over for the time being but also because they had managed to protect the people that mattered, the parliamentary candidates, and because no effective measures had yet been taken against the tendency. From their point of view, they had virtually won the battle.

There were many on the right of the party who also felt that Militant had done very well. One shadow Cabinet political adviser said later: 'Militant had won – game, set and match.'[39] In spite of its supposedly firm majority on the NEC, the right had been almost totally ineffectual, not just because of Militant's legal action and clever tactics but also because of its own internal divisions and lack of a clear strategy. What it had lacked above all was a good dose of democratic centralism.

This would not have mattered if the right had not been divided internally. Some right-wing NEC members took a hard line on everything. Golding, while he wanted strong action, appreciated that this might not be possible. His main preoccupation, as chairman of the Home Policy Committee, was to hammer out an agreed programme on which to fight the election. He would have loved to expel the Militant candidates and full-timers but realised that the legal constraints compelled the party to proceed with caution. Privately Golding hoped that Militant would take the NEC through a long court action so that the evidence could be publicly revealed. Quite a few NEC right-wingers blamed John Golding for not taking more advantage of the majority they had on the NEC and felt very strongly that bad planning on Golding's part allowed Militant to get away. Some regretted that they left it to Golding to co-ordinate their work, and privately one or two later felt that they might be better off without him.

If the right had been determined, there is little doubt that the parliamentary candidates could have been dropped. The NEC can choose to abandon any candidate it likes and can override the wishes of the constituency party concerned. The problem then would have been the reaction of local parties, and ultimately the NEC would probably have had to impose its own candidates upon the constituencies. As far as Militant was concerned, all the right could do was to follow the cautious lead of Jim Mortimer and Michael Foot. Foot was trying to meet pressure from Labour MPs who wanted action against Militant, and felt he had to be seen doing something publicly. Mortimer simply wanted to support his party leader and do his job. Neither man wanted mass expulsions.

Boundary changes meant that eventually only five Militant candidates contested the general election. Michael Foot managed to be seen during the campaign with four of them. On the day the Labour leader went to share a platform in Bradford with Pat Wall the Conservatives published full-page newspaper advertisements in which they reprinted part of Wall's famous 'bloodshed' speech.[40]

Bradford North fell to the Conservatives after Ben Ford stood as an Independent and split the Labour vote. But on the night that Labour seats were falling everywhere, two Militant candidates were returned to Parliament: David Nellist in Coventry South-East and Terry Fields in Liverpool Broadgreen, where he recorded a remarkable 4.8 per cent swing to Labour (though in Broadgreen Labour may have benefited from a split in the Alliance between their official candidate, Richard Crawshaw, and an unofficial

Liberal). Around Britain most Labour supporters were in despair. Not members of Militant, though – they were delighted with their two successes.

John Golding returned to the Commons as MP for Newcastle-under-Lyme with a reduced majority of just under 3,000. But Golding's days as boss of the Labour right were numbered. Earlier in the week of the general election, at the conference of his union, the Post Office engineers, the broad left had taken over the union's Executive after years of control by the right. Prominent among those elected was Phil Holt, convener of the union's broad left and a member of Militant. A month later the union Executive decided that in 1983 it would not be nominating John Golding for election to the NEC of the Labour Party.

Contrast the methods of the new broad left of the Post Office engineers' Executive with those of the right-wingers on the Labour NEC. It had taken Golding months to deal with Militant, but it took just one meeting for Militant and its allies to deal with him.

John Golding was never elected to the NEC again. In 1986 he got his revenge on Militant in his union by beating their candidate Phil Holt, by 41,350 votes to 18,559 in the election for general secretary. But the result also signalled John Golding's effective withdrawal from mainstream Labour Party politics.

12

MILITANT MERSEYSIDE

In the June 1983 election the City of Liverpool was the one place that stood out against the Tory tide. While Britain as a whole recorded a swing of 3.9 per cent from Labour to the Conservatives, Liverpool saw a swing of 2.4 per cent from Conservative to Labour, and for the first time in recent history Liverpool had no Conservative MPs. A similar trend had occurred in the local elections five weeks earlier. While the Conservatives had made small gains in town halls across the country – so persuading Mrs Thatcher to call the general election – to the surprise of many concerned, for the first time in ten years Liverpool elected a Labour council. But then in politics, as in so many things, Liverpool has always been different.

Over a period of fourteen months, between February 1981 and March 1982, the public face of the Labour Party in Liverpool underwent a remarkable transformation. Three of the party's MPs – Richard Crawshaw, Eric Ogden and Jimmy Dunn – all defected to the Social Democrats, making Liverpool an SDP stronghold, at least for the time being. Eric Ogden left after being dropped by his constituency party in the new reselection process introduced by the Labour Party in 1980. Crawshaw and Dunn went before reselection had taken place, but for both men there was a very strong possibility that they would not be chosen again.

At the same time the Liverpool party selected a new generation of left-wing candidates – four of them Militant members. First, Terry Harrison, a Central Committee member, was picked to fight Edge Hill, a Labour seat until 1979. Replacing Crawshaw in Toxteth was a print worker, Tony Mulhearn, president of the Liverpool District Labour Party. In Kirkdale Labour chose Terry Fields, a member of the Executive of the Fire Brigades' Union. And finally in the Conservative seat of Wavertree they picked a young, energetic Militant councillor, Derek Hatton.

In the event only one of those four candidates, Terry Fields, actually stood in June 1983. Boundary changes reduced the number of Liverpool seats from eight to six, and with the threat of expulsions Militant wisely saw the redistribution as an opportunity to cool it a bit, and so three of its candidates withdrew. On election night, though, Terry Fields was elected MP for Liverpool Broadgreen and could boast of a 4.8 per cent swing to Labour.

Most people in Liverpool Labour politics, whatever their political position, agree on one point: the tendency's success can be explained partly by Merseyside's appalling economic conditions. Several older right-wing members of the party say that if they were now unemployed teenagers, they would find Militant attractive.

Economically Merseyside suffered long before many parts of Britain knew what unemployment was. Liverpool – sometimes called the 'Bermuda Triangle' of British capitalism – cannot remember what it was like *without* the dole queues. Even in the days when it was a prosperous port thousands of men had to wander down to the docks every morning to bid for casual work. In the 1970s, as successive recessions hit the rest of Britain, Merseyside's problems multiplied. Of the ten constituencies in England and Wales with the worst unemployment in the 1981 census, four were in Liverpool, all with jobless rates of more than 25 per cent.[1] Now, of course, that figure is far higher. Heroin, vandalism, violent crime, bad housing – all follow on, and in turn help to cause each other. Liverpudlians were not shocked when riots broke out in Toxteth in 1981: what surprised them was that trouble had not occurred before. And extreme economic conditions might be expected to encourage extreme politics.

In 1934, a young Liberal graduate came to Liverpool to work in a shipping company: 'I saw there for the first time in my young life, with my own eyes, what poverty meant ... I saw mass unemployment as the most fearful curse which could befall our people.'[2] Michael Foot's experience persuaded him to become a socialist and to join the Labour Party. Fifty years later unemployment in the same city is driving today's young idealists to join Militant.

But Merseyside's economic plight cannot provide the only reason for Militant's success. Other parts of Britain have suffered just as much as Merseyside – Scotland and the north-east, for example – without anything like the same support for Militant.

And while revolutionary and Marxist groups have always been strong on Merseyside, it is only recently that they have succeeded in the Labour Party. For most of its history the Labour Party in Liverpool has been a very right-wing body, but in itself this partly explains Militant's recent success. Eventually the small group of Trotskyists growing quietly in the Walton constituency in the 1950s and 1960s came to take over the whole city.

Peter Taaffe and Keith Dickinson eventually went to London to work full-time for Militant; Pat Wall moved away because of his job; but Harrison stayed behind looking after the home patch. Until ten years ago he worked as a boilermaker with Cammell Laird in Birkenhead but in 1973 put down his tools to become Militant's first full-time organiser in Liverpool. From the mid-1960s onwards he served on the RSL National Committee. Harrison has also been a chairman of Militant's National Conference.

Harrison has always insisted he is only a freelance journalist. He belongs to the NUJ and strenuously denies being an organiser for Militant. In reality he is Militant's leader on Merseyside and its father-figure – local members even call him 'Grandad'. But Harrison has a good Labour Party record. He has been a delegate to the District Labour Party (DLP) since 1958, and an Executive member since 1965. In the 1979 European elections Harrison stood for Labour in Liverpool, and lost the new Euro-seat on an 11 per cent swing to the Tories, the highest swing in the country. Between 1978 and 1980 he was also a Liverpool councillor.

The other important Militant figure who stayed behind was Tony Mulhearn. Born just before the war, right in the centre of

Liverpool, Mulhearn was from a Roman Catholic family, and on leaving school went into the printing trade. He didn't join the Labour Party until 1963, but then he also quickly got involved in the RSL. Indeed, like Harrison, Mulhearn is named on documents in the Jimmy Deane collection. Through his work in his union, the National Graphical Association, and for the Labour Party, Mulhearn built quite a strong personal base. From 1965 onwards he too served on the DLP Executive and in 1973 was elected vice-president of the District Party, long before Militant had emerged as a major force in Liverpool. For more than a decade Mulhearn was Liverpool's other representative on Militant's Central Committee, and he too chaired the National Conference on occasion. Mulhearn had to give up his Central Committee position when the committee was reorganised a few years ago and membership was confined to Militant full-timers.

Tony Mulhearn happened to join the Labour Party just as an era was closing. In November 1963 Labour's Liverpool boss, Jack Braddock, died. He was succeeded as Labour group leader by Alderman William Sefton, one of Braddock's strongest critics in the group. But just as in 1950 Braddock had taken over a political machine he had once opposed, so now, to some extent, did Bill Sefton.

The 1960s saw Labour and Conservatives alternating in office on the council, pursuing a largely bipartisan policy for the city. But at the end of the decade the Liberals suddenly emerged almost from nothing. The brilliant campaigning skills of a local business-man, Trevor Jones, exploited the growing disillusionment with the traditional parties. The term 'community politics' was introduced into Britain. 'Jones the Vote' was remarkably successful: the Liberals, who had just one councillor in 1967, became the largest single party after the 1973 elections.

For the next ten years no single party had a firm majority on the council. Usually the Liberals held office but had to rely on Conservative support to hold power. Ian Craig, former political editor of the *Liverpool Echo*, thinks that this three-party system, combined with Labour's frequent inability or refusal to take office, forced the Labour Party leftwards.[3] The party in opposition adopted policies that it might have abandoned long ago had it been in power, and the leadership no longer had the spoils of office with which to keep a grip on the party. Above all, there was an important shift in power from the Labour Group to the District Labour Party outside.

Most observers see 1972 as the year that really marked the end of the right's dominance of the Liverpool Labour Party. In the local elections that year the party in Liverpool had fought on a platform of outright opposition to any increase in rents which might be caused by the Heath government's Housing Finance Act. Within weeks of polling day, however, Sefton had abandoned this position. But he could get the required rent increase through council only with support from the Conservatives and Liberals. Twenty-one Labour councillors voted against Sefton; they then broke away and formed a separate Labour group on the council. What was important was that they won the backing of the Labour Party outside, and the Labour left resolved to make the council leadership more accountable in future. Its task was made easier when Sefton lost his council seat in the Liberal landslide the following year.

The early 1970s also saw among local Labour parties the first signs of discontent with their right-wing MPs. Richard Crawshaw in Toxteth, Sir Arthur Irvine in Edge Hill and Eric Ogden in West Derby all had problems.

In Toxteth Richard Crawshaw, an MP of great integrity, had met opposition ever since his first selection in 1962. In 1965 he had been 'nearly crucified' for voting against the Labour government on the defence estimates – an act that would normally impress a local party but not in Crawshaw's case, since he was protesting that not enough money was going to the Territorial Army. In 1971 he voted with the Heath government, and against the Labour whip, in the famous vote on entry to the EEC. Two years later he had to explain to his constituency executive why he had sponsored Dick Taverne, when the rebel MP returned to the Commons after defeating Labour in the Lincoln by-election.

Eric Ogden's relations with his party were a bit better, but in 1975 he was censured for supporting a pay rise for MPs just at the time when the Labour government was introducing another incomes policy.

The MP with the biggest problems, though, was Sir Arthur Irvine, Member for Edge Hill since 1947. Irvine was attacked for spending too much time on his London law practice and too little in his constituency. He visited Edge Hill once a month for surgeries, staying overnight at a local hotel. Irvine's party was the most decrepit of all. Twice – in 1971 and 1972 – it voted not to readopt

Sir Arthur as its candidate. Somehow the MP got the decisions overturned on technical irregularities and survived to fight both elections in 1974.

In 1977 the party finally succeeded in ousting Irvine, by thirty-seven votes to three. The voting figures indicated not only Irvine's unpopularity but also how small his party was. The following year Sir Arthur died suddenly: his family blamed his death on the local party. The subsequent by-election was won by David Alton for the Liberals in a remarkable result. At the general election five weeks later Alton won again.

Sir Arthur blamed his downfall on what he saw as a 'Trotskyist–Liberal alliance'. That Irvine believed Trotskyists and Liberals might work together was a sign of how out of touch he was. In any case the Trotskyist strength in Edge Hill at that time was fairly limited, and the same was true in the other seats where MPs were having trouble. All three constituencies had in key positions Militant supporters who were naturally among each MP's sternest critics, but in every case dissatisfaction with the MP was also felt by a much wider group of people on the left and, in Irvine's case, by many on the right too.

When, after the 1979 general election, Crawshaw, Ogden and Dunn defected to the SDP one by one and were replaced by left-wingers, it was not because Militant had been plotting their downfall, however delighted Militant was to see them go. The MPs had long been out of touch with their parties; they were no longer prepared to keep fighting. The reselection system introduced in 1980 meant they would probably not survive, and with the advent of the SDP in 1981 they left the Labour Party. But for Militant the departures offered just the opportunity it wanted; within a year Militant candidates had been installed in four of Liverpool's eight seats; three of those seats had traditionally been Labour.

Most people say that it was in about 1978 or 1979 that Militant became a serious political force in Liverpool. A few Militant members had served on the council before, but in those two years a block of seven was elected including both Terry Harrison and Derek Hatton. This small triumph for Militant coincided with the last dying gasp of the right-wing old guard.

Since Sefton's departure in 1973, the Labour group had been led by John Hamilton, a quiet, modest left-winger who was a complete contrast to Braddock and Sefton. Hamilton, a Quaker and a bachelor, had a long record of party service and was very popular, though regarded as rather weak: indeed, these two characteristics originally ensured his election. But in 1978, at the first meeting after the local elections, Hamilton was unexpectedly deposed in a coup by a right-winger, Eddie Roderick.

Within hours the local parties were in uproar. Wards and constituencies began to condemn the takeover and called for a new election. A special meeting of the district party was convened – with the highest attendance in years: after a stormy debate Roderick was forced to resign. In the new election several councillors switched their votes and Hamilton got his job back. He has held on to it ever since.

Roderick believes that Militant was largely responsible for the campaign that overturned his election and says that it was behind the resolutions passed by local parties and unions. At the special district party meeting he claims that councillors were warned by Militant speakers that if they did not vote the right way, they would be dropped as council candidates.[4]

Roderick concedes, however, that Militant could not have succeeded without the support of the rest of the Liverpool left and of people who were genuinely outraged by what had happened. But whatever interpretation one puts on it, the incident illustrated the important shift in power that had occurred since the 1972 split. Braddock and Sefton had always been able to outmanoeuvre the district party, but now the council leadership could no longer do so. The district party had become the more powerful of the two bodies. In particular it had learned how to use its power to draw up the list of approved candidates for council elections. Several long-serving right-wing councillors had their careers brought to an abrupt halt through being dropped by the district party, though Roderick himself survived until 1984.

It was in 1980 that the Liverpool Labour Party's future attitude towards the city's financial position first emerged. In 1979, Labour had taken over from the Liberals as the largest party on the council but without an overall majority. In March the following year, Labour leader John Hamilton proposed a budget that included a 50 per cent rate rise, but the first amendment to this came not from the Conservatives or Liberals, but from Hamilton's own back benches. The amendment, which received only nine votes, from Labour left-wingers, argued that as 'responsibility for the plight of the city lies squarely in the lap of the government' the rate rise should be restricted to the rate of inflation, 13 per cent, and that there should be 'no cuts or redundancies'.[5] The mover of the motion, Derek Hatton, had been a councillor for less than a year. Within another year his position would be official party policy.

The 1982 council elections were the first occasion on which Labour had stood on an outright Militant platform with the slogan 'No Cuts in Jobs or Services, No Increases in Rents and No Increases in Rates'. It was a policy that the local party accepted would lead to 'clear confrontation with Mrs Thatcher's government' if Labour won power. The district party's policy document stated:

> The entire strategy of the District Labour Party is based on the premise that the council position should be used as a platform to expose the political bankruptcy of capitalism, educate the working class and provide a political leadership on a local level to ensure a fight back against the Tory policy of cuts in public expenditure.[6]

Ted Grant could not have put it better himself. In the 1982 election campaign the Liberals exploited the 'Labour extremist' card to the full: posters went up saying 'Marxists Out, Liberals In'. But this propaganda did not seem to work, and Labour gained two seats.

The following year the Liberals played down the anti-Militant line, but few voters in Liverpool can have been unaware by then that Militant had a strong position in the local Labour Party. It did not seem to worry them: Labour achieved an outstanding result in 1983, winning twenty-three of the thirty-three seats contested.

Militant supporters now held many of the leading positions in the ruling Labour group. Most notable of their men was Derek Hatton, elected deputy leader in the summer of 1983. Like several other young left-wing socialist leaders suddenly propelled into high office in the early-1980s, including Arthur Scargill, Ken Livingstone and Neil Kinnock, Derek Hatton was a television politician. His ability to sum up his political position in that twenty to thirty second 'clip' that broadcasters treasure, his good looks, his instant availability, and his cultivation of relations with local journalists quickly made him the second most familiar local government leader of all time – after Ken Livingstone. And what was so remarkable was that Hatton wasn't even Labour leader in Liverpool, only the deputy. But within only a year or two in the early 1980s Hatton came to represent Labour and Militant politics in the city.

A Liverpudlian by birth, Derek Anthony Hatton attended one of the city's best schools, the Liverpool Institute, where two of his older colleagues were Paul McCartney and Peter Sissons, the ITN presenter. Before leaving school at fifteen, Hatton had initially had thoughts of becoming an actor, but his mother dissuaded him and he instead joined Plessey as an apprentice telephone technician. That lasted just six months, and a whole series of jobs followed, including insurance, until he joined his father's profession, the fire service. It was after serving as a fireman, in 1971 at the age of twenty-three, that Hatton joined the Labour Party. He says it was seeing the terrible conditions people had to live in, including fifteen people living in one room on one occasion, that drew him to socialism.

Hatton enrolled on a social work course at Goldsmith's

College in London, where one tutor wrote prophetically that he was 'bound to make his mark on a community'.[7] On returning to Liverpool Hatton ran the Brontë Youth Centre in Toxteth, but, as the person in charge, had to leave after an internal inquiry accused him of incompetence and found that £17,000 had inexplicably gone missing.

Hatton moved to Sheffield to become a community worker for the city council. There he came into close contact with a rising Labour councillor, David Blunkett, who helped him out in various battles with right-wing Labour councillors, including Roy Hattersley's mother, Enid. But Hatton was not popular with his Sheffield employers, mainly because of his union activities and his attempts to get colleagues out on strike. When he left the council to return to a job back on Merseyside his reference warned: 'We cannot recommend Mr Hatton without reservation.'[8]

Hatton had returned to join Knowsley Council as a community development officer in Kirkby, a new town with vast council estates and high unemployment. At that time Kirkby had a number of long-standing community associations, run largely by people who are probably best described as 'old guard' Labour right-wingers. It was Hatton's job to work with these groups, encourage them into activities, and give them support. Within a few months, however, Hatton again came into conflict. He was accused of bussing people in to win majorities on the associations' executive bodies. Unable to get his way, he tried to set up his own alternative community organisation. So bad were his relations that two community centres banned him from their premises. There was even a public meeting to complain about his activities.

Hatton's former boss in Knowsley, Mike Hughes, remembers Hatton as an extremely energetic employee. He points out that Hatton's training as a community worker had given him the ability to understand how to control groups of people, to get meetings to do what he wanted them to do – exactly the kind of experience that is useful to a local government politician. However, Hughes soon came into conflict with Hatton as he was spending more and more of his time on politics, and less and less on community development work. In the end, Hughes had to recommend on two separate occasions that Hatton be sacked. By then Hatton was a Liverpool councillor and such a decision would have been extremely embarrassing to Knowsley's councillors, who overruled Hughes.

Hatton first stood for Liverpool Council in May 1978, in Tuebrook, one of the first wards controlled by Militant in Liverpool. He lost by ninety-one votes and took the defeat so badly that he ended up hurling abuse at the Conservative victor, and at the electors of Tuebrook. Hatton has a violent temper.

In Knowsley, meanwhile, the future Liverpool leader had rapidly become involved in the work of the Knowsley NALGO branch, and was soon elected chairman. Another man in the branch, former Militant member Terry McDonald, recalls:

> He brought Knowsley out on strike twice, and used exactly the same sort of tactics he later used in Liverpool, causing disputes over the slightest incident. But the third time he tried to bring us out he failed. People lost faith in him. They thought he was just making things worse.[9]

By this stage Hatton had become fully committed to Militant's politics, and worked extremely hard for the tendency, both in Knowsley and in Liverpool, in NALGO and in the Labour Party. Hatton was not a particularly important member of Militant, simply a very useful one, especially after he was elected to Liverpool Council in 1979 on the same day Margaret Thatcher became Prime Minister. But even then, it seems, long-serving Militant members were finding him irritating. Full-timer Tony Aitman would often criticise Hatton privately, but, nevertheless, he acknowledged that Hatton put in a lot of effort for the organisation.

Hatton's election as council deputy leader after Labour took office in 1983 came as no surprise. Indeed, it was assumed by many that it would not be long before Hatton was challenging John Hamilton for the leadership itself. Hatton's rise from novice councillor to effective leader had been rapid, and greatly aided by the media. His cultivation of local reporters was vital. Whenever journalists wanted a quote they went to him, and he didn't mind if they rang at three in the morning. And Hatton would often turn up unexpectedly at Liverpool's Radio City, for instance, with a story for them. He became known as 'Hatton-the-Mouth' and 'Mr Media'. Boring council debates would always be enlivened by his contributions. Hatton represented the side of Liverpool's Labour politics that made any story interesting – a Marxist holding political office. He was something new in Liverpool, and would often drink with reporters, sometimes in the company of young Liberal councillors, or go to Everton matches with them.

The real Labour leader, John Hamilton, was little different

from any other council leader. Articulate certainly, truthful definitely, and saying much the same things as Hatton, at least *on the record*, but story-wise Hamilton didn't fit. How could this amiable old man with soup stains on his cardigan pose a revolutionary threat to civilisation as Liverpool knew it? There wasn't really time to explain to the listeners and viewers that there was more to Liverpool's new left-wing politics than just Militant.

Remarkably, of fifty-one Labour councillors in the new ruling Labour group in 1983 no more than sixteen were actually Militant members. But through brilliant organisation the tendency was able to exert far more control than their numbers would lead one to expect. This had occurred long before Labour took office, as Eddie Roderick explained:

All political parties, on the Monday before the council meeting on a Wednesday, have a caucus meeting to decide the line of approach at the council. The agenda for the meeting comes out on a Friday. The ten or twelve Militant members [a slight exaggeration] meet on either the Friday or the Saturday and go through the agenda to look for important policy decisions and for important vacancies. They then have a meeting with the broad left of the Labour group [an alliance of all the left-wing councillors] on Sunday morning at Pirrie Labour Club ... those Militants turn up in their full strength. There are generally about twenty people and the ten or eleven Militants there. They carry the majority vote there that commits the broad left for the meeting of the Labour group. On the Monday night at the Labour group of forty-two members the commitment that Militant have made themselves, plus other people they've taken along at the meeting on the Sunday morning, gives them a majority ... so you find that of forty-two Labour councillors, ten Militants control the policy of the Labour group.[10]

Roderick's analysis may have been a rather simplified version of what happened, but his opponents do not substantially deny it. Militant councillors admitted they did get together to discuss forthcoming issues, but caucuses were not new to Liverpool Council. Until recently the Catholic Action group of Labour councillors met regularly. In Braddock's day there were three caucuses in all: Catholic Action, Braddock and his close allies – and the left, which has carried on meeting ever since. Caucusing like this was happening more and more in local government Labour groups: two of the best examples were Manchester Council and the Greater London Council. And, of course, at Westminster caucuses like the Tribune Group had been meeting for years.

The 'caucus-within-a-caucus' operation was also used by Militant in Liverpool's local Labour parties and trade unions. According to Terry McDonald, former chairman of the Liverpool Kirkdale party, Militant members of the Management Committee would agree a line at their meeting, then persuade the Kirkdale broad left to accept it and finally use the broad left majority to win over the General Management Committee itself. It was exactly the method advocated by Trotsky in the 1930s with regard to the Independent Labour Party working within the Labour Party. Essentially it depends on members of each caucus sticking to the agreed line. In the Labour movement there is a long tradition of members of a group voting with a decided position, even if they disagree with it; hence the system of union block votes. But this kind of caucusing means that a minority within a body can be transformed into what is in effect a majority. For Militant the distinction is between 'physical' and 'political' control. 'Physical' control means having an absolute majority; 'political' control means being able to exert effective control, through good organisation and caucusing, without an absolute majority. So long as non-Militant members of the broad left in Liverpool were prepared to carry on abiding by the caucus majority decisions, Militant would continue to exert 'political' control.

Eddie Roderick paid tribute to Militant's good organisation and accepted that the record of Militant councillors' attendance at meetings was as good as his own. Roderick's problem was that other right-wingers were not always as conscientious. In what were often still very small ward parties the absence of one or two individuals could frequently make the difference between failure and success. But Militant did not try simply to ensure a good turn-out. Its caucus meetings decided who would propose, second and speak on motions, which amendments would be accepted or rejected, and even which points should be made at particular moments in the debate.

In Liverpool, Militant also benefited from the fact that past disillusionment in the performance of Labour councillors had, more than in any other city, helped transfer power away from the Labour group to the district party outside. As Peter Taaffe explained in an internal Militant document:

Perhaps there is no other area in the country in which the DLP exercises such control over the affairs of the Labour Group. In effect it appoints the leader and deputy leader of the Labour Group, and has a decisive say in the chairmanship of the major committees in the council ... It is this relationship which has determined the decisive role of the Marxists [i.e. Militant] in the struggle ... on the DLP the Marxists hold sway, and therefore, in effect, their tactics and strategy can determine the course of the battle.[11]

By 1982, Militant almost had a majority on the thirty-strong Executive of the DLP, and in any case could count on some of its opponents being absent and support from other left-wingers to ensure it got its way. In the much larger DLP General Committee, Militant's majority was much less clear-cut. But since the Executive had a strong say in what happened at DLP general meetings and only a minority of delegates usually attended, the tendency again held the ascendancy.

Since 1980 Militant's official Liverpool headquarters has been at 2 Lower Breck Road, Tuebrook, a semi-detached house Militant bought from the local Labour Party for £8,700. Like those of other Militant buildings, the windows are covered by iron grilles, and the door in sheet metal. A large room on the ground floor is let to local Labour parties and other groups for meetings and election work, but no one except members of Militant is ever allowed into the rooms on the top floor.

By the early 1980s, Militant had at least six full-time organisers working from this building. After Terry Harrison, the other important full-timer was Richard Venton, who took Mulhearn's place on the Central Committee. Described as Militant's official Merseyside spokesman, Venton was born and brought up in a Northern Ireland Catholic family, but he never became involved in Ulster politics. He joined both Militant and the Labour Party on coming to Liverpool University in 1972. After his studies, Venton spent a short time teaching before becoming a Militant employee in 1979.

Another important full-time organiser was Tony Aitman, a former vice-chairman of the LPYS. Aitman always insisted he was a freelance journalist, not a Militant organiser, but he had little journalistic work to show for it. His wife Josie looked after Militant's youth work in the area, while Richard Knights was the local industrial organiser.

When Labour came to power in Liverpool in 1983, Militant was already the dominant force within the District Labour Party, but by no means as powerful and as well organised as it would become with three years in office. In some ways Militant had achieved its position by default. The old right wing was dying out, while, unlike the party in other cities, such as Manchester and London, the left had not offered any credible and organised alternative. Groups such as Merseyside Labour Briefing and the Merseyside Labour Co-ordinating Committee were eventually established in Liverpool, but only when it was too late, and they were also very disorganised. Tony Lane explained as long ago as 1981:

A political vacuum opened up in the Labour Party – to be filled, in the absence of anything more coherent, by Young Socialists equipped with the strident, urgent politics of Militant. Following meekly behind, a mere handful of the intuitively left old guard, unable to think of anything better. Militant is heard as Labour's voice because it is the only voice to be heard … Sectarian to a fault, its main activity is making platform speeches and waging warfare within the Labour ranks. Its practice, despite the noise, is traditional and remarkably similar to that of the right-wing old guard.[12]

Even Lane may not have appreciated the extent of the boss politics Liverpool would experience when Labour returned to power in 1983.

13

HATTON'S ARMY

On Everton heights, overlooking the centre of Liverpool, stand monuments to the politicians and policies that so dominated the city's post-war history: two systems-built tower blocks, ten stories high, called the Braddocks. Actually named Jack and Bessie, they were opened in 1958 to house people who'd lived in the local slums of Everton. The council leader and his wife, the local MP, attended an opening ceremony at which the Labour Party leader, Hugh Gaitskell, unveiled a plaque commemorating Jack and Bessie Braddocks's 'outstanding services to the City of Liverpool'.

Today the plaque is cracked and defaced with graffiti. The 'multi-storey dwellings', as they were called in 1958, have suffered from damp, condensation and structural problems. Tenants have no gardens. The grass areas surrounding the blocks are home only for stray dogs and litter. When the lifts break down, which they often do, tenants feel like prisoners. Life inside Jack or Bessie Braddock has not been pleasant.

Less than thirty years after they were built the council tenants are being moved out – to new 'dwellings', proper houses with gardens. In 1987 the Braddocks are due to be pulled down.

In the Braddock era housing was by far the most important political issue in Liverpool. It is just the same today. The Braddocks, on Netherfield Road North, a mile and a quarter north-east of the city centre, are in Liverpool City Council's priority area 4. Under the council's Urban Regeneration Strategy much of the housing in this area is making way for Everton Park, which the council boasts is the largest inner-city park built in Britain this century.

The Urban Regeneration Strategy is one of the most radical and major development programmes carried out by any British city since the war. The council stresses it is not simply a housing programme, but a scheme designed to improve the whole nature of selected 'priority areas'. Yet over the last three years the building and redevelopment work being carried out by Liverpool Council has largely been obscured and ignored by the most dramatic confrontation ever between a local authority and a British government.

Even if Militant had never existed in Liverpool a struggle would have been likely between a Liverpool Labour council and the Thatcher administration. Liverpool has suffered particularly badly from the successive measures introduced by the government to curb local council spending. The drift of population away from the city centre to new towns outside the city boundary and the decline of local industry have badly eroded Liverpool's base for both rate revenue and for assessing government grant. A series of Liberal budgets during the 1970s, passed with Conservative support, kept both the rates and expenditure relatively low, but also lowered the 1978 baseline upon which the Conservative government's financial penalties were assessed. Michael Parkinson, Director of Liverpool University's Urban Studies Unit, explains:

> Labour's frustration was complete when the Conservative government introduced its new grant system in 1981. This was generally unsympathetic to the city's problems of long-term demographic and economic decline. Its target system – which was designed to cut the spending of Labour-controlled cities – was even more unsympathetic to a city which had behaved in a parsimonious fashion in the 1970s, but was required to cut its spending again in the 1980s. Liverpool is more financially restricted than many other Labour-controlled cities … [which] – because of their high-rating policies of the 1970s – had built up substantial services and financial reserves. But Liverpool, which under the Liberals had incurred budget deficits in six years out of ten, could not follow suit.[1]

Parkinson makes a comparison between Liverpool and Manchester, cities that are very similar in size. In the first financial year of both these metropolitan councils, 1974–75, Manchester spent £81 million, Liverpool £79 million. But during the late 1970s the spending of Labour Manchester expanded much more than Liberal-dominated Liverpool, so that for 1984–85 Liverpool's target, based on past spending, was only £216 million, while Manchester's was £245 million, almost 14 per cent more.[2]

For the Liverpool Labour Party in 1983, Liverpool's atrocious housing conditions, among the worst in Europe, could not be neglected. With the council now by far the largest employer on Merseyside, it also felt a certain responsibility not only for maintaining employment levels but expanding them. The policies upon which Labour came to power in 1983 were not simply Militant policies; they were Labour policies agreed upon by most of the Liverpool Labour Party, and fully supported by old-style Bevanites such as John Hamilton.

The 1983 local election result was a major surprise to almost everyone. Labour had expected to do well, but not well enough to secure a majority. Nevertheless, on taking office, Labour set about carrying out its election pledges, pledges that would inevitably lead to a large financial deficit, and that would inevitably lead to confrontation with Whitehall. The 1,200 redundancies previously planned by the Liberals were cancelled, and the council created 1,000 new jobs through Manpower Services Commission schemes. As if to make it clear that a new type of Labour Party was in power the office of Lord Mayor was abolished and replaced by a council chairmanship. The mayor's gold chain of office was sent to a museum, and the council's ceremonial horses sold off.

Militant tried to secure a firm grip on the council from the very beginning. Three months after the election Derek Hatton was elected deputy Labour leader, in place of Eddie Loyden, who had just been elected to Parliament. Many people thought it would not be long before Hatton was actually leader. John Hamilton, meanwhile, was given a new personal assistant, much against his wishes. The Labour leader simply wanted a secretary, somebody to type letters. Instead, Derek Hatton appointed Lynn Caldow for him, a former secretary of the Labour Party in Terry Fields's constituency, Broadgreen, who for several months previously had worked as a Militant full-timer in Liverpool. She could not type, and Hamilton had no tasks for her beyond ordering the occasional rail ticket, but she found plenty to do. At the same time her husband, Barry Caldow, was made the council's chief press officer. Unusually for somebody married to a Militant full-timer, Barry Caldow was not a Militant member, although he had attended readers' meetings, and the press assumed he was in the tendency.

Much of Labour's first year in office was spent preparing the ground for the confrontation it knew lay ahead. The big crunch would come over the budget for the following financial year, 1984–85, and so Derek Hatton and Militant started a process of trying to find support for their strategy.

A new council department was established – the Central Support Unit. In effect it was a propaganda department, similar to those set up by other Labour councils. Its purpose was to win backing for what the council was doing, both among Liverpudlians and the outside world. It was led by Andy Pink, another Militant member, and largely, but not entirely, staffed by Militant members. In time, parts of the municipal buildings and municipal annexe in Dale Street would come to resemble another Militant headquarters.

Rallies, meetings, demonstrations and petitions were arranged to put Labour's case to the Liverpool electorate and, in particular, to the trade unions. This began with a half-day rally at the Phil-harmonic Hall for council shop stewards in September 1983. It was followed by a 20,000-strong demonstration in December. Meanwhile a council newspaper, *Liverpool News*, was distributed throughout the city. Old school signs were taken down and replaced by new red signs proclaiming the fact that Liverpool was 'A Socialist Council'. For Militant this kind of campaigning activity was the key aspect to the whole Liverpool struggle. The crisis would provide the opportunity to politicise people, to raise working-class consciousness, to recruit people to Militant and to improve Militant's standing with the Labour movement. In an internal document written early in 1984 Peter Taaffe explained:

> There is no guarantee, according to the Marxists, that 'success' will result from their stand, if success or otherwise is to be judged by whether the Tory government backs down or not. However, the Marxists have always argued that their criteria for any struggle, particularly a struggle which can be isolated because of the role of the national Labour and trade union leaders, is whether it meets the twin objectives of raising the level of understanding, the conscious-ness, of the proletariat as a whole and also strengthens the position of the Labour movement and of Marxism in the eyes of the broad mass of the working class ...
>
> By this measure, no matter what the outcome in the next weeks and months, the stand of the Liverpool city council has been more than justified.[3]

An important aspect of Militant's strategy involved the council trade unions. Since 1979 the Liverpool council unions had been organised into a Joint Shop Stewards' Committee. Increasing opposition within the council unions to the Liberals' policy had made both blue-collar and white-collar unions sympathetic to Labour. The chairman of the committee was Ian Lowes, a tree-feller, and convenor of the General and Municipal Union's branch 5, covering parks and recreation. Lowes was a Militant member. He had once spent six months in Walton Prison for assaulting two police officers. His girlfriend, councillor Pauline Dunlop, another Militant member, was the new vice-chairman of the Personnel Committee, number two to Derek Hatton. From an early stage Militant's aim was ultimately to get the council workforce in a position where they would be prepared to mount a general strike over Liverpool.

A significant early move in cementing relations between Militant, the council and the unions, was to give the unions the right to nominate people for council jobs. In the past, in theory at least, jobs had been advertised in local Job Centres and given to unemployed people. But it was widely believed by many in Liverpool that in practice people were often appointed to council positions on the basis of who they knew. Matrons of old people's homes might appoint neighbours as cleaners. A caretaker was apparently taken on by one Roman Catholic school after promising the local priest he would dig graves for the church as well. An almost contradictory complaint was Masonic influence on certain council appointments.

Under the new 50 per cent nomination rights system agreed early on in the new Labour administration, unions were allowed to nominate people for half the council jobs. The scheme was generally welcomed by all the council unions, who hoped it would introduce more fairness into the selection procedure. They argued that similar practices already existed in Fleet Street and in parts of the construction industry. Initially the council still had the right to put forward their own nominees for any positions, though shop stewards were not involved in the interview process.

While Militant, in the form of Derek Hatton and Ian Lowes, were establishing good relations between the council and the unions, and had begun a process of politicising both the council workforce and the people of Liverpool, another key councillor was busy with what he regarded as 'the Jewel in Liverpool's Crown', the achievement for which he hoped the new Labour council would be remembered.

The council's Urban Regeneration Strategy, designed as a 'co-ordinated attack upon the decay and dereliction' of Liverpool, was largely the work of one man, councillor Tony Byrne. Seven-teen parts of the city were selected as urban priority areas, where planners and builders would move in and, in what was called 'the total approach', re-plan the environment and build new houses, or modify old ones, over a five-year period. The strategy was based on much of the latest thinking in housing and urban planning, which had learned much from the failures of the 1950s and 1960s.

New parks were designed, such as Everton Park near the city centre. Several sports centres were planned. Residential streets would be narrowed and better lit. The council would help shop-keepers to modernise their properties. No new housing would be more than two storeys high, and there would be access only from the front. Three-storey blocks of flats that had been built only in the early 1970s were subjected to a process of 'top-downing' – the top floors were knocked off and the bottom parts of the buildings rebuilt into bungalows. An important aspect of the Urban Regeneration Strategy was the delineation of space. Everton Park had a stone wall and iron railings built round it. Tenants' gardens were fenced off in a belief that it is important that people should live in defined areas, with as few as possible communal areas, which tend to be neglected. Raised grass banks were planned to separate industry from housing.

Tony Byrne was not a member of Militant. In some ways he was much more left-wing than Militant, though in private he could often be critical of the tendency. His obsession was housing. From a Conservative family, in his youth Byrne had started training to be a Jesuit priest. Later he worked as a draughtsman with English Electric, and had then got involved in Liverpool voluntary organisations. In the 1970s Byrne had often seemed more sympathetic to the Liberals than to Labour, and became a Labour councillor only in 1980. But once on the council he soon mastered the city's financial problems, preparing for the time when Labour returned to office. Indeed, Militant councillors such as Derek Hatton seemed happy to let Byrne look after the complex detail. In appearance he could not be more different from Hatton. Instead of smart suits he always wears scruffy jumpers and training shoes.

During its first year in office Labour managed to survive by stretching the budget left to them by the Liberals. Planned expenditure of £218 million was increased to £232 million, with a deficit for the year of £34 million. It was not until Labour started planning for the following year, 1984–85, that the battles really began. The only way to maintain its election promises was a deficit budget. The alternative, Labour said, was 5,000 redundancies, or a 170 per cent rate rise.

In March 1984, Labour did not have a large enough majority to ensure its proposed deficit budget for 1984–85 would go through. Six right-wing Labour councillors, led by Eddie Roderick, made it clear they would not vote for such a package. The 'sensible six', as they liked to be known, were politically survivors of the Braddock era. Roderick himself was a strong admirer of Braddock; Joe Morgan had been heavily involved in the 1960s high-rise housing developments. Most of the rebels had served on the council for more than twenty years. Some had strong Catholic connections.

On the appointed Budget Day, 29 March, Labour held a Day of Action. The council unions, all of whom except the teachers' union, the NUT, supported the 'illegal' budget, agreed to a one-day strike in order to join Labour's march through the city to the Town Hall. But that afternoon the six rebels ensured that Labour's planned deficit budget wouldn't go through. Labour entered the new financial year with no budget at all, hoping its forces would be reinforced in the forthcoming local elections. Opinion polls showed that the council's stand had considerable support among Liverpudlians, and in May the months of campaigning paid off.

In a 51 per cent poll – very high for local government elections – Labour got 46 per cent of the vote, only very slightly down on its 1983 record. The party increased its number of seats by seven; a deficit budget could now go through, even if the Labour rebels, now reduced to five by Roderick's deselection, voted against.

Throughout the period Liverpool had been in contact with the Environment Secretary, Patrick Jenkin. Jenkin visited Liverpool in June 1984, and on seeing some of Liverpool's housing spoke of 'deplorable conditions which have got to be tackled as a matter of urgency'.[4] That statement was to restrict his room for manoeuvre: it would be difficult for him not to concede something to Liverpool. Government ministers dreaded the idea of having to take the city over. Jenkin lay in bed at night fearing what would happen if he had to send commissioners in by helicopter. He knew that they would meet almost total hostility from the council workforce, that doors would be locked and computer tapes wiped. And the government also feared the possibility of more riots along the lines of Toxteth in 1981. The government was in the middle of a coal dispute, and had no wish to fight on a second front. After weeks of crisis talks between Liverpool's leaders and Jenkin, a financial package was hammered out, and a balanced budget arranged.

Derek Hatton hailed the deal as a victory for Liverpool and for Militant. So too did many Conservative supporters. 'Today in Liverpool municipal militancy is vindicated,' argued *The Times*; 'It is the Tory government which has given away the most,' said the *Daily Mail*, attacking Jenkin; 'He has set a precedent. He has allowed defying the law, or the threat of it, to pay off!' moaned the *Daily Star*.[5]

Liverpool's leaders claimed the settlement was worth between £50 and £90 million. This is impossible to justify. When analysed, the budget was nothing like the victory that Labour claimed. There had been no concessions by Jenkin in terms either of target, grant or penalty, the key aspects of the local government finance system. Furthermore, the council had been forced to accept a 17 per cent rate rise, having previously opposed all rate rises which were more than the rate of inflation, and it had been forced into capitalisation, spending money allocated for housing repairs on day-to-day expenditure. Jenkin had given the council an extra £2.5 million under the Urban Aid programme, and allowed more urban money to go on schemes which otherwise the council would have had to pay for. There was also more housing subsidy to cover interest charges on borrowing for flats which had already been demolished, and the government agreed to pay £1 million for environmental improvements. In total, this was nothing like the money Liverpool wanted, as Michael Parkinson concluded: 'If the government made some concessions in July 1984, Liverpool made far greater ones. It dropped many of its spending plans and did a lot of creative accounting ... The major savings were made by cancelling nearly all of Labour's new policies.'[6]

Patrick Jenkin had also mentioned the possibility of more housing money to come. This money never materialised because of the council's refusal to modify its housing policies, and possibly also because of the government's annoyance that Liverpool had claimed the 1984 settlement as a victory.

The Environment Secretary regretted later that he had given

Liverpool's Labour leaders two days in which to present the package to their party. On the very evening of the day the settlement had been agreed, Derek Hatton emerged from a DLP meeting in jubilation. Liverpool had taken the initiative before Jenkin had had the chance to brief anybody about what the settlement actually involved.

Patrick Jenkin later spoke on television of Liverpool's leaders 'dancing on his political grave'. More than a year later he was sacked, and a major reason for his downfall was probably Liverpool, although he also had problems over the abolition of the GLC and the metropolitan county councils. After the embarrassment Jenkin had suffered from Liverpool boasting about its victory, he made it clear that in 1985 Liverpool would be left to sort its own problems out, and there would be no negotiations. But in the long term the 1984 Liverpool settlement probably did more damage to the Labour Party than the Conservatives. In 1985 the sixteen rate-capped councils and Liverpool, which wasn't rate-capped, would pursue a policy of defiance towards the government, pledging themselves not to set rates until the government had stood down in the same way it had in Liverpool. This stance was to fail dismally.

For Militant, of course, the 1984 Liverpool victory had brought tremendous gains, and the tendency was able to bask in its triumph at the 1984 Labour conference in Blackpool. Through its determination in the composite meeting on local government resolutions, presided over by the General Boilermakers and Allied Trades Union (GMBATU) official Larry Whitty, Militant delegates managed to ensure that two separate Liverpool motions were discussed on the conference floor. The result was four consecutive speeches from Militant Liverpool councillors Derek Hatton, Felicity Dowling, Tony Mulhearn and Paul Luckock. The speeches were interrupted only by the chairman of the Conference Arrangements' Committee, Derek Gladwin, making a timely intervention about an urgent TGWU motion concerning a writ served on the miners' union.

Worse still for Neil Kinnock the motion calling for unlawful defiance of the rate-capping law was unexpectedly passed, and paved the way for the disastrous anti-rate-capping campaign in 1985. A special Labour Party local government conference had already agreed to adopt a strategy of 'non-compliance' with rate-capping earlier in July, only days before the Liverpool settlement, in the expectation that Liverpool was about to get concessions from the government.

Militant knew it could only gain from the Liverpool situation. Militant's membership in the city almost doubled between September 1983 and September 1984, from 180 members to 354, and the Liverpool district was divided into three new districts, covering north Liverpool, south Liverpool and Terry Fields's constituency, Broadgreen. Nationally, Militant membership increased by a third over the same period.

Throughout the first Liverpool budget crisis, Militant full-timers from other areas flocked to the area, and Peter Taaffe himself made a number of visits, though he rarely made any public appearances. Liverpool was Militant's lifeblood; large sections of the newspaper were devoted to it, and *Militant* editorial after editorial.

Militant was at its strongest in Liverpool in the summer and autumn of 1984, when it had gained credit not just in Liverpool but throughout the Labour movement. From then on it was downhill, and Militant seemed to swerve from tactical error to tactical error.

Many in the Militant old guard began expressing disquiet over the position of Derek Hatton. For some of the long-serving Militant cadres Hatton had the wrong image for the tendency; they didn't like the way he seemed to enjoy all the publicity. Hatton had built a reputation for dressing in smart, expensive suits, a fondness he says he acquired as a teenager when doing a Saturday job for Jackson's the Tailor. His daughters' ponies, his late-night revelling in expensive night-clubs and restaurants, his hours under the sunbed, his seat in a private box at Everton – these were not the usual lifestyle of the Militant member, who is normally expected to give every spare penny to the tendency. Militant MP Terry Fields, for instance, had agreed to live on the average wage of a skilled worker, and give the rest to the Labour movement – in effect, most of it to Militant. He remarked on one occasion how a certain other well-known Liverpool Militant supporter didn't seem to live on a worker's wage.

At the same time Hatton had to endure a whole series of allegations in the press. There was the Asda affair, when Hatton had encouraged the approval of planning permission for an Asda hypermarket in the Speke enterprise zone, when Liverpool party policy was in fact against the building of hypermarkets. It so happened that the leading man in Asda's PR firm was Tony Beyga, a Labour councillor in Knowsley, whom the *Liverpool Echo* filmed on holiday with Hatton in Tangiers. In another case a council committee approved planning permission for an amusement arcade to be built by a former Liberal councillor called Joe Farley. Again, Labour policy was against amusement arcades, and Hatton managed to be seen with Farley on an excursion to watch Everton in Czechoslovakia.

Meanwhile, it was reported that Hatton was rarely seen at his employers, Knowsley Council, but attempts to discipline him in Knowsley ran into political obstacles. And some newspapers seemed to enjoy finding Hatton with women who were not his wife.

Such stories were always dismissed by Militant as fabrications, and attempts to smear Hatton. Nevertheless there were those in the highest ranks of the organisation who felt Hatton might be getting out of hand, who believed that his commitment to the tendency might be less than it once was. This was especially true of Ted Grant. Any action to curb the Liverpool deputy leader had to be taken carefully, though. He was now by far the most famous member of the organisation, and still a tremendous asset to Militant. It would be foolish to replace him, and virtually impossible anyway. And if Hatton were to leave Militant, think of the beans he might spill – Hatton's story would be the most damaging allegations ever made about the tendency.

Not long after Labour assumed office in 1983, Militant agreed to project Tony Mulhearn more prominently in Liverpool. He represented more of the kind of image the Militant old guard liked. A policy decision had been taken by the Militant leadership that Tony Mulhearn should get himself elected to the council, and so Mulhearn became a councillor at the 1984 elections. After that Mulhearn took part in the council's negotiations, but he never had the understanding of the council's problems that his colleagues had. Government officials found him shallow. Promoting Mulhearn never really solved Militant's Hatton problem. He and Hatton were too good friends, though behind his back Hatton was not always straight with Mulhearn. It seemed that Terry Fields was the only Militant member able to discipline Hatton. At times some Militant full-timers were so worried about Hatton that they even went so far as to encourage John Hamilton to put himself forward more.

Increasingly the mass of support that Militant had built up among both the electorate and the council workforce began to crumble, largely through tactical errors, caused perhaps by over-confidence. Militant slowly succeeded in antagonising a wide range of separate groups, and in particular the council unions.

The public employees' union, NUPE, felt it was losing out from the nomination rights system to the manual unions, the TGWU and the GMBATU. In 1984 it was agreed that nomination rights would belong only to those unions which had more than a third of the workforce in any particular area. NUPE suffered from this. The union also felt it was not being consulted on important decisions, and that other unions were being given certain privileges.

The other main white-collar union, NALGO, was antagonised by the famous Sampson Bond affair. Bond, a quantity surveyor and a Militant member from north London, was appointed the council's Principal Race Relations Adviser in October 1984, in spite of competition from several far better qualified candidates. When the application forms had come in Derek Hatton had referred to Bond as an 'absolute cracker'. Bond was immediately boycotted by the

Black Caucus, and NALGO also refused to work with him, even to the extent of not putting through his telephone calls. On one occasion members of the Black Caucus stormed into Derek Hatton's office and kept him there until he agreed to reconsider the appointment. Hatton finally agreed, but later withdrew his decision.

The Bond controversy was then used by Hatton as a justification for stepping up his own personal security. A new group of security guards was appointed, the Static Security Force, whose job it was to guard council properties and to protect Hatton. The man appointed to head the force was David Ware, a neighbour of Hatton, whose only qualification was being a former club bouncer. Many in the force had criminal records. Two were councillors with Hatton's employers, Knowsley Council. Not surprisingly, in time the force came to be known as Hatton's Army. It was not only used to protect Hatton; members of the force began turning up at District Labour Party meetings in uniform. They were used to eject people from meetings, and some DLP delegates found them intimidating.

From the time of the Bond appointment, relations between the Labour Party and the black community grew progressively worse. The council's Race Relations Liaison Committee stopped meeting, was eventually abolished and replaced by an Equal Opportunities Committee. At one point a Labour Party march against racism was cancelled when it was learned that the Black Caucus intended to join. A meeting in Toxteth ended in violence and accusations that Militant was using council money to pay young blacks to attend. Bob Lee and other full-timers from Militant's Black and Asian Caucus were drafted into Liverpool.

Eventually Militant set up its own black front organisation, the Merseyside Action Group, and it was proposed that the group's organiser, Carol Darby, be paid by the council.

At times, Militant seemed to be pursuing policies out of sheer vindictiveness against individuals who disagreed with it. One group of gardeners – the Harthill Six – who had refused to take part in a day of action, were demoted to menial jobs. The six went to court to get their old jobs back. When they won the council decided it could no longer afford to maintain the greenhouses where they worked, and the city's prize orchid collection, which they had maintained, was dispersed.

Similarly, the NUT came into conflict with the council when the union refused to participate in another day of action. Because the strike by school caretakers had prevented teachers from doing any teaching that day, the council docked a day's pay from NUT members all the same. The union had to go to court to get it back.

Militant often alienated the very people who should have been allies of a radical Labour council – blacks, voluntary organisations and the council unions. A good example of this unnecessary attitude came in Walton where Laura Kirton gave up her jobs as constituency secretary and agent. She had never been a member of the RSL or Militant, but few people in the city had done more to help the tendency's growth. The young members of Militant, however, decided that Kirton was too old and getting too critical of the tendency's policies. She was axed as a Walton delegate to the District Party and lost her place on the Walton constituency executive.

Militant was also using the council to employ more and more of its own people. In John Hamilton's words: 'You can't get a job here unless you are a Militant.'[7] The promise of a job was held out to young people to get them to join Militant, while people who had been given posts were put under pressure to join the tendency. This recruitment served several purposes at once. It brought the organisation new members; it brought the tendency money in terms of those members' subscriptions, which were based upon a share of their income, and it helped to reinforce Militant's position within the council unions, as Militant members were of course the most active members of the union branches. That in turn reinforced Militant's position within the District Labour Party.

It was all part of a complex power network in Liverpool involving the council, its unions, the District Labour Party, and an organisation that, we are told, does not exist. Instead of council unions and the council in the traditional employer–employee situation, in some cases they were bolstering each other. One GMBATU convenor, Peter Lennard, argues that Militant union officials were offered favourable settlements in order to strengthen their position with their own members; no negotiation was involved, he argues. It was further complicated by certain individuals holding several positions at once. Derek Hatton was not only deputy leader of the council and chairman of its Personnel Committee, but also a member of the DLP Executive, a leading member of the Militant Merseyside Executive, and, as an employee of Knowsley Council, also an active member of NALGO. Ian Lowes was chairman of the Shop Stewards' Committee, convenor of GMBATU branch 5, a Militant member, member of the DLP Executive and married to Pauline Dunlop, a Militant councillor and deputy chair of the Personnel Committee.

The one body which it could be argued was at the centre of this power network was the District Labour Party. There Militant could depend totally on the Executive Committee, since a clear majority of the thirty-two were Militant members. In the General Committee comprising hundreds of delegates from the unions, and the constituency and ward parties, the position was less simple. By 1985, however, Militant could depend upon two unions, the TGWU and the GMBATU, almost entirely. Both had gained most from the council's employment practices. Between them the two unions had eighty-five delegates, more than the constituency and ward parties combined.

Increasingly Militant's opponents began to complain about the way in which the DLP's business was conducted. It was alleged that some unions had more delegates than they were entitled to. Party members trying to become councillors complained that they were excluded from the candidates' panel for refusing to toe the Militant line. DLP meetings became more and more acrimonious. What particularly annoyed Militant's critics was the increasing use of aggregate meetings – involving not just elected delegates, but any party member who chose to come. It was perhaps ironic that while the Labour right have long argued for one-member-one-vote in important party decisions, in Liverpool, when this was put into practice, it seemed to work in Militant's favour. Critics alleged that non-Militant members were intimidated by the overwhelming numbers of people there, or that in some cases so many people turned up that they could not get in. People who opposed the leadership's line had to endure increasing abuse and threats against their well-being.

Above all, there was a climate of fear in the city – to a degree which it is difficult for outsiders to understand. While politicians and council officials would privately complain of what was occurring, few would ever give details in public. They were frightened of losing their political positions, or of losing their jobs. There was perhaps no better example of this than council leader John Hamilton himself.

Hamilton's position was becoming unbearable. He strongly suspected that Militant was listening to his phone calls and opening his mail. Journalists who rang Hamilton's office would sometimes be told he was out and be put through to Hatton instead. Of course, Hamilton found out only later. He had almost no friends in the Liverpool Labour Party. He sometimes considered resignation, but could never bring himself to it. Hamilton felt that by remaining leader, if only nominal leader, he was bringing stability, perhaps preventing some of the worst excesses. At times he seemed to be on the point of speaking out against Militant, and standing up to them, but always drew back at the last moment. He just could not imagine what life would be without his council work.

His predicament is well illustrated by two letters he wrote in March 1984 after a Labour councillor, John McLean, had announced he was resigning just before the important council budget meeting, in order to spend more time on his work as a union official. On 21 March, Hamilton wrote to McLean, saying he appreciated why McLean had taken the decision and wishing him well. 'I would like to thank you for your help and support,' he wrote.[8] Only a day later, 22 March, following a meeting with other council committee chairmen, Hamilton wrote a second letter to McLean. This made no mention of the first letter, and explained that Hamilton and his colleagues had decided unanimously that McLean's act was 'one of outright treachery to the movement and is one which the chairmen feel will not be forgiven by the Labour and Trade Union Movement'.[9] At times Hamilton hated himself for allowing himself to get into the position he was in.

As Liverpool prepared for its second confrontation with the government, it could no longer count on the support it once had. Labour lost two council by-elections, while Patrick Jenkin was making it clear that in 1985 he would not meet Liverpool's leaders. He felt he had been 'kicked in the teeth' once and he was no longer willing to trust Liverpool.

In 1985, Militant was fighting the government in conjunction with the sixteen rate-capped councils who had agreed on a joint strategy of not setting any rate at all in an effort to make the government climb down. Militant and Liverpool argued correctly that the 'no rate' policy adopted by the rate-capped Labour councils would not work. Peter Taaffe wrote later: 'The "no rate" policy was an invention of the "trendy lefts" to avoid giving battle to the Tory government in a clear and unambiguous fashion ... Liverpool felt it had to go along with this tactic, while making clear that it disagreed with it, in the interests of unity in the struggle of all Labour councils that were rate-capped.'[10] At the same time Militant argued that the 'trendies' would not last, that only Liverpool would stick it out to the bitter end.

The only possible outside obstacle to Liverpool's glory in 1985 was Lambeth Council, led by Ted Knight. Lambeth too made it clear that it took the 'no rate' policy seriously, but Knight had a far more precarious majority than Liverpool. Behind the headlines a test of strength was going on between two brands of British Trotskyism. Lambeth had long been the darling of Gerry Healy's Workers' Revolutionary Party. Knight had once been an organiser for Healy's Socialist Labour League (the WRP's predecessor) and was still close to Healy, who printed Knight's newspaper *Labour Herald* on the WRP presses.

When Liverpool abandoned the 'no rate' policy in June 1985, in favour of a 9 per cent rate, which meant an illegal deficit budget, the WRP's *Newsline* proclaimed, 'Lambeth stands firm – Liverpool capitulates.'[11] Privately Militant was quite scathing about its public allies from south London: 'In the case of Lambeth it had all the hallmarks of a hastily prepared and ill-thought-out struggle with all the evidence showing that Ted Knight and his entourage had stumbled into, rather than consciously prepared for, a battle with the Tory government. Knight, who is undoubtedly a WRP sympathiser … was desperately attempting to outflank from the left the Marxists in Liverpool.'[12]

Militant had seemed prepared for an 18 or 20 per cent rate rise at first, but suddenly the tendency concluded that 18 per cent with no concessions from the government was far worse than the previous year's 17 per cent with concessions. So it went for 9 per cent and hoped for government concessions later.

'Oh my God, it's going to go through,' Derek Hatton was heard to say as the budget votes were counted in the council chamber. It seems that the unbalanced June budget was passed by accident: Militant probably hoped that enough right-wing Labour councillors would vote against the budget for it to be defeated. A balanced budget could then have been put through amid accusations that the 'right-wing traitors' had forced the council leadership into a position where they had no other option. The council Labour group turned out to be much more solid than Derek Hatton perhaps hoped. While the June deficit budget took the pressure off Liverpool for a while, it had not solved that year's financial problems, which dragged on far longer than Lambeth's. From June on, Liverpool's crisis worsened by the day, and the coalition of support that the party leadership had built up among the council workforce and the electorate crumbled. Liverpool and Lambeth were eventually forced into a public display of unity, when both of their district auditors took simultaneous action against them for delay in setting a rate, and both councils went to court to appeal.

In Liverpool's case the district auditor decided that the eleven-week delay in setting a rate had deprived the city of £106,000 in interest on government payments that the council would have received earlier. The auditor's decision to press for the councillors to be surcharged and disqualified resulted in a legal case which dragged on for nearly a year, and from Militant's point of view led to more useful campaigning publicity as the councillors took their appeals from one court to another.

In the hectic weeks and months from June to November, Militant was guided in Liverpool by several different motives. First was the belief that in the end the government would have to step in and do something – either in the form of more money to the city, or taking it over with commissioners. The former would be hailed as a victory, the latter was just the kind of highly charged, potentially revolutionary, situation Militant wanted. The second consideration was the need to identify 'traitors' if the council did suffer defeat – be they in the form of the leadership of certain local unions, or the unions nationally, or the leaders of the Labour Party. Thirdly, though, Militant's overwhelming consideration was to recruit forces to its organisation and to politicise people both in Liverpool and beyond, through campaigns, meetings, demonstrations, and, if possible, strike action.

In terms of all three motives Militant stood to gain more the longer the crisis went on. The nearer Liverpool got to chaos the more likely it was that the government would have to intervene in one way or another. The longer the crisis went on the more likely it was that 'traitors' would emerge, and every day the confrontation continued the more publicity Militant received and the more it was able to use the Liverpool issue to recruit to its own organisation.

As part of the increased campaigning, Militant had held a meeting in Liverpool in March to set up yet another body, the National Local Authorities Coordinating Committee. It was attended by delegates from sixty other authorities. The NLACC, whose organising secretary was Ian Lowes, was designed to liaise between council workforces and, in theory, act as a means for securing strike action in other councils when the crunch came in Liverpool.

The so-called A-Team was a further body that helped with the campaigning. The A-Team was a group of about sixty Liverpool Council shop stewards, gathered together by Derek Hatton and seconded from their work, whose task was to visit factories and other workplaces around Liverpool selling the council's case. Receiving generous overtime and good expenses the A-Team was, of course, being paid to spread the Militant cause more than that of its council.

In theory, Militant could not lose. In practice, it did. Over the period from June to November, Militant began to lose its cohesion, though this rarely surfaced publicly. There were increasing differences between Liverpool and the national leadership, and differences between those on the ground in Liverpool. For Peter Taaffe and Ted Grant, Liverpool had got out of control and the organisation made a number of awful tactical errors. At one point Militant Executive member John Pickard had to be sent to Liverpool to sort the comrades out.

The biggest tactical blunder was undoubtedly the scheme announced in September to declare 31,000 redundancies. By the end of August 1985 council officials were warning councillors that since the money would run out at the end of December, they were obliged by law – Labour's own employment law – to issue ninety-day redundancy notices. The plan was taken up by Militant and its allies. The ninety-day leeway would be used to campaign more vigorously than ever before. There was no real intention to make anybody redundant, they argued, it was simply a tactical move. For the two manual unions, the TGWU and GMBATU, this plan had its attractions, since even if the redundancies did actually occur, the 31,000 workforce would be reinstated at the start of the following financial year. With government-aided redundancy pay and Unemployment Benefit some low-paid manual workers would actually be better off from January to March than they would be in employment.

Though some of those behind the redundancies scheme may have genuinely intended that nobody should actually be made redundant, neither the media nor most of the workforce understood that. In any case, it was difficult to see how, if the council had not secured government help at the end of the ninety days, redundancies could be prevented. Most union members were horrified. Some in the white-collar unions feared that with the council's record of employment discrimination there was no guarantee even that the 31,000 who got their jobs back at the end of the financial year would be exactly the same 31,000 who had been made redundant. A NALGO picket prevented the council meeting at which the decision was to be taken from going ahead. The NUT and the head teachers' union went to court to stop the notices. Later NALGO and the teaching unions refused to distribute the redundancy notices to their members, so instead GMBATU shop-stewards took them around the city in a fleet of thirty hired taxis.

The scheme totally divided the Liverpool council workforce. Plans for an all-out strike were narrowly voted down in a series of ballots, though not every union bothered to ballot its members.

The all-out strike had to be dropped in favour of a simple one-day strike, but even that was boycotted by certain unions. Not only were most unions now set against the council, they were set against each other. Many of Hatton's troops, the council work-force, had deserted.

However, it must be recognised that at the same time the council seemed to have maintained, or even increased, its popularity with the Liverpool voters. A poll carried out by Harris Research for ITN's *Channel 4 News* in late September showed that almost equal numbers of voters favoured as disapproved of Liverpool's opposition to the government. Forty-seven per cent of Liverpool voters thought the government was to blame for the Liverpool situation, while only 33 per cent blamed the council. Moreover, 51 per cent said they would vote Labour in the next council elections, 5 per cent up on those who had actually voted Labour at the last poll.[13] A similar opinion poll carried out by MORI for the *Sunday Times* a few days later showed support for the council among Liverpool voters at slightly higher levels still.[14]

In some ways the council had already been forced to retreat by the autumn of 1985, since it was failing to maintain jobs and services. Cuts were already occurring, often, it so happened, in those areas where the council unions had been weakest in their support. In the Social Services department some vacancies had not been filled for months. Schools and colleges found themselves without stationery, books or even toilet rolls. Certain schools had to close for the odd day when they ran out of heating oil. At one Liverpool college equipment was seized when the council hadn't paid for it. Every single item of council expenditure had to be approved by Tony Byrne personally, which, of course, enabled him to delay payment. Even John Hamilton found difficulty in getting rail tickets to travel to meetings in London, though Derek Hatton had no trouble with the council cars – when these were seized by bailiffs on one occasion, the council acted quickly to buy them back. David Blunkett wondered whether it was a case of a campaign being used to maintain jobs and services, or jobs and services being used to maintain a campaign.

At the end of November, Liverpool Council was finally forced to balance its books. Even *Militant* described it as an 'orderly retreat'.[15] This was primarily brought about by £30 million worth of loans from Swiss banks, whereby capital projects would be carried out now and paid for later – a sort of municipal hire purchase. The package also involved the reallocation to Liverpool of spare capital borrowing allowances from other sympathetic Labour councils, a large amount of the dreaded capitalisation, and £3 million of cuts. Liverpool's financial crisis, for 1985–86 at least, was over.

By then Militant had found its 'traitors'. According to Derek Hatton the blame for this 'temporary setback' should lie 'on the shoulders of the national Labour Party leadership and the local trade unions'.[16] Other targets were the leaders of other councils who backed out of their own budget campaigns and had backed the Stonefrost Report, initiated by David Blunkett and several national union leaders, and which recommended rate rises and/or cuts.

Significantly, the 1985 settlement on 22 November had come only days after Militant's 4,000-strong public rally, a show of strength involving fireworks and Derek Hatton, at the Albert Hall in London. From 10 to 17 November the tendency had held its annual Red Week, eight days in which members were told to go all out and bring in new recruits. A circular told Militant branches: 'Like the miners' strike, Liverpool is politicising youth who are seeing for the first time a Labour leadership which has adopted a Marxist programme to fight the Tory government. This provides the best objective conditions for recruitment.'[17]

In the short term Militant had actually made tremendous gains from the 1985 Liverpool crisis in terms of its immediate aim – new recruits. But in the longer term Liverpool had done Militant's credibility and reputation considerable damage. And by now the national Labour leadership, and not just Neil Kinnock but union leaders too, had become embroiled in Liverpool's affairs.

14

THE TENDENCY
TACTICIANS

A few days after the 1983 general election Militant held a rally at the Friends' Meeting House in Euston Road, London. Unlike other Labour Party gatherings following Margaret Thatcher's return to Downing Street, it was not a depressed occasion, but euphoric. The comrades were celebrating the election of Militant's first two Members of Parliament, Terry Fields and David Nellist. 'Our army is on the march ... we've now got two MPs into Parliament,' one speaker proclaimed. A foreigner sitting in the hall that night would never have guessed that the two MPs referred to were actually Labour MPs, that the party they officially stood for had actually recorded its worst ever result in an election, But then, as the Militant constitution dictates (see Appendix 4), Fields and Nellist were Militant MPs first, Labour MPs second.

The mood of that meeting was typical of Militant's whole attitude during the election campaign. All the efforts of Militant members in 1983 had been concentrated on the five seats where

Militant candidates were standing: Brighton Kemptown, Liverpool Broadgreen, Bradford North, Coventry South-East and the Isle of Wight. They came in coaches from around the country, sleeping on comrades' floors. At the same time other more marginal seats were usually ignored by Militant. The tendency specialised in the mass-canvass, whereby dozens of them would descend upon an area, and go from door to door with canvass cards in one hand and plastic bags containing copies of *Militant* in the other. Voters who indicated they would be voting Labour were asked to buy a copy of the paper, and make a donation to the Fighting Fund. Ordinary party members who volunteered their services in these seats were often made to feel quite unwelcome. One group of local party members reported from Brighton Kemptown, where Rod Fitch was standing, that: 'Local Labour activists were deliberately alienated from the campaign and discouraged from canvassing ... the main part of the campaign was to sell the paper and recruit to Militant.'[1]

The 1983 general election saw early signs of hostility towards Militant from others on the left, partly brought about by the way in which it organised its own election campaigns. For a number of reasons the years 1982 and 1983 probably saw Militant at its peak in terms of influence within the Labour Party. Until then Militant was always able to count on the support of most of the broad coalition on the left of the party, though privately many left-wingers were very critical of Militant's tactics and politics. Militant's decision to take the Labour Party to court in 1982 had won no friends either, no matter how just some left-wingers considered their cause. After 1983, though Militant's influence declined within the party nationally, its membership more than doubled in number, and Liverpool made the organisation far better known publicly than it had ever been before.

Militant had dominated the agenda at most meetings on the National Executive in the year running up to the election. It continued to do so afterwards. The NEC meeting in July 1983 postponed any discussion of why Labour had lost the election, and instead proceeded to ban sales of *Militant* at party meetings and to prohibit Militant from using party facilities. That autumn, at the party conference in Brighton, the expulsion of the five members of the Editorial Board was confirmed in a closed session. The separate votes were roughly 5,160,000 to 1,616,000, though for some reason Ted Grant got about 175,000 votes more than his comrades. The public employees' union, NUPE, was the largest union to support Militant, and it was calculated that only about two-thirds of the constituencies supported the tendency. The decision made little difference to the five, however, since party membership played such a small role in their activities. In any case, some of the five continued to receive membership cards from their local parties for several years afterwards. Probably more significant for Militant that week was the election of a new Labour Party leader.

Neil Kinnock's dislike of Militant was far more intense than anything Michael Foot felt. During the 1983 leadership campaign he had not been frightened of making his position clear. More than once he spoke of Militant's 'democratic centralism in antagonism to democratic socialism' and stressed that the party's 'parameters' must be safeguarded: 'If not, we're not a political party, we're a darts club.'[2] More than any previous Labour leader, Neil Kinnock understood what Militant was. His rise within the ranks of the party over the previous twenty years had run parallel with the tendency's. Neil Kinnock's election as Labour leader was not good news for Militant.

Many of those involved in his election campaign had spent their student days fighting Militant in NOLS. This was perhaps best typified by the Red Revue group, who helped to raise money for Kinnock's election campaign. Mainly Scottish students from Glasgow, Red Revue's members are politically the heirs of those on the Icepick Express. Militant's style of public speaking is a constant object of their satire.

At the time of his election Kinnock was making it clear, however, that the expulsion of the Editorial Board would be the end of the matter, that no more action was proposed against Militant. The Militant grip on the party's youth section, and its position in Liverpool, together with Kinnock's background, made that hard to believe, though it may genuinely have been his intention at the time. Moreover, even if the leadership wasn't going to take action against Militant, others would.

The first party to make moves against Militant was Blackburn, where, in 1982, a Militant defector, Michael Gregory, had provided the local Labour MP, Jack Straw, with a dossier of evidence on the tendency's activities. The Blackburn party proceeded to expel six local Militant members named by Gregory. Since then dozens of local parties have moved to expel Militant members from the party – among them Stevenage, Rhondda, Sheffield Attercliffe, Gillingham, Faversham, Cardiff South, Warley West, Newcastle-under-Lyme, Newcastle East, Wrekin, Mansfield, Ipswich, Chorley, Cannock and Burntwood, Eddisbury, Knowsley South, Bromsgrove, Wrexham, Llanelli and Havant. By the spring of 1986 the number of such expulsions totalled nearly forty. Among those affected were Militant Central Committee members Bill Hopwood, Steve Glennon and Bill Mullins. In Wales the TGWU secretary, George Wright, led moves to prevent Militant Central Committee member Chris Peace taking his place on the Welsh Party Executive. The engineering union, the AUEW, banned Militant members from holding union office.

Many of the constituency parties taking action received advice from regional and national Labour Party headquarters. When the expelled members appealed to the National Executive Committee the expulsions were usually upheld by the new Appeals and Mediations Committee under the chairmanship of AUEW right-winger Ken Cure. The expulsions were usually carried out on the basis of the NEC's January 1983 definition of Militant membership as 'involvement in financial support for and/or the organisation of and/or the activities of the Militant Tendency'.[3]

What is especially interesting is that many of these constituency parties could not be described as particularly right wing. For instance, analysis of the records shows that by far the majority of them voted for Tony Benn, Eric Heffer and Dennis Skinner in the annual elections to the National Executive. What the series of expulsions indicated was a decreasing tolerance of Militant among party activists, and a growing understanding of the nature of the tendency's organisation and methods.

At the same time the broad left coalition within the party was breaking up, in what became known as the 'realignment of the left'. It was a process that was greatly influenced by the debates taking place within the Communist Party, and by the events of the miners' strike. On the one hand was the so-called 'soft-left' grouping, broadly loyal to Neil Kinnock, to which people like Ken Livingstone, Michael Meacher, Tom Sawyer and David Blunkett gravitated. On the other side was the so-called 'hard-left' around Tony Benn, Eric Heffer (who began to work more closely with Benn), Dennis Skinner and Arthur Scargill. The group of people who were prepared to support Militant, or at least defend them, was shrinking. Livingstone and Blunkett, while opposed to purges, publicly became more critical of Militant, particularly after coming into contact with Liverpool's leaders in local government circles. By rejecting the Stonefrost Report, Liverpool managed to snub Blunkett, Livingstone and several trade union leaders all at once. Livingstone came to describe Derek Hatton as 'possibly one of the most attractive faces of the Labour Party since Oswald Mosley'.[4] An important sign of this change in attitude came earlier in the left-wing union NUPE, which in May 1985 voted by a majority of two-to-one in favour of the Labour Party expelling Militant members found to be in breach of the constitution. Militant had lost its largest defender in the trade union movement. Significantly, the NUPE motion had been proposed by the delegation from Liverpool.

Militant's plan to expand in the trade unions made little progress. In the two medium-sized unions where Militant had made some impact it suffered setbacks. In the Civil and Public Services Association the Broad Left grouping, which had helped Militant achieve nine places on the CPSA National Executive, split in November 1984, after an alliance of Communist Party members and Labour left-wingers staged a premeditated walk out from the Broad Left conference in protest at Militant's tactics. Militant remains a force within the union though, largely based on the large CPSA branch at the DHSS computer centre in Newcastle, which it controls. In July 1986 Militant made a dramatic advance with the surprise election of Militant member, John Macreadie, as CPSA general secretary. The result was put in doubt, however, by an inquiry into the conduct of the election.

In the National Communications Union (formerly the Post Office Engineering Union) the coup against John Golding in 1983 was reversed the following year. In 1986 Golding easily defeated Militant member, Phil Holt, in the election for the union's general secretaryship. Holt, though, won the union's nomination for the Labour NEC elections.

In the major unions Militant has made little impact at national level. Though of course Militant is strong in the Liverpool branches of both the TGWU and the GMBATU, these unions, and the AUEW, police themselves well and officials are often able to stop Militant's progress in advance. The only other significant union where Militant has made much impact has been the shop workers' union, USDAW. In 1985 Militant got its man, Bill

Connor, selected as the USDAW Broad Left candidate for general secretary. Connor secured 27 per cent of the vote, compared with 46 per cent for the victor, Garfield Davies.

One union where Militant had high hopes was the miners' union, the NUM, particularly during the 1984–85 strike. The tendency suffered, however, from the lack of an open Broad Left group operating within the union, while the closed left-wing grouping has long been dominated by Communists and Labour left-wingers who are not exactly sympathetic to Militant's Trotskyism. David Hopper, recently elected general secretary of the Durham miners, is a former Militant member. During the strike Militant published occasional editions of *Militant Miner* and its members were often out on the picket lines, but the union will be an extremely tough nut to crack.

Militant's other area of work in the unions, the Broad Left Organising Committee, seems to have made little progress either. BLOC's annual conferences each April have been more and more dominated by Militant. This might look good for Militant, but as experience in the CPSA and the NCU has shown, Militant can't operate on its own, and depends on broad alliances with the rest of the left to make progress.

Militant's failure to build upon its previously strong position in the Labour movement after 1983 is perhaps best illustrated in the round of selections and reselections in preparation for the coming election. In two constituencies where Militant had stood candidates in 1983 there was a strong backlash against the tendency.

On the Isle of Wight, when Militant candidate Cathy Wilson

had received a mere 2.4 per cent of the vote – probably the lowest vote ever recorded by Labour in a parliamentary election – Militant got the blame. The reaction against Militant in the local party was compounded when the tendency used the election canvass cards to go on a recruitment drive among the few voters who had promised to vote Labour. Party agent Robert Jones, who had joined Militant for political survival, left the tendency and then led moves first to oust Militant members from local party offices, and then to expel them from party membership. In Brighton Kemptown the party chose a non-Militant candidate to succeed Rod Fitch, though Militant still remained strong in the constituency and Central Committee member Ray Apps continued to be selected as party conference delegate. Similarly, in Coventry South-East, Militant MP David Nellist faced opposition within his constituency, which even led to an NEC inquiry into the conduct of the general election campaign. Eventually though, Nellist secured reselection fairly easily, partly because he was widely recognised as a good constituency MP. In fact Nellist's main opponent was a former IMG member.

In several constituencies where Militant had high hopes, it narrowly failed to get its men selected as parliamentary candidates. In Glasgow Provan James Cameron was beaten by seventy-three votes to seventy-two, while in Pollok, on the other side of the city, Militant full-timer David Churchley failed to win by nine votes. In Gateshead East, Malcolm Graham lost by only two. However, in both Glasgow Pollok and Gateshead East, Militant succeeded in antagonising the rest of the left by tactically voting for right-wing candidates in the early stages of the voting procedure in order to give their own men an easier run.

A Militant challenge to Frank Field in Birkenhead was easily beaten off, largely through good organisation on Field's part. In Derbyshire North-East a Militant member, John Dunn, secured the valuable miners' union nomination, but then, for the first time in memory, the party chose not to select the NUM nominee.

In Knowsley North, next door to Liverpool, Robert Kilroy-Silk was challenged by Tony Mulhearn. But it was more than a simple battle between the sitting MP and Militant. Robert Kilroy-Silk had many critics in Knowsley. He was seen as a careerist: shortly after being elected to Parliament in 1974, he had declared on television his ambition to become Prime Minister. He annoyed some party workers by saying he would live in the constituency and then bought a house in a leafy part of Buckinghamshire. Many Knowsley left-wingers, not just Militant, felt he was not the ideal MP for the deprived council estates of Kirkby. For his part Kilroy-Silk complained of intimidation by Mulhearn's supporters and alleged that some people were not entitled to be delegates. The selection was held up both by an inquiry into Knowsley's affairs and the Liverpool investigation. When the selection does take place, even if Tony Mulhearn is not allowed to stand, Kilroy-Silk is likely to be challenged by another left-winger, Keva Coombes, former leader of Merseyside Council.

In Bradford North, however, Pat Wall easily secured the nomination again. The NEC was reluctant to endorse Wall at first. In June 1986 he was interviewed by the Executive and accepted after assurances that he no longer had any connection with Militant. Although Wall has had disagreements with the Militant leadership recently, and illness has curtailed his political work, there is no evidence that he has left Militant.

Militant's one real gain in the selection process was in Peter Tatchell's area, Bermondsey, where the deputy leader of Southwark Council, John Bryan, was selected. He will have to oust the Liberal Simon Hughes to become Bermondsey's MP.

Overall Militant had done far worse in the selection round than it had hoped, and its enemies had feared. Militant's representation in the next parliament is unlikely to be more than three or four.

In the increasingly desperate search for new members, Militant set up new front organisations to speed its recruitment among young people. The LPYS's Youth Trade Union Rights Campaign worked among YTS trainees, and met within increasing opposition from the Labour Party hierarchy. In April 1985 YTURC organised a strike among school students in protest about the Youth Training Scheme. It met with limited support, but received considerable publicity. Liverpool Council gave its pupils 'immunity' for the day so that they could join the protest. Nationally the strike caused the Labour Party considerable embarrassment since YTURC was officially an LPYS operation, and had an office at Walworth Road; Neil Kinnock called YTURC 'dafties'. Shortly afterwards the NEC told YTURC to find accommodation elsewhere. A result of the strike was the establishment of another Militant front organisation, the School Students' Union.

In the other area where Militant was hoping to recruit, further education colleges, it set up an organisation called Further Education Labour Students (FELS). FELS was designed partly to help Militant win back control of the official university-dominated Labour student organisation, NOLS, and partly to compensate for the fact that Militant couldn't tackle NOLS; but FELS, too, was soon disowned by the Labour Party. During the course of 1985 four Militant front organisations – SALEP, the Chile Socialist Defence Campaign, YTURC and FELS – had been repudiated by the NEC, in what was a deliberate campaign to attack Militant.

At the same time party officials had begun planning to undermine Militant in the LPYS. Aware that Labour had performed particularly badly among young voters in 1983, Neil Kinnock could not ignore the Militant domination of his own youth section. The leadership was supported in its plans by the vehemently anti-Militant leadership of NOLS. The LPYS budget was progressively cut back, and the money reallocated to NOLS, while the party launched a number of initiatives designed to bypass the LPYS. These included a Youth Campaigns Committee, a Youth Arts for Labour Group and events such as the Labour Listens to Youth festival in London in November 1985. In particular high hopes have been placed upon Red Wedge, a group of musicians, comedians and actors brought together by Billy Bragg and Paul Weller in support of the Labour Party. In 1986 Red Wedge staged a series of concerts designed to attract young people to the party 'without thrusting politics down their throats'. Militant has found it difficult to work out how to react to Red Wedge: on the one hand some tendency leaders argue that such entertainment distracts from revolutionary politics, and yet on the other hand Militant recognises the appeal of Red Wedge. In the pages of *Militant* itself Red Wedge has received only limited coverage, while Andy Bevan (a supporter of the venture) and the Young Socialists' NEC representative, Frances Curran (an opponent), have disagreed in public about it.

Another part of the leadership's youth strategy is eventually to get rid of Andy Bevan as Youth Officer. As Bevan is convenor of the Walworth Road trade unions, and seen by party staff as a good shop steward, it will be difficult to sack him outright. A job of equal status elsewhere has yet to be found. Another suggested reform has been the reduction of the upper age for LPYS membership from twenty-five down to twenty-one, in order to reduce further the importance of the organisation.

By the time of the 1985 Labour Party conference in Bournemouth, Militant seemed to be less of the force within the party that it once was. Though stronger in actual numbers than ever before, Militant was having increasing difficulties in controlling those numbers. The emphasis on growth, at times even the coercion upon people to join, led to an influx of new members who were not paying their subscriptions as they should, who were not selling the paper – or even buying it – and who had none of the long traditional grounding in Militant politics. In short Militant was suffering from an increasing lack of commitment, and if members were being recruited faster than ever before, more were also leaving than ever before. Everywhere within the movement

Militant was either being contained, or even, in some cases, on the decline – in the constituencies, the unions, and the LPYS. Everywhere, that is, except Liverpool.

There, by September 1985, the city's financial crisis had become so dire that the council had begun issuing the redundancy notices to its divided workforce. Indeed, some of the notices were actually going out by taxi in the week that many of Liverpool's leaders were away at the Labour conference in Bournemouth. The apparently ludicrous situation of a council issuing redundancy notices to preserve jobs was seized upon.

Neil Kinnock had kept an eye on the events in Liverpool without making any significant political intervention. The opposition leader's office had maintained close contacts with many people in Liverpool, including the council leader, John Hamilton, members of the Black Caucus, and even the city's Anglican and Roman Catholic church leaders. After the redundancies decision, however, Kinnock decided to go for Derek Hatton and his colleagues. Militant's guard was down. The opportunity would be the leader's speech at the coming party conference in Bournemouth, and work was begun preparing the speech's key passages.

Not since Hugh Gaitskell has a Labour Party leader dominated his conference in the way that Neil Kinnock did in Bournemouth in October 1985. The Labour leader arrived amid predictions that it would be a bad week. His efforts to defeat a motion from the miners calling for reimbursement of fines and legal costs incurred during the coal dispute seemed to have failed. Yet by Friday the defeat on that motion seemed largely to have been forgotten. What was remembered instead was Kinnock's repudiation of the politics of Arthur Scargill, and the 'impossible promises' of Derek Hatton:

> I'll tell you what happens with impossible promises. You start with far-fetched resolutions. They are then pickled into a rigid dogma, a code, and you go through the years sticking to that, out-dated, misplaced, irrelevant to the real needs, and you end in the grotesque chaos of a Labour council – a *Labour* council – hiring taxis to scuttle around a city handing out redundancy notices to its own workers.

At that point Eric Heffer walked off the platform and out through the hall – a move he much regretted later. Heffer's walkout turned it into a moment of high political drama. 'You're telling lies,' Derek Hatton shouted from the floor. With most of the audience behind him though, Kinnock pressed on: 'You can't play politics with people's jobs ... The people will not, cannot, abide posturing. They cannot respect the gesture-generals or the tendency-tacticians.'[5]

Those words won wide applause inside the hall and outside. For a potential Labour Prime Minister needing to establish his leadership credentials, and needing to show he could be just as tough and firm as Margaret Thatcher, the speech had helped do the trick. At the time Kinnock was reluctant to talk about disciplinary action against Derek Hatton and his colleagues, but in effect he was committed. Overnight Kinnock's personal rating in the opinion polls shot up. To maintain that electoral popularity, action would have to be taken against Militant.

Some of Kinnock's natural allies on the National Executive had been worried by what he had said in his conference speech. David Blunkett was concerned that Kinnock's attack had failed to acknowledge Liverpool's very genuine financial problems. The next day, in the local government debate, Blunkett acted as conciliator. In a dramatic moment in the middle of Blunkett's summing-up speech, Derek Hatton was summoned to the rostrum and agreed to withdraw his motion calling for industrial action in support of surcharged councillors. In return Blunkett agreed to initiate an independent inquiry into Liverpool's financial problems. It is difficult to say who had gained more. Blunkett had gained the image of conciliator-supreme, while Hatton had been saved from the overwhelming defeat his motion would have suffered. Kinnock was very annoyed that Blunkett had not let Hatton be defeated by the conference vote.

The day before Neil Kinnock's conference attack, Liverpool's Militant leaders had suffered another onslaught, from a rather unusual quarter. In an article in *The Times*, Liverpool's Roman Catholic archbishop, Derek Warlock, and Anglican bishop, David Sheppard, had accepted that Liverpool's case had not been 'adequately heard by Whitehall', but said the city's 'confrontation', 'has to a great extent been manufactured by the Militant leadership of the city council'.[6] The timing of the bishops' article was no coincidence.

Two weeks later the new leaders of the TGWU and GMBATU, Ron Todd and John Edmonds, led a team of union leaders to Liverpool to look at the council's books. That visit led to the Stonefrost

Report, which proposed several ways in which Liverpool's financial problems could be resolved. Among the several options were an 11 per cent rate rise, a pound a week rent increase, and capitalisation. The Stonefrost Report was rejected almost straight away by the council, and generally misinterpreted by Militant.

The decision angered both the Labour leadership and the union leaders who had helped commission it, as well as David Blunkett and other Labour council leaders who had been involved. Already the redundancy notices fiasco and the failure of the union leaders to secure a solution to the Liverpool crisis convinced more and more people that something had to be done. Action was delayed in order to encourage Liverpool to sort out its financial problems. When Liverpool finally produced its settlement based upon the Swiss bank loans, the time had come to act.

After consultation with Neil Kinnock, Ron Todd and John Edmonds had written to the NEC demanding an inquiry. By twenty-one votes to five the NEC agreed that Larry Whitty and an eight-strong delegation look into Liverpool. Neil Kinnock made it clear privately that at the least he expected Mulhearn and Hatton to be expelled. On television that evening the Labour leader referred to Militant as 'a maggot in the body of the Labour Party' and added later that the future for Militant in Liverpool looked 'very bleak – very short term'.[7]

It would not be quite as short-term as Neil Kinnock had hoped. The inquiry, which had hoped to finish its work by the end of January, dragged on into February. For nearly three months it met about once a week, often for a whole day or even two at a time.

Six meetings were held in Liverpool, mainly at the AUEW offices in the city centre, while several other meetings were held in London at Walworth Road, and on one occasion at the Union of Communication Workers' office in Clapham. The team received thousands of pages of written evidence: particularly long submissions were sent in by the Liverpool branch of NUPE, the Liverpool Black Caucus and the Merseyside Labour Co-ordinating Committee (the LCC evidence was also printed in *Tribune*). Dozens of individual party members wrote in with complaints about Militant and the district party leadership. Yet at the same time an even greater number of Liverpool party members, mostly, but not exclusively Militant members, wrote to say they had no evidence of malpractices in the DLP and that in their experience district party meetings were conducted properly. Militant had clearly organised this mass write-in, but nearly every such letter was handwritten, with no evidence of a dummy letter having been circulated.

In all the team questioned 120 witnesses, all of them, without exception, Labour Party members. At one point a Liverpool solicitor, Rex Makin, had asked to see the team on behalf of several clients, but the inquiry team decided against hearing him on the grounds that Makin is not a Labour Party member and was thought to be sympathetic to the Liberals. It was agreed that no matter what non-party witnesses might have to say, politically it would be too damaging to allow their evidence. All the leading DLP members were seen several times each, sometimes together, sometimes individually: Derek Hatton even asked to bring along a witness to his final appearance, who turned out to be Eric Heffer.

Some people were prepared to give evidence to the inquiry team only if it was done in the strictest confidence. They feared reprisals by Militant. One leading witness was so frightened he would be spotted entering the AUEW offices that instead the team had to see him secretly early one morning at their hotel in Bootle.

One of the most important witnesses was Derek Hatton's former mistress, Irene Buxton, who had been the most damaging interviewee in a *World In Action* programme Granada TV had broadcast about Hatton only a few weeks before. Buxton had written to the inquiry, inviting them to come and see her. Since leaving Liverpool she had gone to live in Potterton, a small village near Aberdeen, and remarkably only a few miles from another village called Hattoncrook. Buxton had been trying to avoid journalists ever since the *World In Action* programme, and so when Charles Turnock, Larry Whitty and the Scottish Labour Party secretary, Helen Liddell, flew to Aberdeen, they saw her in the Station Hotel. As she had for Granada, Buxton told the three visitors exactly how Militant is organised in Liverpool, with details of Hatton's role in the organisation. A tape of the interview was played to the rest of the team later. Another important witness was Steve Kelly, a Granada researcher who had worked on the *World In Action* programme. Kelly, a former journalist on *Tribune*, provided them with copies of documents from the Deane Collection, and furnished them with a list of twenty-six people he believed to be Militant full-timers in Liverpool. His evidence, which was partly based on his own questioning of Buxton, was quite influential when it came to drawing up the list of people to be considered for disciplinary action.

However, Irene Buxton was the only former Militant member the inquiry team spoke to. So even by the end of its investigations the team still had an incomplete picture of Militant's organisation in Liverpool, and still didn't have a clear idea of exactly who the key Militant personnel were. One very revealing witness, however, was Peter Lennard, one of those who had 'scuttled round' in taxis handing out redundancy notices. The convenor of GMBATU branch 80, Lennard had worked closely with Ian Lowes on the Shop Stewards' Committee, but only a few weeks before seeing the inquiry team had suddenly turned violently against Militant when he discovered it was trying to secure jobs for Militant members in those areas of the council that were covered by his branch. Lennard was a powerful witness.

Almost from the beginning of its investigation it had been clear that the eight NEC members would be divided over how many people should be expelled, if any. Left-wingers Audrey Wise and Margaret Beckett were against any expulsions, while right-wingers Charles Turnock, Tony Clarke and Betty Boothroyd wanted several dozen to go. The initiative effectively lay with two soft-left unionists – Eddie Haigh of the Dyers and Bleachers section of the TGWU, and Tom Sawyer of NUPE. Sawyer had been quite shocked by what he discovered in Liverpool, and angry about the way in which NUPE members had been discriminated against by the council. Sawyer says that what he had seen in Liverpool had had a very fundamental effect on the way he thought about socialism, and ideas such as freedom and truth. It was Sawyer, together with Haigh, who effectively determined what the team's majority report would contain. 'Tom was really marvellous,' commented one right-winger later.

The inquiry's forty-four-page majority report had taken much longer to compile than originally intended. It emerged at the end of February only days before the National Executive meeting, after weeks of media speculation, much of it wrong. The report dealt mostly with alleged breaches of the rules of the District Labour Party, and concluded that there were 'very serious irregularities in the functioning and practices' of the Liverpool party 'which have put it in breach of the party's rules'. The report accused the DLP of interfering in the day-to-day affairs of the city council, particularly in the matter of appointments and industrial relations. The report condemned the practice of holding DLP 'aggregate' meetings, talked of an 'air of intimidation' at meetings 'including verbal intimidation and threats and acts of physical intimidation', and said there had been abuses in the composition of delegations to the DLP.[8]

Some of the complaints in the report, especially those about the way the DLP conducted its affairs, were extremely trivial, though. That the DLP was acting unconstitutionally by having two vice-presidents instead of one, or in discussing subjects not relevant to its local government role, such as Nicaragua, was hardly earth-shattering. There cannot be a Labour Party in the country that does not bend its rules in small ways such as this. The presence of minor allegations such as these may have reduced the impact of the much more serious complaints.

The report's recommendations fell into two parts. First it

called for various reforms in the operation of the DLP, including the appointment of two new temporary full-time organisers and the adoption of new Rules and Standing Orders by a reconstituted party later in the year. Second, the team recommended that Larry Whitty should draw up charges against sixteen individuals on the basis of their involvement in the abuses and breaches of the party rules, and their involvement in Militant. The sixteen were: Derek Hatton, Tony Mulhearn, Terry Harrison, Felicity Dowling (the DLP secretary), Tony and Josie Aitman, Cheryl Varley (sabbatical officer for the Liverpool further education colleges' students' unions), Richard Knights, Richard Venton, councillors Pauline Dunlop, Paul Astbury and Harry Smith, Ian Lowes, Sylvia Sharpey-Shafer, Roger Bannister, and Carol Darby (the organiser of the Merseyside Action Group). Dunlop, Astbury, Smith, Sharpey-Shafer, Bannister and Darby had not been agreed on by Tom Sawyer and Eddie Haigh.

One notable absentee from the list of names was Dave Cotterill, a Militant Central Committee member who had been transferred to Liverpool from Newcastle early in 1985. Others who might have considered themselves lucky to escape were Laurence Coates, who had spent a lot of time in the Liverpool area, and Cathy Wilson, the former Militant candidate on the Isle of Wight, who had moved to Merseyside in 1985. Some members of the team felt it would be wrong to try to expel Wilson since she was disabled, and Militant might have played on this for publicity purposes.

One man disappointed not to have been included was Tony Byrne, who felt himself to have been just as involved in the affairs of the DLP as anybody. At one stage Byrne had been on the list of some inquiry members. Others considered for action, on the grounds that they held offices in the DLP, were John Hamilton, who served as treasurer, and Eddie Loyden, one of the two vice-presidents. Hamilton, though, had made clear to inquiry members his lack of involvement in events in Liverpool, while Loyden, an MP, had often been absent. Furthermore, to try to expel people other than Militant members would have opened up accusations that Militant was only the first target, and that the rest of the left would be next.

A minority report from the two left-wing members of the team, Audrey Wise and Margaret Beckett, supported some of the majority's proposals for reorganising the party, but rejected the idea of any expulsions.

A mass demonstration was planned by Militant outside Walworth Road on the day the National Executive considered the two reports, 26 February. Only a few hundred turned up, though, compared with the 2,000 Militant had expected. Among them were six of those threatened with expulsion. By far the most striking shot on the television screens that day was Neil Kinnock walking through a crowd of protestors who were screaming 'scab'. It was a deliberate act by Kinnock. He could easily have entered quietly through the back of the premises, but wanted not only to stand up to Militant, but also to be *seen* to be standing up to them. After more than eight hours, the majority report was approved by nineteen votes to ten and Larry Whitty was asked to draw up charges against the sixteen.

While Larry Whitty was busy doing this, Militant was also active, on several fronts. First, Lynn Walsh was consulting Militant's lawyers to see if there were any ways the expulsions could be frustrated. Second, the tendency was doing its best to make the most of the publicity the pending expulsions would bring. Plans were announced for a petition aimed at getting 1 million signatures opposing the leadership's proposals against Militant. A series of meetings was already under way around the country. Many of them drew large crowds: more than 1,000 to hear Derek Hatton and Bob Wylie in Glasgow, and meetings of several hundred people in Edinburgh, Newcastle, Manchester, Sheffield, London and Liverpool. Above all, Militant intended to use the issue to pursue what had increasingly become its number one aim, almost to the exclusion of anything else – recruitment. A Central Committee resolution sent out to all branches on 17 March spoke of the 'colossal opportunities now presented by the twin attacks of the bourgeois state and the trade union and Labour leadership on the Marxists in Liverpool … There are thousands, tens of thousands, of workers literally knocking at our door at the present time.' Claiming that Militant membership was now more than 8,100, it put forward a new aim: 'The task is posed point blank: doubling our size. Our immediate aim is to reach the agreed target within the next three months. The objective circumstances have never been more favourable.'[9]

Branches were told to go out on the doorsteps of target council estates, selling the paper and holding meetings, in the search for new members. 'We have been preparing for over ten years for this situation,' the Central Committee document concluded. 'Now the blows have been struck by the bureaucracy it is time to act. We need, in the words of Trotsky, "to be bold when the hour for action arrives". That time has come.'[10]

Over the coming weeks there were plenty of opportunities for publicity. The longer the expulsions process could be dragged on the more publicity there would be. The National Executive was due to meet again on 26 March, and Militant planned to be out on the streets at 6.30 that night, immediately after the evening television news bulletins, in which it predicted the expulsions issue would again be the major item. It was right.

Before the National Executive met, however, Militant applied to the High Court for an injunction against the proceedings on the grounds that it had not been given natural justice. The tendency had already gone to court once over the inquiry, in January, securing a guarantee from the Labour Party that action would not be taken until the Liverpool councillors' appeal against surcharge and disqualification had been heard. This time Militant's lawyers argued, among other things, that the eight members of the inquiry team, when attending the National Executive, would be acting as prosecution and jury and that it was unfair to consider evidence heard in secret when Militant had no chance to reply. The day before the NEC met, the Vice-Chancellor, Sir Nicolas Browne-Wilkinson, found largely in favour of Militant, and ordered that the inquiry team could not attend the National Executive, and that the NEC should not consider evidence given in confidence. That evening the left-wingers on the NEC held their traditional pre-NEC caucus.

When the National Executive gathered to start its disciplinary hearings, the list had been cut down to twelve from sixteen through lack of evidence against Josie Aitman, Pauline Dunlop, Sylvia Sharpey-Shafer and Paul Astbury. The meeting began with more than an hour of procedural wranglings, during which time Tony Benn and Eric Heffer had tried to get the matter postponed. Then, when the hearings actually started and the first of the accused, Felicity Dowling, was sent away to consider the revised charges against her, seven left-wing NEC members, led by Eric Heffer, walked out in protest at the way the hearing was being conducted. Without the eight inquiry team members and the seven left-wingers the meeting was suddenly inquorate. Neil Kinnock was furious. The seven strenuously denied afterwards that they had planned the move before the meeting, but it is hard to believe. Certainly Derek Hatton seemed to expect it. When told by a party official that Eric Heffer and Tony Benn had walked out, Hatton anxiously enquired, 'What, only them?'

Meanwhile, while waiting for their hearings, Hatton and Mulhearn had pulled off another publicity coup. The twelve had been asked to wait in Larry Whitty's office, on the grounds that it was the only available room big enough to hold all of them. Once inside, however, Hatton and Mulhearn opened the window that looks out over the front of the building and waved to their cheering supporters below. The resulting picture, seen on all the television bulletins and on newspaper front pages the next day, made it look as if Hatton and Mulhearn had taken the Labour Party over, rather than that they were waiting to be expelled from it. Officials admitted later it was a bad mistake. It provided more of exactly the kind of publicity Militant wanted, and the Labour Party didn't.

So it dragged on. The party did not seem to have properly learned the lessons of 1982 and 1983. It was now clear that the party had not been careful enough in taking legal advice, first on the question of setting up the inquiry team and second in clarifying the status of confidential evidence. Ironically, had the team known that it would not have been allowed to sit on the NEC while it was considering the report, the report would actually have been more firm in recommending expulsions. The legal advice Larry Whitty had obtained towards the end of the inquiry was that the report was bombproof. It wasn't.

In preparing the charges for the proposed expulsions, Whitty suffered from a shortage of concrete evidence proving people were actually members of Militant. The inquiry had received reams of documentary material but very little of it was conclusive. The purchase contract on the Militant Liverpool headquarters was used against Mulhearn, Harrison and Aitman; signed articles in *Militant* were quoted, and advertisements for Militant meetings at which some of the twelve had been speakers. The latter was particularly inconclusive: Militant gleefully pointed out that Tom Sawyer himself had spoken at a Militant meeting in 1977. Nobody could accuse him of being a member of the tendency. The most effective evidence against the twelve would have been signed statements from former Militant members. The only such person the inquiry had been in contact with was Irene Buxton, but her oral evidence about who exactly ran Militant in Liverpool and her allegations about Hatton, Mulhearn and their colleagues were not used directly against them. Party officials were keen not to get involved in court cases where party witnesses such as Irene Buxton would be cross-examined. Yet this is probably what Militant feared most. The shortage of hard evidence meant that later Richard Knights, who had been a Militant full-timer for several years, had his charges dropped too.

From the beginning there had been a difference in emphasis as to what the inquiry should be doing. Neil Kinnock wanted to get people for their involvement in Militant. For Larry Whitty and David Blunkett, the Militant issue was less important: they thought the inquiry should really examine possible breaches in the party rules. The second view gained the upper hand. As a result the Liverpool inquiry's report was dominated by party procedural matters, yet at the same time the team gathered insufficient material about the involvement of particular individuals in Militant.

Meanwhile, Militant had been having considerable success in stopping the increasing numbers of expulsions taking place in the constituencies. Plans to expel ten Militant members in Stevenage had to be dropped after Militant secured an injunction on the grounds that those concerned had not been given natural justice. Cardiff South was even forced to reinstate three Militant members after it had spent £4,000 losing a court action brought by Militant. Militant employed good lawyers and had the necessary money, though many of those fighting expulsions in the courts managed to do so with legal aid, something not available to local

Labour parties. Eventually party head office was forced to advise parties to drop any planned expulsions until the rules could be made watertight and such action would be easier.

Like Jim Mortimer before him, Larry Whitty had originally been keen not to get obsessed about Militant. Here he was, appointed to his new job as the party's leading official, with the primary aim of getting Labour ready for the next election. Like Mortimer, Whitty also considered himself to be on the left of the party and did not really approve of expulsions. Yet, within months of his appointment, just like Mortimer, he was finding himself dragged more and more into the Militant business. Again Militant was taking up large amounts of Whitty's time and leaving him increasingly frustrated. It was also costing the party tens of thousands of pounds.

The remaining eleven people on the National Executive's list were due to face hearings on Wednesday 21 and Thursday 22 May 1986. However, after two days of hearings, lasting twenty-seven hours, only three on that list had been expelled – Tony Mulhearn, Tony Aitman and Ian Lowes. A fourth, councillor Harry Smith, had the charges against him dropped after giving an undertaking that he would no longer have anything to do with Militant. Most of the two days had been taken up with legal and procedural arguments as those facing expulsion threatened to obtain yet another High Court injunction. Around a third of the time was wasted by procedural matters that could probably have been foreseen and avoided.

Derek Hatton, meanwhile, had returned to Liverpool at the end of the first day, telling the NEC he had been summoned to an urgent council meeting the next day. It may have been urgent, but council leader John Hamilton knew nothing about it – Hamilton happened to travel down to London for a meeting of the Association of Metropolitan Authorities on the same day Hatton said his own presence was urgently required in Liverpool. Hatton took a totally different approach to the hearings from Mulhearn. Mulhearn employed lawyers and had spent days preparing an elaborate defence of his position, which impressed the National Executive, but was not enough to save him. Hatton saw no need for a lawyer. 'Derek relies on his own abilities,' commented one Militant official.

Before the National Executive could meet again to consider Hatton and the other six on their list, the party in Liverpool made it clear it would not accept the existing expulsions anyway. Liverpool Garston voted by forty-six votes to two to ignore the decision about its member, Tony Mulhearn, and Mulhearn continued attending the council Labour Group, while at the same time Walworth Road's newly appointed Liverpool organiser, Peter Kilfoyle, was excluded.

In June, Derek Hatton was eventually expelled, along with Richard Venton, Roger Bannister and Terry Harrison, in two days of hearings lasting twenty-three hours. For the second time both Neil Kinnock and Roy Hattersley missed Prime Minister's Question Time. The vote to expel Hatton was 12–6 after Hatton had chosen to attend another council meeting in Liverpool instead, and lawyers acting on his behalf unsuccessfully tried to secure an injunction to stop the hearing going ahead. Even by the end of June matters were far from resolved though. Two of the accused had still to be heard, and the Liverpool constituency parties still threatened not to recognise the NEC decisions. Militant had made the party hierarchy look foolish at times. The parallels between the party's action against Militant in 1982–83 and that in 1986 were quite striking.

Conclusion
NEIL KINNOCK'S FALKLANDS

The Militant problem, as one front-bench colleague remarked, became Neil Kinnock's Falklands. Once the campaign had been started there was no turning back, at least not without considerable loss of face. It was a costly exercise involving considerable effort for a seemingly small objective. Yet, just as the Falklands War had helped rescue Margaret Thatcher from unfavourable opinion polls and an unimpressed electorate, so the Militant issue helped boost Neil Kinnock's popularity. The Falklands had cemented Thatcher's image as a tough leader, and so for Kinnock might his action against Militant.

Yet sending the task force to recapture the Liverpool Labour Party was a risky exercise. It might be impossible to recover from defeat. Casualties would be embarrassing, and delay would cause questions to be asked. And would victory in the immediate campaign solve the problem in the long term? Would the cost of a Fortress Liverpool be too great?

The evidence is that the action taken by successive Labour leaders against Militant has done little *in itself* to weaken the organisation. The tendency is not going to pack up just because a few of its leading members are expelled. Both in Britain and in other countries, expelled Militant members have simply carried on their work inside the socialist party without the benefit of party membership. Indeed, in the long term the expulsion of several Militant members from Liverpool could well do the organisation more good than harm. Even after the long NEC meetings to expel Derek Hatton and his colleagues from the party, they were promising to let the issue drag on for several months more. On past practice those expelled had the right of appeal to the 1986 Labour Party conference in Blackpool (ironically, Militant has the same right of appeal against expulsion in its own constitution – see Appendix 4). That in itself promised to take up several hours of the Labour Party's annual gathering. And the tendency was still threatening to pursue legal action. Its ability to pay legal costs seems to know no constraints. The free publicity would continue. And for Militant almost any publicity is good publicity.

In spite of expulsions and disqualifications, Liverpool will remain a problem for Labour for a long time. In spite of all the adverse publicity, the May 1986 local elections saw the Liverpool Labour Party retain its control of Liverpool Council, with exactly the same number of seats as before. Liverpool Liberals made gains, but only at the expense of the Conservatives, who were reduced to a mere seven seats. Close analysis of the Liverpool figures, however, revealed that Labour's vote had in fact fallen from the 46 per cent recorded in 1983 and 1984 to 42 per cent. The only leading Militant member whose seat was up for election, Felicity Dowling, suffered a 10 per cent swing against her – the highest anti-Labour swing in the city.

Nevertheless, in the light of the city's continuing crises, the pending disqualification of most Labour councillors by the courts, and the condemnation of Liverpool's Militant leaders by the Labour hierarchy, it was still a remarkably good result. Three successive sets of local elections, in 1983, 1984 and 1986, together with several opinion polls, had indicated that the Liverpool Labour Party's Militant policies were quite popular with the Liverpool electorate.

Furthermore, Militant is likely to retain a strong position in the Liverpool Labour Party even when the inquiry team's recommendations have been carried out in full. The election of Tony Mulhearn and several Militant colleagues to the officer posts in the new Liverpool Labour Party Temporary Co-ordinating Committee in March 1986 illustrated the problem for the Labour leadership. Even when the Liverpool party is reorganised, with two full-time organisers appointed by Walworth Road, and several leading figures have been expelled, other Militant members are ready to take their places. For instance, a long-standing Militant member and former councillor, Ted Mooney, was elected the Temporary Co-ordinating Committee's treasurer, and another tendency member, Phil Rowe, became its secretary. It was thought that Mooney would be Militant's candidate for Mulhearn's job as DLP president once Mulhearn was finally expelled.

Attempts by the TGWU and the GMBATU to reorganise their branches in Liverpool will not eradicate Militant's union power bases overnight. Meanwhile, the Liverpool Labour Left group, set up in October 1985 with Neil Kinnock's backing to pose a left-wing alternative to Militant, is still weak. With hundreds of Militant members in Liverpool, killing off the tendency there will be an almost impossible operation. Moreover, if Militant's influence and strength in Liverpool does eventually decline, it will not be because of the action taken by the Labour leadership, but because of the tendency's own tactical errors over the past few years, and its remarkable record of antagonising large sections of the Merseyside Labour movement.

The same is true on a national scale. Undoubtedly Militant is in trouble. For the first quarter of 1986, for instance, the tendency's Fighting Fund raised only £41,653, the lowest total for many quarters.[1]

The decision made by Militant around 1981 to concentrate on recruitment is one of the root causes of the tendency's current problems. Instead of bringing members in gradually, giving each one the slow initiation process, there was a sudden dash for growth. 'Get 'em in first, educate 'em later', was the new philosophy. In its immediate objectives the strategy brought quick results in terms of a large increase in membership. But there were also major organisational difficulties in terms of members' commitment, their contributions, and their tendency to quit. Furthermore the new strategy entailed a much higher profile for Militant. Every opportunity had to be seized to win new recruits for the organisation

– election campaigns, work in YTURC and among school students, campaigns in unions such as the CPSA, above all Liverpool. That meant treading on other people's toes and antagonising left-wingers who might normally have defended the tendency. The older, experienced cadres seemed to get overwhelmed by the younger Hatton-worshipping comrades, who had little of the experience and diplomacy of practical politics and who rarely stopped to think about who they might be offending. In the four years since 1982, Militant has managed to upset nearly all of its former allies on the left. And nowhere illustrates this better than Liverpool.

In the climate of realignment on the left, such errors will be seized on by those wanting to distance themselves from the tendency. Those who have long had differences on policy matters are now taking the opportunity to point them out. The statement issued by three left-wing NEC members in May 1986, attacking Militant politically, illustrated the tendency's increasing isolation on the left. Michael Meacher, Eric Clarke of the NUM (one of the seven who had walked out of the March NEC), and Margaret Beckett, co-author of the Liverpool minority report, had all opposed the idea of expulsions. 'From Northern Ireland, through nuclear weapons to positive discrimination,' the three argued, 'the policies advocated by Militant are often reactionary and outdated. On issues like women's organisation or black sections, even though opinion on the left may be divided, Militant can be relied on to vote solidly with the right.'[2]

Many in the Labour Party now believe the party's rules need to be changed radically if the NEC is to avoid the kind of legal difficulties it encountered in both 1982–83 and 1986. Many in the party support the idea of an independent tribunal, totally separate from the NEC, to deal with disciplinary matters. In addition the leadership feels that the party ought to introduce a 'bringing into disrepute' rule to tackle Militant, similar to those in many union rulebooks, since the problems of proving somebody is a member of Militant are just too great. It is then of course a question of how such a rule is interpreted.

Militant is going to find life much more difficult in future, although not really because of the recent well-publicised onslaught upon it by the Labour leadership. Indeed, if anything, the Liverpool inquiry and hearings may have helped bolster the tendency, giving it an issue to campaign on, at a time when the organisation was showing cracks and signs of weakness.

Nevertheless, from Neil Kinnock's point of view the attack on the Liverpool party will probably turn out to have been worthwhile, simply because of the 'Falklands' factor, the need to be *seen* to take tough action, *à la* Thatcher.

The expulsion of Derek Hatton and Tony Mulhearn will be viewed in the eyes of the public as tackling Militant, although in reality the end of their careers in public life will have more to do with the Liverpool district auditor than the Labour National Executive. Moreover, such expulsions will do nothing to tackle the thousands of other Militant members, or to prise away Militant's grip on the Labour Party Young Socialists.

Although Militant's difficulties coincide with action by the leadership, they have little to do with it in reality. Militant's problems have more to do with internal factors and wider political currents – the so-called realignment of the left.

Neil Kinnock may *appear* to win his Falklands War, but in this war there can be no clear-cut victory; his troops will endure constant guerrilla attack. There will be no surrender document – not even an internal one!

With the presence of Militant members in Parliament and now in the leadership of the biggest civil service union, the CPSA, Militant looks set to stay in the headlines for some time to come.

Militant's march, though faltering a little, has not yet been halted.

AFTERWORD

Militant did indeed make headlines for several years after this book was last published in 1986. Two years later, they even staged what they said was their biggest-ever gathering, with 8,000 people at Alexandra Palace in north London (though one should treat Militant figures with scepticism). Local Labour parties continued to take action against leading Militant activists, and the tendency reckoned that, by 1991, 219 people had been expelled from the party.

In response, Militant concentrated more on its work in outside protest organisations. Perhaps the greatest of these was the anti-poll tax movement against the Thatcher government's community charge on all individual residents as a replacement to the local authority rating system that taxed properties. Militant played a leading role in protests and formed anti-poll tax unions, initially in Scotland (where the tax was introduced first), but later elsewhere. The tendency had a policy of encouraging supporters not to pay the charge, and the Militant MP Terry Fields was jailed for sixty days for non-payment, while several other Militant members went to prison for similar offences around the same time.

Militant also formed the All Britain Anti-Poll Tax Federation, which organised the famous demonstration in London in March 1990 that led to violent clashes with the police in Trafalgar Square and degenerated into one of the worst political riots in post-war history. Militant would subsequently claim credit for the fall of Margaret Thatcher at the end of 1990, since the poll tax – seen very much as her policy – was a prime factor in the disquiet among Conservative MPs (and the tax was rapidly abolished by her successor John Major). However, most analysts would argue that Tory divisions over Europe were the more immediate cause of Thatcher's downfall.

The following year, 1991, saw the most dramatic changes in Militant's history. First, buoyed by the success of its anti-poll tax work, the organisation decided to set up a new independent structure in Scotland – Scottish Militant Labour – which began operating more openly than its English and Welsh counterparts. Then, for the first time, Militant began to challenge the Labour Party in elections, standing against official Labour candidates. This first occurred with five broad-left candidates in the 1991 council elections in Liverpool. Later that year, after the death of Eric Heffer, Militant failed to stop Labour picking as its candidate for the subsequent by-election Peter Kilfoyle, the organiser who had worked against the tendency on Merseyside for several years. Instead, they put up Militant member Lesley Mahmood as the 'Walton Real Labour' candidate. She came a poor third in the by-election, with 6.5 per cent of the vote. It was a dismal outcome in the very seat where Militant had started forty years before, and a sign that Militant was in serious decline.

These were difficult times, of course, for Marxists of every type. Militant had always been strong critics of the USSR and its grip on Eastern Europe, but the fall of the Berlin Wall in 1989 and the consequent collapse of Communist parties in Eastern Europe were hugely symbolic. In the public mind, full-blooded socialism had been seen not just to have failed, but in particular, parties run along strict Marxist–Leninist lines had finally been exposed as corrupt, tyrannical, inefficient and deeply unpopular. And the collapse of Communism almost everywhere in Europe followed other trends that made Militant's work more difficult, such as the decline in heavy industry, the weakening of trade unions, and a loss of public confidence in the virtues of the state. Where the left had made progress in recent times, it was often around social causes such as feminism, anti-racism and gay rights – issues on which Militant had often been seen as unsympathetic.

It was no surprise, therefore, that 1991 also saw the most serious divide in Militant's history. Amazingly, given the habit of British Trotskyist groups to split and split again over minor issues of doctrine, it was the first serious breakaway from the RSL (or Militant) in four decades.

Ted Grant had found himself increasingly at odds with Peter Taaffe and the rest of the leadership. Grant had voted for the new Scottish organisation, but had opposed non-payment of the poll tax and the standing of candidates against Labour, and he urged that the RSL should remain an 'entrist' group within the Labour Party (even though he himself had been excluded from Labour membership for the past eight years). Taaffe and the majority, however, argued that life had become increasingly difficult within the Labour Party, in part because of disciplinary action against the tendency. When they made an impact anywhere, Labour organisers quickly took action against them. Yet, there was little point in lying low.

The Militant Executive Committee met in July 1991 to consider two opposing resolutions. The majority motion – to leave the Labour Party – was agreed by forty-six votes to three. Grant's minority resolution, maintaining the status quo – entrism – was lost by forty-three votes to three. At an RSL conference in Bridlington that autumn, the new position – known as the 'Open Turn', or 'Scottish Turn' – was endorsed by 93 per cent of the delegates.

Ted Grant was then expelled by the RSL, along with his supporters, including Alan Woods and Rob Sewell. With no appreciation of the irony, the *Militant* newspaper accused Grant and his friends of 'plans to launch a monthly magazine, moving as soon as possible, to a fortnightly and a weekly. They now have their own small premises and their own staff and are raising their own funds.'[†] That, of course, was exactly what Militant itself had been accused of doing within the Labour Party for thirty years. Militant leaders who complained of witch-hunts by the Labour hierarchy had now ruthlessly expelled their 78-year-old figurehead from the party he had founded, built, inspired and led.

The majority group, still led by Peter Taaffe, changed its name to Militant Labour and retained the British franchise of the

---

† *Militant*, 24 January 1992.

Committee for a Workers' International. In 1997, the organisation adopted its current name – the Socialist Party – while the *Militant* newspaper, after thirty-three years, became *The Socialist*. In Scotland, Socialist Militant Labour became the Scottish Socialist Party (SSP), and continued to operate at arm's length from its sister party south of the border. The chief Militant organiser in Liverpool during the 1980s, Richard 'Richie' Venton, moved to Scotland to run the SSP and teamed up with the charismatic Tommy Sheridan, a poll tax refusenik who was jailed in 1992 for his role in a public protest. In character, Sheridan was a kind of Scottish Derek Hatton.

The Grant faction, meanwhile, readopted the old title of Socialist Appeal, after the newspaper they relaunched (which continues to this day); they also formed a new overseas body, the International Marxist Tendency. Grant died in 2006 at the age of ninety-three (when his obituaries finally revealed for the first time that he had been born with the name Isaac Blank), but his close friend Alan Woods remains active in the organisation. After Woods held several meetings with the late Venezuelan president Hugo Chávez, some observers suggested he was one of the Venezuelan leader's closest advisers, especially when Chávez revealed on television that he was reading one of Woods's books 'in great detail'.

What of the Militant MPs? The contingent in the Commons rose to three with the election of Pat Wall for Bradford North at the 1987 election, though Wall died three years later. The Labour high command was surprisingly slow to take action against the other two Militant MPs, partly because of their local popularity. Both Terry Fields and Dave Nellist were deselected as Labour candidates a few months before the 1992 election, though there was some delay in Nellist's case after he was picked as the *Spectator* magazine's 'Backbencher of the Year'. At the election, both men stood in their old seats as independents. Nellist came third with almost 29 per cent of the vote in Coventry South-East, yet only 351 votes behind the Labour winner; Fields fared less well, with just 14 per cent in Liverpool Broadgreen. Fields never stood for election again; nor, before he died in 2008, did he ever join his Militant colleagues in their new Socialist Party. Nellist, in contrast, joined Taaffe's new party and has stood under various Socialist labels for one of the Coventry seats at every election since then. He enjoyed a genuine popularity in the city and from 1998 to 2012 he was also a socialist councillor in Coventry, even helping a couple of party colleagues to win seats on the council.

Elsewhere, however, the Socialist Party has performed very badly in elections since Militant left the Labour Party in 1991, even though it has generally stood in alliance with other socialist groups. In 2010 and 2015, the party stood as part of the Trade Unionist and Socialist Coalition (TUSC). In 2010, thirty-eight TUSC candidates got just 12,275 votes between them, while four Socialist Party candidates standing as Socialist Alternative got a further 3,298 votes. In 2015, 136 TUSC candidates won just 36,327 votes in all – fewer than 270 each, on average.

In Scotland, however, Militant's heirs were markedly more successful at first, thanks in part to the dynamic role of Tommy Sheridan in running the anti-poll tax campaign. In Glasgow Pollok in 1992 – while he was still in prison – he got almost 20 per cent of the vote. Scottish Militant Labour joined with others to form the Scottish Socialist Alliance, which in turn became the Scottish Socialist Party (SSP) in 1998, with Sheridan as convenor. In the first Scottish Parliament elections in 1999, Sheridan was elected for the Glasgow area, and in 2003 the party fared even better, winning six MSPs under the proportional representation system.

But the SSP fell apart over when Tommy Sheridan was involved in an astonishing sex scandal, the repercussions of which dragged on for more than ten years. The *News of the World* alleged that Sheridan had not only had two extra-marital affairs, but also attended swingers' parties in Manchester. Sheridan's libel action against the tabloid paper split the SSP executive, with a majority giving evidence against him and a small minority in his favour. He won the trial, and £200,000 in damages, but when the *News of the World* began gathering evidence to appeal, Sheridan's case began to unravel. In 2010, he was convicted of perjury and jailed for three years. Forced out of the leadership by these battles, Sheridan quit the party and formed a breakaway group, Solidarity, but it has enjoyed no success. And the SSP is now a shadow of its former self – its four candidates gained just 895 votes at the 2015 general election.

In Liverpool, meanwhile, in 1987, the year after the leading Militant figures were expelled from the Labour Party, the district auditor succeeded in his efforts to have forty-seven left-wing Labour councillors disqualified from office for five years and surcharged £333,000. In the decades since then, the Liverpool Labour Party has in some ways returned to the politics of the pre-Militant era. None of Liverpool's five Labour MPs are even very left wing these days, and none of them nominated Jeremy Corbyn for Labour leader in 2015. Liverpool is now run by another boss figure, Joe Anderson, who became the city's first elected mayor in 2012. In his previous role as Labour leader of the council, Anderson introduced the post of elected mayor without holding a public referendum (unlike all other English cities, where elected mayors were adopted by popular consent).

In the 2012 mayoral election, TUSC stood Tony Mulhearn, who since his expulsion from the Labour Party had spent several years as a taxi driver in the city. He came fifth, with less than 5 per cent, though with a few more votes than the Conservative.

Derek Hatton left Militant as long ago as 1988, claiming that membership was incompatible with his business activities – and, he might have added, his lifestyle. In the mid-1990s, Hatton was twice put on trial. In the first case, in 1993, as a result of police Operation Cheetah, he was accused of lining his pockets by helping businessmen secure favourable land deals on council sites in Liverpool. Two years later, he was in the dock accused of an insurance swindle against the Norwich Union. In both trials Hatton was acquitted, and later complained of being the victim of an establishment 'vendetta' over his work with Militant.

Hatton's entrepreneurial activities have included developing internet sites, helping firms set up bike-to-work programmes, and he has sold villas and other property in Cyprus. Hatton has also operated in public relations; been a presenter with Talk Sport and other radio stations; worked as a male model; acted as an after-dinner speaker; and, in 1991, he even appeared as King Rat in pantomime. He is now a multi-millionaire.

At least two former members of Militant – Greg Pope and Ian Pearson – became MPs in the Blair–Brown years, with Pope serving as a whip, and Pearson rising to become a Treasury minister.

Andrew Glyn, the Oxford University tutor who'd acted for several years as Militant's economist before he left the organisation around 1985, died in 2007. Most of Glyn's obituaries ignored his work for Militant – as if it was an embarrassment to be airbrushed from history – but the tributes did mention his two most distinguished students – brothers from north London whom he'd known since they were children. Both David and Ed Miliband had been attracted to Glyn's college, Corpus Christi, by his presence there, and later described him as a huge influence on their politics. David Miliband, who years later edited a book with Glyn on the subject of inequality, had economics tutorials from him while Glyn was still running the Oxford Militant branch. Ed Miliband, who described Glyn as 'a friend', was taught by him several years after he'd split with the organisation.

Other Militant figures have also enjoyed considerable success after leaving the tendency, assisted by the formidable organisational and speaking skills they acquired during their years inside the RSL. In 1998, this author teamed up with former Militant full-timer Andy Walsh (another of those jailed for refusing to pay the poll tax), who had become chairman of the Independent Manchester United Supporters' Association (IMUSA) in a successful campaign against BSkyB's proposed takeover of United. Today, Walsh is chief executive of FC United of Manchester, the non-league club formed in 2005 by disillusioned United fans who were unhappy with the club subsequently being bought by the Glazer family. Another Militant figure, Kevin Miles, who played a major role in the All Britain Anti-Poll Tax Federation, now runs the Football Supporters' Federation. Phil Frampton campaigns against child abuse, having written an excellent book about his childhood as a Barnardo boy. Bob Wylie and Cheryl Varley went on to successful careers as BBC journalists. Wylie has now moved into public relations and is producing corporate videos.

Between 2007 and 2015, there were several stories about Derek Hatton rejoining the Labour Party and even standing for Parliament again. In 2015, he even claimed to have been given a new Labour membership card and announced he would be backing Jeremy Corbyn, though Labour HQ quickly said it was a mistake and purged him from the voting list. However, the Labour deputy leadership contender Tom Watson was also embarrassed to discover on his crowd-sourcing fund-raising website that Hatton had donated £100 to his campaign. By a strange twist, it had been Watson's job, as a teenage member of staff at Labour headquarters in 1986, to welcome the Liverpool Militants to the building and look after them during the famous hearings for their expulsion. What's more, Watson discovered that next to Hatton's name in the donors' list was Larry Whitty, who'd been Labour Party general secretary at the time of the expulsions.

Jeremy Corbyn's election as Labour leader gave the Socialist Party, like every group on the left, new impetus. In August 2015, a month before Corbyn was formally elected, *The Socialist* added the strap 'formerly Militant' to its masthead, with the distinctive old orange logo. It was as if Militant had almost become respectable, or at least a selling point.

Yet, Jeremy Corbyn's extraordinary success poses big dilemmas for both sides. Should the Socialist Party and the wider left-wing coalition to which it belongs, TUSC, now cease independent activity and rejoin Corbyn's new left-wing party? If they don't, TUSC and the Socialist Party are likely to fare even more poorly in elections, and become even more of an irrelevance. For the time being, the two organisations have decided to see how Labour evolves under the new Labour leader.

For Corbyn himself, the problem is even more acute. How can the former convenor of the campaign against the witch-hunt now prevent people from holding Labour membership cards when he passionately believed they never should have been expelled from the party in the first place? The case for re-admission would be even stronger were these former Militant members to pledge not to stand against Labour again in elections.

Yet, if the successors to Militant are welcomed back, Jeremy Corbyn would then face the questions that troubled Michael Foot, Neil Kinnock and their predecessors. Can the Labour Party afford to have no ideological boundary on its left flank? Are socialists of any stripe welcome to join, even those committed to achieve power by revolutionary means rather than through the ballot box? And can a party again tolerate an organisation in its midst that operates as secretly and dishonestly as Militant long did – the ultimate party within a party?

Appendix 1

MILITANT CANDIDATES STANDING FOR THE LABOUR PARTY NATIONAL EXECUTIVE, 1971-83

Between 1971 and 1983 Militant candidates stood annually in contests for the seven constituency seats on the National Executive. They were never successful, nor did they even come close. But this section is always dominated by prominent MPs, and Militant candidates have frequently received more votes than any other candidate who is not an MP or a former MP. Over the years such well-known MPs as Joe Ashton, Bob Cryer, David Ennals, Stuart Holland, Les Huckfield, Gerald Kaufman, Stan Orme, Merlyn Rees, John Smith and Peter Shore have sometimes polled fewer votes than Militant candidates. In this period the lowest number of votes needed to secure election has ranged from 225,000 to 290,000. Apart from a handful of parties with a very high membership, each constituency has 1,000 votes. Since 1983 the votes of each constituency delegate have been publicly recorded and Militant has stopped standing candidates.

Year	Candidate	Votes polled
1971	Ray Apps	31,000
1972	Pat Craven	51,000
1973	David Skinner[2]	144,000[1]
	Ray Apps	81,000
1974	Ray Apps	54,000[1]
1975	Maureen Golby	75,000[1]
1976	David White[3]	57,000[1]
	John Ferguson	56,000[1]
1977	Pat Wall	67,000[1]
	Ray Apps	66,000[1]
1978	Nick Bradley[4]	97,000[1]
	Ray Apps	57,000[1]
	Pat Wall	51,000[1]
1979	Ray Apps	73,000
	Pat Wall	69,000
1980	Pat Wall	45,000
	Ray Apps	43,000
1981	Ray Apps	46,000
	Pat Wall	45,000
1982	Pat Wall	103,000[1,5]
1983	Terry Fields MP[6]	
	Pat Wall[6]	

Notes

1. The highest vote(s) for any candidate(s) not an MP or a former MP.
2. Skinner was not a Militant member, but was promoted by Militant as one of its candidates. His vote was probably exceptionally high because he was one of the disqualified Clay Cross councillors.

3. Although White, a GLC councillor, said he was a supporter of Militant's policies, and was supported by Militant, it is not clear whether he was actually a Militant member.

4. Retiring LPYS NEC member.

5. Terry Fields polled 1,305,000 votes in the trade union section.

6. Recorded votes for the first time – withdrew in the cause of 'left unity'.

Source: Labour Party Annual Conference Reports, 1971–83.

Appendix 2
MILITANT CANDIDATES IN ELECTIONS

The following abbreviations are used below: AP – Alliance Party; Con – Conservative; DLTUP – Derry Labour and Trade Union Party; DUP – Democratic Unionist; Ecol – Ecology Party; IIP – Irish Independence Party; Ind – Independent; IWRP – Isle of Wight Residents' Party; Lab – Labour; Lib – Liberal; Lib/All – Liberal Alliance; LTUG – Labour and Trade Union Group; NA – Noise Abatement; NF – National Front; OUP – Official Unionist Party; PSF – Provisional Sinn Féin; RC – Republican Clubs; SDLP – Social Democratic and Labour Party; SDP – Social Democratic Party; SDP/All – SDP Alliance; WP – Workers' Party.

MAY 1979 GENERAL ELECTION
National Lab–Con swing: 5.2 per cent

Crosby

Candidate	Votes polled	% of total
Page (Con)	34,768	56.9
Mulhearn, Tony	15,496	25.4
Hill (Lib)	9,302	15.2
Hussey (Ecol)	1,489	2.4

Swing to Con: 5.2 per cent.

Croydon Central

Candidate	Votes polled	% of total
Moore (Con)	26,457	52.5
White, David	18,499	36.7
Johnson (Lib)	5,112	10.1
Others	354	0.7

Swing to Con: 7.7 per cent. A larger than average swing in a seat once held by Labour.

Isle of Wight

Candidate	Votes polled	% of total
Ross (Lib)	35,889	48.2
Fishburn (Con)	35,537	47.7
Wilson, Cathy	3,014	4.0

Labour's vote fell from 13 to 4 per cent, partly as a result of long-term erosion by the Liberals.

Londonderry

Candidate	Votes polled	% of total
Ross (OUP)	31,592	49.7
Logue (SDLP)	19,185	30.2
Barr (AP)	5,830	9.2
McAteer (IIP)	5,489	8.6
Melough (RC)	888	1.4
Webster, Bill (DLTUP)	639	1.0

JUNE 1979 ELECTIONS TO THE EUROPEAN PARLIAMENT

Liverpool

Candidate	Votes polled	% of total
Hooper (Con)	49,646	45.2
Harrison, Terry	42,419	38.7
Clark (Lib)	17,650	16.1

The swing to the Conservatives of 11 per cent, based on the general election figures of only a month before, was the largest in the country. It was partly a result of the lowest turnout in the UK, 23.7 per cent.

JUNE 1983 GENERAL ELECTION

National Lab–Con swing: 3.9 per cent

Bradford North

Candidate	Votes polled	% of total
Lawler (Con)	16,094	34.3
Wall, Pat	14,492	30.9
Birkby (SDP/All)	11,962	25.5
Ford (Lab Ind)	4,018	8.6
Others	387	0.8

Pat Wall would have won this normally safe Labour seat had not the deselected MP, Ben Ford, stood as an Independent.

Brighton Kemptown

Candidate	Votes polled	% of total
Bowden (Con)	22,265	51.1
Fitch, Rod	12,887	29.6
Burke (SDP/All)	8,098	18.6
Budden (NF)	290	0.7

Swing to Con: 2.2 per cent. From 1964 to 1970 this was a Labour seat.

Coventry South-East

Candidate	Votes polled	% of total
Nellist, David	15,307	41.1
Arnold (Con)	12,625	33.9
Kilby (Lib/All)	9,323	25.0

Swing to Con: 4.2 per cent. David Nellist took over the seat from retiring Labour MP, William Wilson.

Isle of Wight

Candidate	Votes polled	% of total
Ross (Lib/All)	38,407	51.0
Bottomley (Con)	34,904	46.3
Wilson, Cathy	1,828	2.4
McDermott (IWRP)	208	0.3

Thought to be Labour's worst ever vote in a parliamentary election. Back in 1964 Labour polled 31.6 per cent of the votes, more than twice the Liberal vote.

Liverpool Broadgreen

Candidate	Votes polled	% of total
Fields, Terry	18,802	40.9
Dougherty (Con)	15,002	32.6
Pine (Ind Lib)	7,021	15.3
Crawshaw (SDP/All)	5,169	11.2

Swing to Lab: 4.8 per cent. The swing to Labour was probably aided by a split between the official SDP/Alliance candidate and an unofficial Liberal. Liverpool had an overall 2.4 per cent swing to Labour.

Belfast East

Candidate	Votes polled	% of total
Robinson (DUP)	17,631	45.3
Burchill (OUP)	9,642	24.8
Napier (AP)	9,373	24.1
Donaldson (PSF)	682	1.8
Tang, Muriel (LTUG)	584	1.5
Prendiville (SDLP)	519	1.3
Cullen (WP)	421	1.1
Boyd (NA)	59	0.2

A tiny share of the vote for Militant's Northern Irish section in a strongly Protestant seat, but it was a higher vote than the SDLP and compared favourably with the other left-wing parties.

Appendix 3
THE MILITANT LEADERSHIP

EXECUTIVE COMMITTEE

Peter Taaffe (general secretary)

Clare Doyle (treasurer)

Keith Dickinson

Ted Grant

Brian Ingham

Peter Jarvis

John Pickard

Rob Sewell

Roger Silverman

Lynn Walsh

Alan Woods

CENTRAL COMMITTEE

The above members plus:

Ray Apps; Bryan Beckingham; Jeremy Birch; Ed Bober; Nick Brooks; Muriel Browning; Laurence Coates; Dave Cotterill; Pat Craven; Margaret Creear; Bob Edwards; Robert Faulkes; Phil Frampton; Steve Glennon; Peter Hadden; Terry Harrison; Alan Hartley; Bill Hopwood; Jon Ingham; Wayne Jones; Bob Labi; Gerry Lerner; Steve Morgan; Bill Mullins; Chris Peace; Kevin Ramage; Tony Saunois; Alex Thraves; Richard Venton; Mike Waddington; Ed Waugh; Bill Webster; Bob Wylie.

Appendix 4
THE CONSTITUTION OF THE REVOLUTIONARY SOCIALIST LEAGUE/MILITANT (1962)

NAME:

Revolutionary Socialist League [RSL]. British Section of the Fourth International.

AIM:

Basing itself on the principles embodied in the first four Congresses of the Communist International and the World Conferences of the Fourth International the RSL strives to win the leadership of the working class for the establishment of a Workers' Government in Britain, and in collaboration with the world working and toiling masses to abolish classes and build the World Socialist order of society.

MEMBERSHIP:

Any person who accepts the principles and constitution of the RSL and who participates in its activities under the direction of its organs is eligible for membership.

Every member must be a member of a Branch but in exceptional conditions where no Branch exists may become a national member working under the control of the Executive Committee [EC].

Applications for membership must be made to the Branch except in those cases stated above, and must be ratified by the District Committee [DC] or Executive Committee. All so accepted will become probationary members for a period of three months.

Probationary members are entitled to the rights of members but may not be delegates or officers of the organisation. The length of probation may be extended or the member excluded.

BRANCHES:

The Unit of the RSL is the Branch which is based upon an industrial or area group of not less than three. Where the Branch is of sufficient size it may divide itself in agreement with the DC or EC. The Branch shall elect officials who will be responsible for the direction of local activity.

DISTRICT COMMITTEE:

Where more than one Branch exists within an area a District Committee shall be set up. The DC shall be composed of at least two members from each Branch and shall be responsible for the direction of all activities within the District.

NATIONAL COMMITTEE:

A National Committee [NC] shall be elected at the time of the

National Conference composed of twelve members – with at least one member drawn from each area. The National Committee shall have the authority of the National Conference in between such Conferences.

EXECUTIVE COMMITTEE:

An EC shall be elected at the National Committee and shall have the authority of that body in between its meetings. It shall be composed of at least seven members and must meet at least twice a month or when convened by the Secretariat. Each member must have a special responsibility or task.

NATIONAL CONFERENCE:

A National Conference of the membership represented by Delegates from Branches, District Committees, the Executive Committee members and other units as formed from time to time shall meet at least once per year.

The members or delegates from the EC and DCs shall be present in a consultative capacity, though they may be elected as Branch delegates.

Resolutions for the National Conference must be in the hands of the EC at least two months before the Conference and must be submitted to the membership not less than six weeks before the Conference. Emergency resolutions and amendments may be submitted up to the time of the Conference itself.

No binding mandate can be imposed on any delegate. The decisions on all questions shall be by a simple majority.

SPECIAL POWERS:

A control Commission can be elected by the National Committee as and when required. In the event of an emergency the National Committee shall have power to amend the Constitution.

MEMBERSHIP CONTRIBUTIONS:

Members' dues shall be a minimum of five shillings per week except in special cases where they may be fixed at a higher or lower level by the Branch Treasurer in agreement with the National Treasurer. In addition to the basic dues members will be required to contribute at least six pence per week for the International.

Members two months in arrears shall not have the right to vote. Members three months in arrears shall be considered lapsed after due notice from the treasurer.

Two-fifths of the dues shall be retained by the local Branch, three-fifths shall be sent to the National Treasurer.

Branches shall issue monthly reports of finances. The NC shall submit a balance sheet of all finances to the National Conference.

DEMOCRATIC RIGHTS AND DISCIPLINE:

All decisions of the governing bodies are binding upon all members and subordinate units. Any member violating these decisions shall be subjected to disciplinary action.

While co-operating in the carrying out of all democratic decisions all minorities have the right to present their viewpoint within the organisation, verbally and by means of the Internal Bulletin.

Any member subjected to disciplinary action is entitled to

appeal to the higher bodies and to the National Conference, the disciplinary action is meanwhile upheld. Members also have the right to appeal against the decision of the National Conference to the governing bodies of the Fourth International.

All officials of the party shall be subject to recall by the body appointing them. All property of the party vested in trustees and such shall be under the complete jurisdiction of the party.

All members holding public office, paid or otherwise, shall come under the complete control of the party and its organs.

All members of the RSL are required to enter the mass organisations of the working class under the direction of the party organs for the purpose of fulfilling the aims of the party.

Adopted by the National Conference March 1962.

Source: Deane Collection, Manchester Polytechnic

Appendix 5
THE CONSTITUTION OF THE COMMITTEE FOR THE WORKERS' INTERNATIONAL (CWI) (1974)

1 The objective of the CWI is to create a single worldwide organisation linking together all the proletarian and revolutionary militants in the world who accept its principles and programme, on the basis of the traditions of democratic centralism at local, national and international level, and of united action.

2 The CWI consists of affiliated national sections whose aim is the creation over the next period of mass revolutionary workers' parties.

3 Every section is based on the platform and accords with the structure defined and established by the conferences of the CWI.

4 The conferences of the CWI are the highest body of the organisation, and its decisions are binding on national sections.

5 An international conference will be held at least every two years, and if possible annually. Each fully affiliated national section will be represented equally by three voting delegates, regardless of the

size of the section. Individual members of affiliated organisations who come from countries where no section yet exists may attend as full delegates, to a maximum of three from each country.

6 Additional members of national sections, and sympathisers from countries where no section yet exists, may attend the conference with the approval of a majority of voting delegates, with full speaking rights and consultative votes.

7 An International Executive Committee (IEC) shall be established, consisting of one member nominated by each of the most important national sections. The IEC will meet every three months, and will have the power to co-opt additional members.

8 Each national section must pay to the IEC the equivalent of £5 per member per year.

9 An international bulletin will be published every three months, to which each section must contribute regular material.

10 The most important documents of each section must be circulated to the other affiliated organisations.

11 The IEC may call seminars, camps, cadre schools, etc., to which all members and sympathisers are invited.

12 This Constitution comes into force on 21 April 1974 and may be amended by a simple majority of voting delegates at future conferences.

Adopted unanimously by delegates from established organisations in Britain, Ireland, Sweden and Germany, and by individual members from Spain, Ceylon, Pakistan, Jamaica and Iraq.

Source: 'CWI Bulletin No. 1' (Militant int. doc.), July 1974, pp 2–3.

Appendix 6
THE GROWTH OF MILITANT MEMBERSHIP, 1965–86

These figures are Militant's own internal claims, and there is strong reason to believe they may be exaggerated.

1965	100	1979	1,621
1971	217	1980	1,850
1972	354	1981	2,545
1973	464	1982	3,438
1974	517	1983	4,313
1975	775	1984	c.6,000
1976	1,030	1985	c.7,000
1977	1,193	1986	8,100+
1978	1,433		

NOTES AND
REFERENCES

Where the source is an internal Militant document I have indicated this by the words 'Militant int. doc.' The tendency's internal documents have not been published anywhere in full, although P. Shipley (*The Militant Tendency*, Foreign Affairs Publishing Co., London, 1983) has published lengthy extracts from some of them. The best publicly available collection of Militant internal documents is in the archives of the Labour Party headquarters. LPACR refers to the Labour Party Annual Conference Report, the account of conference proceedings published each year a few months afterwards. NEC Report refers to the annual report submitted to the conference by the Labour Party National Executive Committee.

The Harvester Press has an almost complete run of *Militant*, together with some of the pre-Militant 'Grantite' publications, in its microfilm collection, 'The Left in Britain' (Harvester/Primary Social Sources, Brighton) available in many academic libraries. But since this material was supplied by Militant itself, it lacks many of the earlier publications from the RCP and RSL. Some of the 'Grantite' publications from the 1930s, 1940s and 1950s can be found in the Haston Collection at the University of Hull, in the Deane Collection at Manchester Polytechnic, and in a library of Trotskyist literature at the University of Warwick.

1 'I CALL THIS AN OUTRAGE' (PP 1–13)

1   NEC Papers, April 1954.
2   *Tribune*, 13 August 1954.
3   *Tribune*, 18 June 1982, 25 June 1982 and 1 October 1982.
4   *Lenin on Britain*, Martin Lawrence, London, 1934, p. 257.
5   D. Hyde, *I Believed*, William Heinemann, London, 1950, pp 65–6.
6   Ibid.
7   Quoted in B. Reed and G. Williams, *Denis Healey and the Policies of Power*, Sidgwick and Jackson, London, 1971, p. 25.
8   *Socialist Outlook* was never on the Proscribed List, though.
9   *Tribune*, 13 August 1954.
10 S. Hoggart and D. Leigh, *Michael Foot: a Portrait*, Hodder and Stoughton, London, 1981, p. 112.
11 Speech reported in *The Times*, 13 October 1952.
12 See I. Mikardo, *New Socialist*, March/April 1982.
13 L. Hunter, *The Road to Brighton Pier*, Arthur Barker, London, 1959, p. 8.
14 Ibid, p. 7.
15 Author's calculation based on P. Norton, *Dissension in the House of Commons*, Macmillan, London, 1975.

2 THE PERMANENT REVOLUTIONARY (PP 14–31)

1   I. Deutscher, *The Prophet Outcast*, Oxford University Press, Oxford, 1979, pp 43–4.
2   L. Trotsky, 'The Lever of a Small Group' (1933), *Writings of Leon Trotsky 1933–34*, Pathfinder, New York, 1975, pp 125–6.
3   L. Trotsky, 'Interview with Collins' (1936), *Writings of Leon Trotsky 1935–36*, Pathfinder, New York, 1977, pp 379, 382.
4   T. Ali, *The Coming British Revolution*, Jonathan Cape, London, 1972, p. 139.
5   *New Leader*, 8 March 1935. For further details on Grant's arrival see S. Bornstein and A. Richardson, *Against the Stream, A History of the Trotskyist Movement in Britain 1924–38*, Socialist Platform, London, 1986, pp 169–70.
6   M. Haston (formerly Lee), interview with author.
7   *Preparing for Power*, Workers' International League, London, 1942, p. 9.
8   War Cabinet papers, The Trotskyist Movement in Great Britain', 13 April 1944, available at Public Records Office.

9 Ibid.
10 Ibid.
11 F. Ward, interview with author.
12 S. Bornstein, unpublished interview with Tom Forester.
13 T. Grant, rough draft of 'Letter to the Members', sent to J. Deane, February 1949, Deane Collection, Manchester Polytechnic.
14 F. Ward, interview with author.
15 *Workers Press*, 15 January 1986.
16 F. Ward, interview with author.
17 *International Socialist*, February 1952.
18 For instance, *Militant*, 16 September 1983.

3 THE LIVERPOOL CONNECTION (PP 32-47)

1 See S. Bornstein and A. Richardson, *Against the Stream, A History of the British Trotskyist Movement in Britain 1924–38*, Socialist Platform, London, 1986, p. 282.
2 See the published guide to the Jimmy Deane Collection, Manchester Polytechnic, Manchester, 1983.
3 T. Lane, *Marxism Today*, November 1978.
4 *New Statesman*, 31 July 1964.
5 R. Baxter, 'The Liverpool Labour Party, 1918–1963', unpublished DPhil thesis, Oxford, 1969.
6 See P. Wall, *The Guardian*, 16 August 1982.
7 Simon Frazer, former secretary of the Liverpool Labour Party and Trades Council, quoted in P. J. Waller, *Democracy and Sectarianism: A Political and Social History of Liverpool 1868-1939*, Liverpool University Press, Liverpool, 1981, p. 348.
8 R. Baxter, op. cit.
9 J. Braddock, letter to M. Phillips, 3 April 1959, Labour Party archives.
10 T. Grant, letter to J. Deane, 14 August 1954, Deane Collection, Manchester Polytechnic.
11 T. Grant, letter to J. Deane, 12 January 1955, Deane Collection, Manchester Polytechnic.
12 L. Kirton, interview with author.
13 J. Deane, interview with author.
14 T. Grant, letter to J. Deane, 14 June 1956, Deane Collection, Manchester Polytechnic.
15 *Workers' International Review*, April/May 1957.
16 E. Heffer, letter to J. Deane, 31 March 1957, Deane Collection, Manchester Polytechnic.
17 *Socialist Fight*, January 1958.
18 *Socialist Fight*, June 1963.
19 *Militant*, January 1970.
20 F. Chapple, *Sparks Fly!*, Michael Joseph, London, 1984, p. 60.
21 'Problems of Entrism', (RSL int. doc.), March 1959.
22 'Entrism' (Militant int. doc.), November 1973.

23 E. Hillman, interview with author.
24 E. Hillman, *Notes on Council Work*, February 1961, Deane Collection, Manchester Polytechnic.
25 T. Harrison, interview with author.
26 L. Kirton, interview with author.

4 ENTER MILITANT (PP 48–68)

1 As reported by J. Deane, interview with author.
2 *Militant*, October 1964.
3 Ibid.
4 Ibid.
5 Ibid.
6 Ibid.
7 *The Week*, no. 3, January 1964.
8 Minutes of RSL–IG leadership meeting, Sevenoaks, 13 September 1964, Deane Collection, Manchester Polytechnic.
9 Quoted by N. Beloff in *The Observer*, 31 August 1975.
10 Letter to G. Kennedy, 6 October 1964, quoted in Beloff, op. cit.
11 Letter to G. Kennedy, December 1964, quoted in Beloff, op. cit.
12 Letter to G. Kennedy, January 1965, quoted in Beloff, op. cit.
13 Bob Pennington, quoted in Beloff, op. cit.
14 *Militant*, May 1965.
15 Z. Layton-Henry, *Journal of Contemporary History*, 1976, p. 275.
16 P. Abrams and A. Little, *British Journal of Sociology*, 1965, p. 321.
17 Report of the Committee of Enquiry into Party Organisation (the Simpson Committee), Labour Party, 1968, pp 11–14.
18 N. Vann, interview with author.
19 Ibid.
20 Ibid.
21 'British Perspectives and Tasks' (Militant int. doc.), March 1972.
22 Claimed in 'CWI Bulletin', no. 1 (Militant int. doc.), July 1974.
23 LPACR, 1972, pp 178–93.
24 LPACR, 1973, pp 170–88.
25 LPACR, 1971, p. 156; 1972, p. 174; 1973, p. 159.
26 'British Perspectives and Tasks 1974' (Militant int. doc.), June 1974, p. 37.
27 Ibid, p. 19.
28 Ibid, p. 21.

5 POLICIES AND PERSPECTIVES (PP 69–95)

1 A. Glyn, *Capitalist Crisis – Tribune's 'Alternative Strategy' or Socialist Plan*, Militant, London, 1983 edn, p. 71.
2 P. Taaffe, 'What We Stand For', Militant, February 1986, pp 2–4.
3 L. Trotsky, *The Transitional Programme* (1938), *Documents of the Fourth International*, Pathfinder, New York, 1973, p. 183.
4 Glyn, op. cit., p. 70.

5   'Bulletin of Marxist Studies' (Militant int. doc.), spring 1985, p. 8.
6   'Bulletin of Marxist Studies' (Militant int. doc.), summer 1985, p. 9.
7   *Militant International Review,* January 1973.
8   T. Grant, *British Perspectives: A Supplement to Capitalism at an Impasse,* Militant, London, November 1985.
9   T. Grant, *Capitalism at an Impasse: Marxist Perspectives for Britain,* Militant, London, January 1985, p. 7.
10 T. Grant, *British Perspectives: A Supplement to Capitalism at an Impasse,* Militant, London, November 1985.
11 'British Perspectives and Tasks 1972', (Militant int. doc.), p. 8.
12 T. Grant, *British Perspectives: A Supplement to Capitalism at an Impasse,* Militant, London, November 1985.
13 Glyn, op. cit., p. 68.
14 T. Grant, *British Perspectives: A Supplement to Capitalism at an Impasse,* Militant, London, November 1985.
15 'Bulletin of Marxist Studies' (Militant int. doc.), spring 1985, p. 8.
16 T. Pearse (P. Taaffe), 'Bulletin' (Militant int. doc.), January/February 1980.
17 *Sunday Times,* 7 March 1982.
18 'British Perspectives and Tasks 1974' (Militant int. doc.), June 1974, p. 33.
19 'Programme of the International' (Militant int. doc.), 3rd edn, January 1980, p. 16.
20 *Militant International Review,* no. 15, 1978.
21 'World Perspectives 1984' (Militant int. doc.), p. 44.
22 Ibid.
23 *Militant,* 21 May 1982.
24 *Militant,* 7 May 1982.
25 *Militant,* 25 September 1981.
26 TP (P. Taaffe), 'Bulletin' (Militant int. doc.), November/December 1979, p. 4.
27 'Bulletin of Marxist Studies' (Militant int. doc.), summer 1985, p. 14.
28 Ibid, p. 15.
29 *Northern Ireland: A Marxist Analysis,* Militant, London, 1984, p. 23.
30 'World Perspectives 1984' (Militant int. doc.), p. 36.
31 *Militant Irish Monthly,* April 1986.
32 'British Perspectives 1977' (Militant int. doc.), 1977, p. 29.
33 'British Perspectives and Tasks, 1972' (Militant int. doc.), p. 17.
34 T. Grant, *Capitalism at an Impasse: Marxist Perspectives for Britain,* Militant, London, January 1985, p. 25.
35 'Bulletin of Marxist Studies' (Militant int. doc.), summer 1985, p. 10.
36 Ibid, p. 5.
37 Ibid, p. 8.
38 *The Miners' Unfinished War,* Militant, London, 1986, p. 2.
39 T. Grant, *British Perspectives: A Supplement to Capitalism at an Impasse,* Militant, London, November 1985.
40 'Bulletin of Marxist Studies' (Militant int. doc.), summer 1984, p. 2.
41 'Bulletin of Marxist Studies' (Militant int. doc.), spring 1985, p. 8.
42 A. Woods and T. Grant, *Lenin and Trotsky – What They Really Stood For,* Militant, 1976 edn, pp 147–8.

6 OPERATION ICEPICK (PP 96–114)

1   NEC Papers, January 1977.
2   B. Clarke, interview with author.
3   See *Militant*, 8 April 1983 or 4 April 1986.
4   See D. Kogan and M. Kogan, *The Battle for the Labour Party*, Kogan Page, London, 1983.
5   LPACR, 1939, p. 322.
6   Lord Underhill, interview with author.
7   Ibid.
8   NEC Papers, November 1975.
9   Ibid.
10 Ibid.
11 For instance, B. Castle, *The Castle Diaries*, Weidenfeld & Nicolson, London, 1980, p. 565.
12 Ibid.
13 *The Times*, 12 December 1975.
14 *The Observer*, 31 August 1975.
15 *The Observer*, 21 September 1975.
16 *The Times*, 21 July 1975.
17 See P. McCormick, *Enemies of Democracy*, Temple Smith, London, 1979.
18 Bradley lost 37–20 to a former Tribunite MP, James Dickens, who then resigned as candidate just before the 1979 election, when the Newham party refused to give overwhelming support to his election manifesto.
19 'British Perspectives and Tasks 1975' (Militant int. doc.), 1975, p. 14.
20 *Daily Telegraph*, 15 January 1977.
21 The title seems to have been used first by the *Daily Express*, 24 November 1976.
22 *Daily Telegraph*, 24 November 1976.
23 NEC Papers, January 1977.
24 *The Times*, 26 November 1976.
25 *The Guardian*, 13 December 1976.
26 Ibid.
27 *The Times*, 1, 2, 3, 4, 6 December 1976.
28 Report of the Special Committee to Examine the Documents on Entrism, LPACR, 1975, pp 383–5.
29 Reported in interviews with author by former members of Youth Committee.

7 THE ORGANISATION (PP 115–36)

1   Quoted in *Daily Mirror*, 26 September 1984.
2   *Liverpool Daily Post*, 11 December 1981.
3   'Entrism' (Militant int. doc.), November 1973.
4   Party Constitution and Standing Orders, Labour Party.

8 MILITANT'S MONEY (PP 137–55)

1   J. Kay and M. King, *The British Tax System*, OUP, Oxford, 1978, p. 199.
2   Accounts of WIR Publications Limited, 1976–7, available at Companies House.
3   T. Harrison, interview with author.

4   See letter from P. Taaffe to Labour Party general secretary, published in NEC Report, 1982, pp 136–9, together with *Militant*, 14 January 1983, and 13 January 1984. The 1984 and 1985 figures calculated from quarterly reports in *Militant*. Building Fund figures from *Militant*, 13 May 1986.

5   For instance, *Militant*, 13 December 1974.

6   *Militant*, 25 October 1974.

7   *Militant*, 1 November 1974.

8   A. Woods and T. Grant, *Lenin and Trotsky – What They Really Stood For*, International Publishers, Colombo, 1972, pp 153–72.

9   WIR Publications Limited, Articles of Association.

10 Cambridge Heath Press Limited, Articles of Association.

11 WIR Publications Limited, Register of Shareholders.

12 Accounts of WIR Publications Limited and Cambridge Heath Press Limited, although the accounts do not state specifically that the loans are from one company to the other, and there are other small loans by WIR Publications Limited.

13 WIR Publications Limited, annual accounts.

14 P. Taaffe's reply to Labour Party questionnaire, April 1980, printed in full in B. Baker, *The Far Left*, Weidenfeld & Nicolson, London, 1981, pp 36–9.

15 WIR Publications Limited, annual accounts 1973–81.

16 Taaffe, op. cit.

17 For instance, *Militant*, 5 January, 23 February 1973.

18 Interview with author.

19 Interview with author.

20 Interview with author.

21 *Militant*, 22 March 1985.

22 Claimed by ex-member Michael Gregory in his report to the Blackburn Labour Party, January 1983. Not published but reported in *The Times*, 21 February 1983, and *The Guardian*, 12 March 1983.

23 M. Gregory written evidence on Blackburn, R. Webb written evidence on Brixton and D. Nelson, interview with author.

24 P. Tatchell, *The Battle for Bermondsey*, Heretic Books, London, 1983, p. 120.

25 Accounts of London Region of NOLS, 1977–78.

26 Labour Co-ordinating Committee press release, 7 April 1985.

27 'Fighting Fund – Some Crucial Tasks' (Militant int. doc.), March 1986.

28 L. Walsh, interview given on BBC *Newsnight* in December 1985. An untransmitted exchange about Militant's finances went as follows: Q: It does come to substantial sums of money doesn't it, I mean, say, around 1 million a year or a little bit more? *Walsh*: Yes, but that's because of the dedication of our supporters and we believe that, despite criticism, it's a demonstration of our growing support.

29 Report of Houghton Committee on aid to political parties, HMSO, Cmnd 6601, 1976.

30 Estimate based upon annual accounts in 1985 NEC Report, Labour Party, London, 1985, and Houghton estimate of constituency party incomes.

31 Author's estimate based on conversations with Liberal Party officials.

32 Fabian Society Annual Report, 1984–85.

33 Accounts of Tribune Publications Limited, 1984–85.

9 MILITANT ABROAD (PP 156–76)

1 'CWI Bulletin No.1' (Militant int. doc.), July 1974, p. 10.
2 Ibid, p. 10.
3 G. Edwards (T. Grant), 'Bulletin of Marxist Studies' (Militant int. doc.), summer 1985, p. 11.
4 *Militant*, 26 April 1974.
5 'CWI Bulletin No.1' (Militant int. doc.), July 1974, p. 11.
6 'International Bulletin' (Militant int. doc.), February 1977.
7 'Bulletin of Marxist Studies' (Militant int. doc.), summer 1984, p. 6.
8 B. Toresson, quoted in M. Linton, *The Swedish Road To Socialism*, Fabian Society, London, 1985, p. 13.
9 M. Linton, op. cit., p. 13.
10 'CWI Bulletin No.1' (Militant int. doc.), July 1974, p. 16.
11 Documents of the Second National Consultative Conference of the African National Congress, Lusaka, June 1985.
12 *Daily Telegraph*, 3 May 1985.

10 THE MILITANT LIFE (PP 177–90)

1 As reported by ex-members who attended.
2 As reported by ex-member.
3 D. Mason, interview with author.
4 Ibid.
5 Ibid.
6 Ibid.
7 T. McDonald, interview with author.
8 Ibid.
9 Ibid.
10 Ibid.
11 Ibid.
12 Ibid.
13 R. Hart, interview with author.
14 Ibid.
15 M. Barnes, letter to *New Statesman*, 1 February 1980.
16 Barnes, interview with author.
17 Ibid.
18 Barnes, letter.
19 Barnes, interview.
20 Barnes, letter.
21 Barnes, interview.
22 Ibid.

11 THE SACRIFICIAL LAMBS (PP 191–221)

1 T. Forester, *New Society*, 10 January 1980.
2 *Daily Mirror*, 14 January 1980.
3 *Sunday Times*, 16 December 1979.

4   *New Society*, op. cit.
5   *New Statesman*, 18 January 1980.
6   BBC 2 *Newsnight*, 31 January 1980.
7   NEC Report, 1980, p. 7.
8   Lord Underhill, interview with author.
9   Both quoted in *Sunday Times*, 20 January 1980.
10 For instance, ITN's main news bulletin had a longer extension on the night of the deputy leadership election in 1981 than on the evening of the elections in 1983.
11 'British Perspectives and Tasks 1974' (Militant int. doc.), June 1974, p. 20.
12 *The Sun*'s headline 'Furious Foot Disowns Red Pete – Militant Will Never Be an MP' (4 December 1981) is one example of many. Long after Tatchell had made it clear that he was not a supporter of Militant, some papers referred to him as 'militant-tending' or having 'militant tendencies'. See P. Tatchell, *The Battle for Bermondsey*, Heretic Books, London, 1983, pp 58–61.
13 Tatchell, op. cit., pp 89, 96.
14 *Tribune*, 25 February 1983. See also article by Audrey Wise giving details of trivial items in regional staff's evidence.
15 F. Field, evidence to Labour Party enquiry.
16 *Sunday Times*, 7 March 1982.
17 Ibid.
18 *Daily Mail* and *Daily Telegraph*, 8 March 1982.
19 NEC Report, 1982, pp 133–42.
20 *Labour Weekly*, 25 June 1982.
21 Ibid.
22 *The Times*, 28 June 1982.
23 LPACR 1982, pp 40–53, for whole debate.
24 Ibid.
25 Ibid.
26 Ibid.
27 *Tribune*, 28 January 1983.
28 *The Guardian*, 28 October 1982.
29 NEC Report, 1982, p. 137.
30 R. Evans, interview with author.
31 Interview with author.
32 Militant's 'Application for Registration'; see *Militant*, 22 October 1982.
33 NEC Papers, November 1982.
34 NEC Papers (revised), November 1982.
35 *The Times*, 16 December 1982.
36 *The Guardian*, 16 December 1982.
37 NEC Papers, January 1983.
38 Ibid.
39 Interview with author.
40 For instance, *Daily Express*, 28 May 1983.

12 MILITANT MERSEYSIDE (PP 222–42)

1 *OPCS Monitor*, Office of Population Censuses and Surveys, October 1982.
2 M. Foot, *Sunday Mirror*, 23 November 1980.
3 I. Craig, interview with author.
4 E. Roderick, interview with author.
5 Minutes of Special Meeting of Liverpool City Council, 19 March 1980.
6 Report of the Policy/Programme Sub-Committee of the Liverpool District Labour Party, 1982.
7 Quoted in Granada TV's *World In Action*, 16 December 1985.
8 Ibid.
9 T. McDonald, interview with author.
10 E. Roderick, interview.
11 T. Pearce (P. Taaffe), 'Bulletin of Marxist Studies' (Militant int. doc.), summer 1984, p. 3.
12 T. Lane, *Marxism Today*, February 1981.

13 HATTON'S ARMY (PP 243–73)

1 *New Society*, 11 October 1985.
2 *See* M. Parkinson, *Liverpool on the Brink*, Policy Journals, Hermitage, 1985, p. 89.
3 T. Pearce, (P. Taaffe) 'Bulletin of Marxist Studies', (Militant int. doc.), summer 1984, p. 3.
4 *The Times*, 8 June 1984.
5 *The Times*, *Daily Mail* and *Daily Star*, 11 July 1984.
6 M. Parkinson, *Liverpool on the Brink*, Policy Journals, Hermitage, 1985, pp 117–18.
7 *New Society*, 29 November 1985.
8 Letter from J. Hamilton to J. McLean, 21 March 1984.
9 Letter from J. Hamilton to J. McLean, 22 March 1984.
10 T. Pearce, (P. Taaffe) 'Bulletin of Marxist Studies', (Militant int. doc.), summer 1985, p. 3.
11 *Newsline*, 12 June 1985.
12 T. Pearce (P. Taaffe) 'Bulletin of Marxist Studies', (Militant int. doc.), summer 1985, p. 3.
13 ITN *Channel 4 News*, 24 September 1985.
14 *Sunday Times*, 29 September 1985.
15 Militant Editorial Board statement, 23 November 1985.
16 Quoted in *The Guardian*, 23 November 1985.
17 Circular from Militant headquarters to branches, 17 October 1985.

14 THE TENDENCY TACTICIANS (PP 274–304)

1 Letter to *Labour Leader*, August 1983.
2 Fabian Society Labour leadership debate, Central Hall, Westminster, 29 July 1983.
3 NEC Report 1983, p. 23.
4 *Tribune*, 7 March 1986.

5   LPACR, 1985, p. 128.
6   *The Times*, 1 October 1985.
7   *Labour Weekly*, 29 November 1985.
8   *Labour Weekly*, 7 March 1986.
9   Internal circular from Militant central committee to branches, 17 March 1986.
10 Ibid.

15 CONCLUSION (PP 305-12)

1   *Militant*, 9 May 1986.
2   *Tribune*, 9 May 1986.

BIBLIOGRAPHY

Ali, Tariq, *The Coming British Revolution*, Jonathan Cape, London, 1972

Baker, Blake, *The Far Left*, Weidenfeld & Nicolson, London, 1981

Baxter, Robert, *The Liverpool Labour Party, 1918–1963*, DPhil thesis, Oxford, 1969

Benn, Tony, *Arguments for Socialism*, ed. Chris Mullin, Jonathan Cape, London, 1979

Bornstein, Sam, and Richardson, Al, *Against the Stream, A History of the British Trotskyist Movement in Britain 1924–38*, Socialist Platform, London, 1986.

Bornstein, Sam, and Richardson, Al, *Two Steps Back*, Socialist Platform, Ilford, 1983

Braddock, Jack and Bessie, *The Braddocks*, Macdonald, London, 1963

Bradley, Ian, *Breaking The Mould? The Birth and Prospects of the Social Democratic Party*, Martin Robertson, Oxford, 1981

Callaghan, John, *British Trotskyism, Theory and Practice*, Blackwell, Oxford, 1984

Castle, Barbara, *The Castle Diaries, 1974–76*, Weidenfeld & Nicolson, London, 1980

Chapple, Frank, *Sparks Fly! A Trade Union Life*, Michael Joseph, London, 1984

Cook, Chris, and Taylor, Ian, *The Labour Party: an Introduction to its History, Structure and Politics*, Longman, London, 1980

Crossman, Richard, *The Backbench Diaries of Richard Crossman*, ed. Janet Morgan, Hamish Hamilton and Jonathan Cape, London, 1981

Deutscher, Isaac, *The Prophet Outcast: Trotsky 1929–1940*, Oxford University Press, Oxford, 1963

Duncan, Pete, *Paved with Good Intentions: The Politics of Militant*, Clause 4, London, 1981

Foot, Michael, *Aneurin Bevan: 1897–1945*, MacGibbon & Kee, London, 1962

Foot, Michael, *Aneurin Bevan: 1945–1960*, Davis-Poynter, London, 1973

Gaitskell, Hugh, *The Diary of Hugh Gaitskell 1945–1956*, ed. P. Williams, Jonathan Cape, London, 1983

Glyn, Andrew, *Capitalist Crisis: Tribune's Alternative Strategy or Socialist Plan*, Militant, London, 1978

Groves, Reg, *The Balham Group*, Pluto, London, 1974

Hain, Peter, *The Democratic Alternative: a Socialist Response to Britain's Crisis*, Penguin, Harmondsworth, 1983

Harris, Kenneth, *Attlee*, Weidenfeld & Nicolson, London, 1982

Harris, Robert, *The Making of Neil Kinnock*, Faber, London, 1984

Haseler, Stephen, *The Tragedy of Labour*, Basil Blackwell, Oxford, 1980

Hindess, Barry, *The Decline of Working Class Politics*, MacGibbon & Kee, London, 1971

Hodgson, Geoff, *Labour at the Crossroads*, Martin Robertson, Oxford, 1981

Hoggart, Simon, and Leigh, David, *Michael Foot: A Portrait*, Hodder and Stoughton, London, 1981

Hunter, Leslie, *The Road to Brighton Pier*, Arthur Barker, London, 1959

Jenkins, Mark, *Bevanism: Labour's High Tide*, Spokesman, Nottingham, 1979

Jenkins, Robert, *Tony Benn: A Political Biography*, Writers and Readers, London, 1980

Kogan, David, and Kogan, Maurice, *The Battle for the Labour Party*, 2nd edn, Kogan Page, London, 1983

Lee, Jennie, *My Life With Nye*, Jonathan Cape, London, 1980

McCormick, Paul, *Enemies of Democracy*, Temple Smith, London, 1979

Mitchell, Austin, *Four Years in the Death of the Labour Party*, Methuen, London, 1983

Nightingale, Martyn, *et al.*, *Merseyside in Crisis*, Merseyside Socialist Research Group, Birkenhead, 1980

Parkinson, Michael, *Liverpool on the Brink*, Policy Journals, Hermitage, 1985

Pelling, Henry, *A Short History of the Labour Party*, Macmillan, London, 1961

Pelling, Henry, *The British Communist Party*, Adam and Charles Black, London, 1975

Pimlott, Ben, *Labour and the Left in the 1930s*, Cambridge University Press, Cambridge, 1977

Shipley, Peter, *Revolutionaries in Modern Britain*, Bodley Head, London, 1976

Shipley, Peter, *The Militant Tendency*, Foreign Affairs Publishing Co., London, 1983

Spiers, John (ed.), *The Left in Britain: A Checklist and Guide*, The Harvester Press, Brighton, 1976

Taaffe, Peter, *What We Stand For*, Militant, London, 1981 and 1986

Tatchell, Peter, *The Battle for Bermondsey*, Heretic Books, London, 1983

Thayer, George, *The British Political Fringe*, Anthony Blond, London, 1965

Tomlinson, John, *Left, Right: The March of Political Extremism in Britain*, John Calder, London, 1981

Upham, Martin, *The History of British Trotskyism to 1949*, Ph.D. thesis, University of Hull, 1980

Walker, Denver, *Quite Right, Mr. Trotsky!*, Harney and Jones, London, 1985

Waller, P. J., *Democracy and Sectarianism: A Political and Social History of Liverpool* 1868–1939, Liverpool University Press, Liverpool, 1982

Weighell, Sidney, *On the Rails*, Orbis, London, 1983

Widgery, David, *The Left in Britain 1956–68*, Penguin, Harmondsworth, 1976

Williams, Philip, *Hugh Gaitskell: A Political Biography*, Jonathan Cape, London, 1979

Willis, Ted, *Whatever Happened to Tom Mix? The Story of One of My Lives*, Cassell, London, 1970

Woods, A., and Grant, T., *Lenin and Trotsky: What They Really Stood For*, Militant, London, 1969

Young, Alison, *The Reselection of MPs*, Heinemann Educational, London, 1983

INDEX